Blaming the Victim

BLAMING THE VICTIM

BY

WILLIAM RYAN

PANTHEON BOOKS

A DIVISION OF RANDOM HOUSE

NEW YORK

All rights reserved under International and Pan-American Copyright
Conventions. Published in the United States by Pantheon Books,
a division of Random House, Inc., New York, and simultaneously in Canada by Random House of Canada Limited, Toronto.

Library of Congress Catalog Card Number: 69-15476

ISBN: 0-394-41726-7

Manufactured in the United States of America by
The Book Press, Brattleboro, Vermont
Design by Vincent Torre

98765432

For my wife Phyllis, whose love has sustained me, whose character has inspired me, and with whom I have shared gratefully the feelings, the values, the perceptions, the ideas, and the actions that have given rise to this book.

Acknowledgments

This book reflects influence and enlightenment from many persons. Some are acknowledged in the footnotes, but there were others—members of what was called The Movement, particularly of the Massachusetts Freedom Movement, SCLC, CORE, and the Welfare Rights Movement—whose influence flowed from words and acts and personal examples. Foremost among them was the late Dr. Martin Luther King.

Among those to whom I am especially indebted for experiences and insights that led me to write this book are Thomas Blair, James Breeden, Noel Day, John Harmon, Alan Gartner, Laura Morris, the late Doris Bland Franklin, Ledonia Wright, Paul Chapman, and my wise and wonderful daughter, Elizabeth.

Contents

Introduction   xi

1. The Art of Savage Discovery: How to Blame
   the Victim   3

2. Savage Discovery in the Schools:
   The Folklore of Cultural Deprivation   30

3. Mammy Observed: Fixing the Negro Family   61

4. The Prevalence of Bastards: Illegitimate Views
   of Illegitimacy   86

5. Learning to Be Poor: The Culture of
   Poverty Cheesecake   112

6. The Hydraulics and Economics of Misery:
   The Society for the Preservation of Disease   136

7. Taking People Out of Oak Street: Slums, Suburbs and Subsidies   164

8. Illegal Order: The Administration of Injustice   185

9. Counting Black Bodies: Riots, Raids and Repression   211

10. In Praise of Loot and Clout: Money, Power and
     Social Change   236

     Notes   279

     Index   291

Introduction

I am addressing this book to one set of persons I know and am concerned about in the hope that it will help them to know and understand more fully another set of persons I know and am concerned about. The latter group are the obvious victims of the racism and of the social and economic injustice that infect all parts of American life. The former appear to have escaped victimization. They have decent jobs and houses and send their children to decent schools. More important, they have not been made insensitive by their own good fortune. As I picture the person I hope will be reading these words, he already knows in some detail about the obvious victims, he knows that there are poor families, slums, discrimination, miseducation, exploitation. He not only knows, but he is concerned, and his concern is not abstract. He acts—at the polls, in civic groups, in church organizations. He wants change. He wants an end to racism and injustice. And, despite the pessimism of many, I still cling to the belief that this group of concerned citizens who act on their concern hold the key, the only key, to nonviolent change in American life.

But, in another sense, this concerned citizen has not escaped; he too is a victim. He has been miseducated and misled by an *ideology,* a mythology, a set of officially-certified nonfacts and respected untruths, and this ideology—which has been infused into the very cells of his brain—prevents him from seeing the process of victimization as a total picture.

In part this is so because his attention is constantly occupied with the details of truly sad and touching stories about individuals. He knows, or has read, or has heard, a hundred or a thousand such stories, but he has no way of fitting them together. The standard content of popular American social thought (as well as the set of categories and dimensions by which that content is structured), as it has been filtered into the intellectual apparatus of the reasonably well-read, average citizen, is insufficient and irrelevant to the task of understanding the pattern that these stories form.

For years, with some sense of despair, I have been observing this process. Let me illustrate. A woman I know read Jonathan Kozol's *Death at an Early Age* and Herbert Kohl's *36 Children.* She was moved and outraged. She heard other stories in conversations with friends about the specifics of life in a ghetto classroom. She was horrified, and her horror was genuine and deep. But when I talked with her, it became clear that what horrified her was that particular series of stories; what appalled her was that there are individual teachers— even in large numbers—who can behave so badly to individual children. She does not fully grasp the fact that ghetto education is not merely an infinite series of teachers acting badly, but is, more importantly, a social institution of American life, a mechanism for destroying black children. Moreover, like other modern engineering miracles, this mechanism uses interchangeable parts: it can substitute one individual teacher for another and still achieve its purpose with no difficulty.

This woman's failure to grasp the total picture leaves her an easy subject for disorientation, and at another time she can support the operations of that engine of destruction with equal sincerity because those operations have been defined plausibly to her as benevolent (like the series of fraudulent programs that are constantly being initiated "to benefit inner-city children").

What is even worse, she participates directly in the process of victimization although she does so unintentionally. A number of the white middle class parents my wife and I know are men and women with the best of intentions whose sincerity and devotion is attested to by their grim determination to keep their children in the New Haven public schools: these parents of our daughter's schoolmates spend many nights and weekends working to improve those schools. They are nevertheless completely acquiescent to the operation of one of the most rigid and mindless tracking systems in the country—it explicitly defines and labels their children as educable and college-bound while the children of the poor and the black are dismissed as "unprepared" or "academically untalented."

These same concerned persons might see a set of pictures of cracked walls, falling plaster, leaking toilets and broken staircases; they might even strip away the protective distance behind the static photograph and visit slum tenements and become nauseated and enraged. They might very well speak out against the slum landlords and condemn the laxity of city officials. But then they are easily hoodwinked into supporting an urban renewal program, the staff of which clouds their vision with quite believable rhetoric about rehabilitation, slum clearance, and badly-needed social services to the "unacculturated" slumdweller. They remain completely blind to the truth that urban renewal is one of the very creators of the slums that have so outraged them.

Good intentions and vigorous actions to improve social conditions are constantly being crippled, sabotaged, and deflected by insidious forces that have already pre-shaped the channels of thought. Because those who intend good and act with vigor also believe certain things to be true about the poor, the black, and the victimized. And, so believing, they are easily tempted into accepting the mythology of Blaming the Victim.

This book is about that mythology and that ideology. My purpose is, first, to persuade the reader that many of his friends and neighbors—and perhaps even he himself—have been tricked into believing many lies and, second, to provide him with a viewpoint and a method of analysis that can armor him against future tricks and future lies.

In this discussion I will try to resist the constant temptation to make this book more "interesting," more "entertaining," more "readable." I will not tell a long series of heartbreaking stories—although, God knows, I know enough of them to fill a book. Others have done that and done it well. I will attempt to be informative: I will aim more frequently for the head than for the heart although it is my firm hope that the heart can be touched more profoundly by way of that detour.

The book grows out of my own experience, both professional and personal. As a psychologist and a social scientist, I have spent some years in clinical work and more recently have engaged in research and planning for the solution of urban social problems. Over these years I have found myself forced, painfully and gradually, to discard one supposed social fact after another, facts that made up some of the core of my own professional identity. My own process of relearning and rethinking has been accelerated by many, many years of activity as a citizen on the battleground of what used to be called the civil rights movement. During these years, I have come to know some of the people who have been victimized and lied about—at meetings, on picket lines, in confrontations with landlords, in living room talks, and at coffee sessions around kitchen tables. The realities I have experienced are very different from the myths and untruths dealt out by politicians and bureaucrats and even by some of my fellow social scientists.

I have now come to believe that the ideology of Blaming the Victim so distorts and disorients the thinking of the average concerned citizen that it becomes a primary barrier to effective social change. And, further, I believe that the injustices and inequalities in American life can never be understood (and, therefore, can never be eliminated) until that ideology is exposed and destroyed.

Since I believe that the quality of my own life, and that of the lives of my wife and daughter and friends, is polluted daily by these injustices, I want that change to come and I want to help to destroy that mythology.

I will not be telling you moving stories, then. Rather, I will be debating with those who have been lying to you. And I will try to tell you some truths as I, at least, have learned them to be true.

Blaming the Victim

1
The Art of Savage Discovery

How to Blame the Victim

I

Twenty years ago, Zero Mostel used to do a sketch in which he impersonated a Dixiecrat Senator conducting an investigation of the origins of World War II. At the climax of the sketch, the Senator boomed out, in an excruciating mixture of triumph and suspicion, "What was Pearl Harbor *doing* in the Pacific?" This is an extreme example of Blaming the Victim.

Twenty years ago, we could laugh at Zero Mostel's caricature. In recent years, however, the same process has been going on every day in the arena of social problems, public health, anti-poverty programs, and social welfare. A philosopher might analyze this process and prove that, technically, it is comic. But it is hardly ever funny.

Consider some victims. One is the miseducated child in

the slum school. He is blamed for his own miseducation. He is said to contain within himself the causes of his inability to read and write well. The shorthand phrase is "cultural deprivation," which, to those in the know, conveys what they allege to be inside information: that the poor child carries a scanty pack of cultural baggage as he enters school. He doesn't know about books and magazines and newspapers, they say. (No books in the home: the mother fails to subscribe to *Reader's Digest*.) They say that if he talks at all— an unlikely event since slum parents don't talk to their children—he certainly doesn't talk correctly. (Lower-class dialect spoken here, or even—God forbid!—Southern Negro. (*Ici on parle nigra*.) If you can manage to get him to sit in a chair, they say, he squirms and looks out the window. (Impulse-ridden, these kids, motoric rather than verbal.) In a word he is "disadvantaged" and "socially deprived," they say, and this, of course, accounts for his failure (*his* failure, they say) to learn much in school.

Note the similarity to the logic of Zero Mostel's Dixiecrat Senator. What is the culturally deprived child *doing* in the school? What is wrong with the victim? In pursuing this logic, no one remembers to ask questions about the collapsing buildings and torn textbooks, the frightened, insensitive teachers, the six additional desks in the room, the blustering, frightened principals, the relentless segregation, the callous administrator, the irrelevant curriculum, the bigoted or cowardly members of the school board, the insulting history book, the stingy taxpayers, the fairy-tale readers, or the self-serving faculty of the local teachers' college. We are encouraged to confine our attention to the child and to dwell on all his alleged defects. Cultural deprivation becomes an omnibus explanation for the educational disaster area known as the inner-city school. This is Blaming the Victim.

Pointing to the supposedly deviant Negro family as the

"fundamental weakness of the Negro community" is another way to blame the victim. Like "cultural deprivation," "Negro family" has become a shorthand phrase with stereotyped connotations of matriarchy, fatherlessness, and pervasive illegitimacy. Growing up in the "crumbling" Negro family is supposed to account for most of the racial evils in America. Insiders have the word, of course, and know that this phrase is supposed to evoke images of growing up with a long-absent or never-present father (replaced from time to time perhaps by a series of transient lovers) and with bossy women ruling the roost, so that the children are irreparably damaged. This refers particularly to the poor, bewildered male children, whose psyches are fatally wounded and who are never, alas, to learn the trick of becoming upright, downright, forthright all-American boys. Is it any wonder the Negroes cannot achieve equality? From such families! And, again, by focusing our attention on the Negro family as the apparent *cause* of racial inequality, our eye is diverted. Racism, discrimination, segregation, and the powerlessness of the ghetto are subtly, but thoroughly, downgraded in importance.

The generic process of Blaming the Victim is applied to almost every American problem. The miserable health care of the poor is explained away on the grounds that the victim has poor motivation and lacks health information. The problems of slum housing are traced to the characteristics of tenants who are labeled as "Southern rural migrants" not yet "acculturated" to life in the big city. The "multiproblem" poor, it is claimed, suffer the psychological effects of impoverishment, the "culture of poverty," and the deviant value system of the lower classes; consequently, though unwittingly, they cause their own troubles. From such a viewpoint, the obvious fact that poverty is primarily an absence of money is easily overlooked or set aside.

The growing number of families receiving welfare are

fallaciously linked together with the increased number of illegitimate children as twin results of promiscuity and sexual abandon among members of the lower orders. Every important social problem—crime, mental illness, civil disorder, unemployment—has been analyzed within the framework of the victim-blaming ideology. In the following pages, I shall present in detail nine examples that relate to social problems and human services in urban areas.

It would be possible for me to venture into other areas— one finds a perfect example in literature about the underdeveloped countries of the Third World, in which the lack of prosperity and technological progress is attributed to some aspect of the national character of the people, such as lack of "achievement motivation"—but I plan to stay within the confines of my own personal and professional experience, which is, generally, with racial injustice, social welfare, and human services in the city.

I have been listening to the victim-blamers and pondering their thought processes for a number of years. That process is often very subtle. Victim-blaming is cloaked in kindness and concern, and bears all the trappings and statistical furbelows of scientism; it is obscured by a perfumed haze of humanitarianism. In observing the process of Blaming the Victim, one tends to be confused and disoriented because those who practice this art display a deep concern for the victims that is quite genuine. In this way, the new ideology is very different from the open prejudice and reactionary tactics of the old days. Its adherents include sympathetic social scientists with social consciences in good working order, and liberal politicians with a genuine commitment to reform. They are very careful to dissociate themselves from vulgar Calvinism or crude racism; they indignantly condemn any notions of innate wickedness or genetic defect. "The Negro is *not born* inferior," they shout apoplectically. "Force of circumstance," they explain in reasonable tones, "has *made* him inferior." And they dismiss with self-righteous contempt any claims that the poor man in America is plainly unworthy or shiftless or enamored of idleness. No, they say, he is "caught in the cycle of poverty." He is trained to be poor by his culture and his family life, endowed by his environment (perhaps by his ignorant mother's outdated style of toilet training) with those unfortunately unpleasant characteristics that make him ineligible for a passport into the affluent society.

Blaming the Victim is, of course, quite different from old-fashioned conservative ideologies. The latter simply dismissed victims as inferior, genetically defective, or morally unfit; the emphasis is on the intrinsic, even hereditary, defect. The former shifts its emphasis to the environmental causation. The old-fashioned conservative could hold firmly to the belief that the oppressed and the victimized were born that way—"that way" being defective or inadequate in character or ability. The new ideology attributes defect and inadequacy to the malignant nature of poverty, injustice, slum life, and racial difficulties. The stigma that marks the victim and accounts for his victimization is an acquired stigma, a stigma of social, rather than genetic, origin. But the stigma, the defect, the fatal difference—though derived in the past from environmental forces—is still located *within* the victim, inside his skin. With such an elegant formulation, the humanitarian can have it both ways. He can, all at the same time, concentrate his charitable interest on the defects of the victim, condemn the vague social and environmental stresses that produced the defect (some time ago), and ignore the continuing effect of victimizing social forces (right now). It is a brilliant ideology for justifying a perverse form of social action designed to change, not society, as one might expect, but rather society's victim.

As a result, there is a terrifying sameness in the programs

that arise from this kind of analysis. In education, we have programs of "compensatory education" to build up the skills and attitudes of the ghetto child, rather than structural changes in the schools. In race relations, we have social engineers who think up ways of "strengthening" the Negro family, rather than methods of eradicating racism. In health care, we develop new programs to provide health information (to correct the supposed ignorance of the poor) and to reach out and discover cases of untreated illness and disability (to compensate for their supposed unwillingness to seek treatment). Meanwhile, the gross inequities of our medical care delivery systems are left completely unchanged. As we might expect, the logical outcome of analyzing social problems in terms of the deficiencies of the victim is the development of programs aimed at correcting those deficiencies. The formula for action becomes extraordinarily simple: change the victim.

All of this happens so smoothly that it seems downright rational. First, identify a social problem. Second, study those affected by the problem and discover in what ways they are different from the rest of us as a consequence of deprivation and injustice. Third, define the differences as the cause of the social problem itself. Finally, of course, assign a government bureaucrat to invent a humanitarian action program to correct the differences.

Now no one in his right mind would quarrel with the assertion that social problems are present in abundance and are readily identifiable. God knows it is true that when hundreds of thousands of poor children drop out of school—or even graduate from school—they are barely literate. After spending some ten thousand hours in the company of professional educators, these children appear to have learned very little. The fact of failure in their education is undisputed. And the racial situation in America is usually acknowledged to be a number one item on the nation's agenda. Despite years of marches, commissions, judicial decisions, and endless legislative remedies, we are confronted with unchanging or even widening racial differences in achievement. In addition, despite our assertions that Americans get the best health care in the world, the poor stubbornly remain unhealthy. They lose more work because of illness, have more carious teeth, lose more babies as a result of both miscarriage and infant death, and die considerably younger than the well-to-do.

The problems are there, and there in great quantities. They make us uneasy. Added together, these disturbing signs reflect inequality and a puzzlingly high level of unalleviated distress in America totally inconsistent with our proclaimed ideals and our enormous wealth. This thread—this rope—of inconsistency stands out so visibly in the fabric of American life, that it is jarring to the eye. And this must be explained, to the satisfaction of our conscience as well as our patriotism. Blaming the Victim is an ideal, almost painless, evasion.

The second step in applying this explanation is to look sympathetically at those who "have" the problem in question, to separate them out and define them in some way as a special group, a group that is *different* from the population in general. This is a crucial and essential step in the process, for that difference is in itself hampering and maladaptive. The Different Ones are seen as less competent, less skilled, less knowing—in short, less human. The ancient Greeks deduced from a single characteristic, a difference in language, that the barbarians—that is, the "babblers" who spoke a strange tongue—were wild, uncivilized, dangerous, rapacious, uneducated, lawless, and, indeed, scarcely more than animals. Automatically labeling strangers as savages, weird and inhuman creatures (thus explaining difference by exaggerating difference) not infrequently justifies mistreatment, enslavement, or even extermination of the Different Ones.

Blaming the Victim depends on a very similar process of identification (carried out, to be sure, in the most kindly, philanthropic, and intellectual manner) whereby the victim of social problems is identified as strange, different—in other words, as a barbarian, a savage. Discovering savages, then, is an essential component of, and prerequisite to, Blaming the Victim, and the art of Savage Discovery is a core skill that must be acquired by all aspiring Victim Blamers. They must learn how to demonstrate that the poor, the black, the ill, the jobless, the slum tenants, are different and strange. They must learn to conduct or interpret the research that shows how "these people" think in different forms, act in different patterns, cling to different values, seek different goals, and learn different truths. Which is to say that they are strangers, barbarians, savages. This is how the distressed and disinherited are redefined in order to make it possible for us to look at society's problems and to attribute their causation to the individuals affected.

II

Blaming the Victim is an ideological process, which is to say that it is a set of ideas and concepts deriving from systematically motivated, but *unintended,* distortions of reality. In the sense that Karl Mannheim[1] used the term, an ideology develops from the "collective unconscious" of a group or class and is rooted in a class-based interest in maintaining the *status quo* (as contrasted with what he calls a *utopia,* a set of ideas rooted in a class-based interest in *changing* the *status quo*). An ideology, then, has several components: First, there is the belief system itself, the way of looking at the world, the set of ideas and concepts. Second, there is the systematic distortion of reality reflected in those ideas. Third is the condition that the distortion must not be a conscious, intentional process. Finally, though they are not intentional, the ideas must serve a specific function: maintaining the *status quo* in the interest of a specific group. Blaming the Victim fits this definition on all counts, as I will attempt to show in detail in the following chapters. Most particularly, it is important to realize that Blaming the Victim is not a process of *intentional* distortion although it does serve the class interests of those who practice it. And it has a rich ancestry in American thought about social problems and how to deal with them.

Thinking about social problems is especially susceptible to ideological influences since, as John Seeley has pointed out,[2] defining a social problem is not so simple. "What is a social problem?" may seem an ingenuous question until one turns to confront its opposite: "What human problem is *not* a social problem?" Since any problem in which people are involved is social, why do we reserve the label for some problems in which people are involved and withhold it from others? To use Seeley's example, why is crime called a social problem when university administration is not? The phenomena we look at are bounded by the act of definition. They become social problems only by being so considered. In Seeley's words, "*naming* it as a problem, after naming it as a *problem*."

It is only recently, for example, that we have begun to *name* the rather large quantity of people on earth as the *problem* of overpopulation, or the population explosion. Such phenomena often become proper predicaments for certain solutions, certain treatments. Before the 1930's, the most anti-Semitic German was unaware that Germany had a

11

"Jewish problem." It took the Nazis to *name* the simple existence of Jews in the Third Reich as a "social problem," and that act of definition helped to shape the final solution.

We have removed "immigration" from our list of social problems (after executing a solution—choking off the flow of immigrants) and have added "urbanization." Nowadays, we define the situation of men out of work as the social problem of "unemployment" rather than, as in Elizabethan times, that of "idleness." (The McCone Commission, investigating the Watts Riot of 1966, showed how hard old ideologies die; it specified both unemployment *and* idleness as causes of the disorder.) In the near future, if we are to credit the prophets of automation, the label "unemployment" will fade away and "idleness," now renamed the "leisure-time problem," will begin again to raise its lazy head. We have been comfortable for years with the "Negro problem," a term that clearly implies that the existence of Negroes is somehow a problematic fact. *Ebony* Magazine turned the tables recently and renamed the phenomenon as "The White Problem in America," which may be a good deal more accurate.

We must particularly ask, "To whom are social problems a problem?" And usually, if truth were to be told, we would have to admit that we mean they are a problem to those of us who are outside the boundaries of what we have defined as the problem. Negroes are a problem to racist whites, welfare is a problem to stingy taxpayers, delinquency is a problem to nervous property owners.

Now, if this is the quality of our assumptions about social problems, we are led unerringly to certain beliefs about the causes of these problems. We cannot comfortably believe that *we* are the cause of that which is problematic to us; therefore, we are almost compelled to believe that *they*—the problematic ones—are the cause and this immediately prompts us to search for deviance. Identification of the deviance as the cause of the problem is a simple step that ordinarily does not even require evidence.

C. Wright Mills analyzed the ideology of those who write about social problems and demonstrated the relationship of their texts to class interest and to the preservation of the existent social order.[3] In sifting the material in thirty-one widely used textbooks in "social problems," "social pathology," and "social disorganization," Mills found a pervasive, coherent ideology with a number of common characteristics.

First, the textbooks present material about these problems, he says, in simple, descriptive terms, with each problem unrelated to the others and none related in any meaningful way to other aspects of the social environment. Second, the problems are selected and described largely according to predetermined norms. Poverty is a problem in that it deviates from the standard of economic self-sufficiency; divorce is a problem because the family is supposed to remain intact; crime and delinquency are problematic insofar as they depart from the accepted moral and legal standards of the community. The norms themselves are taken as givens, and no effort is made to examine them. Nor is there any thought given to the manner in which norms might themselves contribute to the development of the problems. (In a society in which everyone is assumed and expected to be economically self-sufficient, as an example, doesn't economic dependency almost automatically mean poverty? No attention is given to such issues.)

Within such a framework, then, deviation from norms and standards comes to be defined as failed or incomplete socialization—failure to learn the rules or the inability to learn how to keep to them. Those with social problems are then viewed as unable or unwilling to adjust to society's standards, which are narrowly conceived by what Mills calls "independent middle class persons verbally living out Protestant ideas in small town America." This, obviously, is a precise description of the social origins and status of almost every one of the authors.

In defining social problems in this way, the social pathologists are, of course, ignoring a whole set of factors that ordinarily might be considered relevant—for instance, unequal distribution of income, social stratification, political struggle, ethnic and racial group conflict, and inequality of power. Their ideology concentrates almost exclusively on the failure of the deviant. To the extent that society plays any part in social problems, it is said to have somehow failed to socialize the individual, to teach him how to adjust to circumstances, which, though far from perfect, are gradually changing for the better. Mills' essay provides a solid foundation for understanding the concept of Blaming the Victim.

This way of thinking on the part of "social pathologists," which Mills identified as the predominant tool used in *analyzing* social problems, also saturates the majority of programs that have been developed to *solve* social problems in America. These programs are based on the assumption that *individuals* "have" social problems as a result of some kind of unusual circumstances—accident, illness, personal defect or handicap, character flaw or maladjustment—that exclude them from using the ordinary mechanisms for maintaining and advancing themselves. For example, the prevalent belief in America is that, under normal circumstances, everyone can obtain sufficient income for the necessities of life. Those who are unable to do so are special deviant cases, persons who for one reason or another are not able to adapt themselves to the generally satisfactory income-producing system. In times gone by these persons were further classified into the worthy poor—the lame, the blind, the young mother whose husband died in an accident, the aged man no longer able to work—and the unworthy poor—the lazy, the unwed mother and her illegitimate children, the malingerer. All were seen, however, as individuals who, for good reasons or bad, were personal failures, unable to adapt themselves to the system.

In America health care, too, has been predominantly a matter of particular remedial attention provided individually to the more or less random group of persons who have become ill, whose bodily functioning has become deviant and abnormal. In the field of mental health, the same approach has been, and continues to be, dominant. The social problem of mental disease has been viewed as a collection of individual cases of deviance, persons who—through unusual hereditary taint, or exceptional distortion of character—have become unfit for normal activities. The solution to these problems was to segregate the deviants, to protect them, to give them *asylum* from the life of the community for which they were no longer competent.

This has been the dominant style in American social welfare and health activities, then: to treat what we call social problems, such as poverty, disease, and mental illness, in terms of the individual deviance of the special, unusual groups of persons who had those problems. There has also been a competing style, however—much less common, not at all congruent with the prevalent ideology, but continually developing parallel to the dominant style.

Adherents of this approach tended to search for defects in the community and the environment rather than in the individual; to emphasize predictability and usualness rather than random deviance; they tried to think about preventing rather than merely repairing or treating—to see social problems, in a word, as social. In the field of disease, this approach was termed public health, and its practitioners sought the cause of disease in such things as the water supply, the sewage system, the density and quality of housing conditions. They set out to prevent disease, not in individuals, but in the total population, through improved sanitation, inoculation against communicable disease, and the policing of housing conditions. In the field of income maintenance, this secondary style of solving social problems focused on poverty as a predictable event, on the regularities of income deficiency. And it concentrated on the development of standard, generalized programs affecting total groups. Rather than trying to fit the aged worker ending his career into some kind of category of special cases, it assumed all sixty-five-year-old men should expect to retire from the world of work and have the security of an old age pension, to be arranged through public social activity. Unemployment insurance was developed as a method whereby all workers could be protected against the effects of the normal ups and downs of the business cycle. A man out of work could then count on an unemployment check rather than endure the agony of pauperizing himself, selling his tools or his car, and finding himself in the special category of those deserving of charity.

These two approaches to the solution of social problems have existed side by side, the former always dominant, but the latter gradually expanding, slowly becoming more and more prevalent.

Elsewhere[4] I have proposed the dimension of *exceptionalism-universalism* as the ideological underpinning for these two contrasting approaches to the analysis and solution of social problems. The *exceptionalist* viewpoint is reflected in arrangements that are private, voluntary, remedial, special, local, and exclusive. Such arrangements imply that problems occur to specially-defined categories of persons in an unpredictable manner. The problems are unusual, even unique, they are exceptions to the rule, they occur as a result of individual defect, accident, or unfortunate circumstance and must be remedied by means that are particular and, as it were, tailored to the individual case.

The universalistic viewpoint, on the other hand, is reflected in arrangements that are public, legislated, promotive or preventive, general, national, and inclusive. Inherent in such a viewpoint is the idea that social problems are a function of the social arrangements of the community or the society and that, since these social arrangements are quite imperfect and inequitable, such problems are both predictable and, more important, preventable through public action. They are not unique to the individual, and the fact that they encompass individual persons does not imply that those persons are themselves defective or abnormal.

Consider these two contrasting approaches as they are applied to the problem of smallpox. The medical care approach is exceptionalistic; it is designed to provide remedial treatment to the special category of persons who are afflicted with the disease through a private, voluntary arrangement with a local doctor. The universalistic public health approach is designed to provide preventive inoculation to the total population, ordered by legislation and available through public means if no private arrangements can be made.

A similar contrast can be made between an exceptionalistic assistance program such as Aid to Families with Dependent Children and the proposed universalistic program of family allowances based simply on the number of children in a family. The latter assumes that the size of a family should automatically be a consideration in income supplementation, since it is in no way taken into account in the wage structure, and that it should be dealt with in a routine and universal fashion. The AFDC program, on the other hand, assumes that families need income assistance only as a result of special, impoverishing circumstances.

Fluoridation is universalistic; it is aimed at preventing caries in the total population; oral surgery is exceptionalistic, designed to remedy the special cases of infection or neglect that damage the teeth of an individual. Birth control is universalistic; abortion exceptionalistic. It has been said that navigational aids have saved far more lives than have rescue devices, no matter how refined they might be. The compass, then, is universalistic, while the lifeboat is exceptionalistic.

The similarity between exceptionalism and what Mills called the "ideology of social pathologists" is readily apparent. Indeed, the ideological potential of the exceptionalist viewpoint is unusually great. If one is inclined to explain all instances of deviance, all social problems, all occasions on which help is provided to others as the result of unusual circumstances, defect, or accident, one is unlikely to inquire about social inequalities.

This is not to devalue valid exceptionalistic services. Despite fluoridation, some instances of caries and gum disease will require attention; despite excellent prenatal care, handicapped children will occasionally be born; husbands will doubtless continue to die unexpectedly at early ages, leaving widows and orphans in need. And at any given moment, the end products of society's malfunctioning—the miseducated teenager, the unskilled adult laborer, the child brain-damaged as a result of prenatal neglect—will require service that is predominantly exceptionalistic in nature.

The danger in the exceptionalistic viewpoint is in its impact on social policy when it becomes the dominant component in social analysis. Blaming the Victim occurs exclusively within an exceptionalistic framework, and it consists of applying exceptionalistic explanations to universalistic problems. This represents an illogical departure from fact, a method, in Mannheim's words, of systematically distorting reality, of developing an ideology.

Blaming the Victim can take its place in a long series of American ideologies that have rationalized cruelty and injustice.

Slavery, for example, was justified—even praised—on the basis of a complex ideology that showed quite conclusively how useful slavery was to society and how uplifting it was for the slaves.[5] Eminent physicians could be relied upon to provide the biological justification for slavery since after all, they said, the slaves were a separate species—as, for example, cattle are a separate species. No one in his right mind would dream of freeing the cows and fighting to abolish the ownership of cattle. In the view of the average American of 1825, it was important to preserve slavery, not simply because it was in accord with his own group interests (he was not fully aware of that), but because reason and logic showed clearly to the reasonable and intelligent man that slavery was good. In order to persuade a good and moral man to *do* evil, then, it is not necessary first to persuade him to *become* evil. It is only necessary to teach him that he is doing good. No one, in the words of a legendary newspaperman, thinks of himself as a son of a bitch.

In late-nineteenth-century America there flowered another ideology of injustice that seemed rational and just to the decent, progressive person. But Richard Hofstadter's analysis of the phenomenon of Social Darwinism[6] shows clearly its functional role in the preservation of the *status quo*. One can scarcely imagine a better fit than the one between this ideology and the purposes and actions of the robber barons, who descended like piranha fish on the America of this era and picked its bones clean. Their extraordinarily unethical operations netted them not only hundreds of millions of dollars but also, perversely, the adoration of the nation. Behavior that would be, in any more rational land (including today's America), more than enough to have landed them all in jail, was praised as the very model of a captain of modern industry. And the philosophy that justified their thievery was such that John D. Rockefeller could actually stand up and preach it in church. Listen as he speaks in, of all places, Sunday school:

> The growth of a large business is merely a survival of the fittest. . . . The American Beauty rose can be produced in the splendor and fragrance which bring cheer to its beholder only by sacrificing the early buds which grow up around it. This is not an evil tendency in business. It is merely the working-out of a law of nature and a law of God.[7]

This was the core of the gospel, adapted analogically from Darwin's writings on evolution. Herbert Spencer and, later, William Graham Sumner and other beginners in the social sciences considered Darwin's work to be directly applicable to social processes: ultimately as a guarantee that life was progressing toward perfection but, in the short run, as a justification for an absolutely uncontrolled laissez-faire economic system. The central concepts of "survival of the fittest," "natural selection," and "gradualism" were exalted in Rockefeller's preaching to the status of laws of God and Nature. Not only did this ideology justify the criminal rapacity of those who rose to the top of the industrial heap, defining them automatically as naturally superior (this was bad enough), but at the same time it also required that those at the bottom of the heap be labeled as patently *unfit*—a label based solely on their position in society. According to the law of natural selection, they should be, in Spencer's judgment, eliminated. "The whole effort of nature is to get rid of such, to clear the world of them and make room for better."

For a generation, Social Darwinism was the orthodox doctrine in the social sciences, such as they were at that time. Opponents of this ideology were shut out of respectable intellectual life. The philosophy that enabled John D. Rockefeller to justify himself self-righteously in front of a class of Sunday school children was not the product of an academic quack or a marginal crackpot philosopher. It came directly from the lectures and books of leading intellectual figures of the time, occupants of professorial chairs at Harvard and Yale. Such is the power of an ideology that so neatly fits the needs of the dominant interests of society.

If one is to think about ideologies in America in 1970, one must be prepared to consider the possibility that a body of ideas that might seem almost self-evident is, in fact, highly distorted and highly selective; one must allow that the inclusion of a specific formulation in every freshman sociology text does not guarantee that the particular formulation represents abstract Truth rather than group interest. It is important not to delude ourselves into thinking that ideological monstrosities were constructed by monsters. They were not; they are not. They are developed through a process that shows every sign of being valid scholarship, complete with tables of numbers, copious footnotes, and scientific terminology. Ideologies are quite often academically and socially respectable and in many instances hold positions of exclusive validity, so that disagreement is considered unrespectable or radical and risks being labeled as irresponsible, unenlightened, or trashy.

Blaming the Victim holds such a position. It is central in the mainstream of contemporary American social thought, and its ideas pervade our most crucial assumptions so thoroughly that they are hardly noticed. Moreover, the fruits of this ideology appear to be fraught with altruism and humanitarianism, so it is hard to believe that it has principally functioned to block social change.

I I I

A major pharmaceutical manufacturer, as an act of humanitarian concern, has distributed copies of a large poster warning "LEAD PAINT CAN KILL!" The poster, featuring a photograph of the face of a charming little girl, goes on to explain that if children *eat* lead paint, it can poison them, they can develop serious symptoms, suffer permanent brain damage, even die. The health department of a major American city has put out a coloring book that provides the same information. While the poster urges parents to prevent their children from eating paint, the coloring book is more vivid. It labels as neglectful and thoughtless the mother who does not keep her infant under constant surveillance to keep it from eating paint chips.

Now, no one would argue against the idea that it is important to spread knowledge about the danger of eating paint in order that parents might act to forestall their children from doing so. But to campaign against lead paint *only* in these terms is destructive and misleading and, in a sense, an effective way to support and agree with slum landlords—who define the problem of lead poisoning in precisely these terms.

This is an example of applying an exceptionalistic solution

to a universalistic problem. It is not accurate to say that lead poisoning results from the actions of individual neglectful mothers. Rather, lead poisoning is a social phenomenon supported by a number of social mechanisms, one of the most tragic by-products of the systematic toleration of slum housing. In New Haven, which has the highest reported rate of lead poisoning in the country, several small children have died and many others have incurred irreparable brain damage as a result of eating peeling paint. In several cases, when the landlord failed to make repairs, poisonings have occurred time and again through a succession of tenancies. And the major reason for the landlord's neglect of this problem was that the city agency responsible for enforcing the housing code did nothing to make him correct this dangerous condition.

The cause of the poisoning is the lead in the paint on the walls of the apartment in which the children live. The presence of the lead is illegal. To use lead paint in a residence is illegal; to permit lead paint to be exposed in a residence is illegal. It is not only illegal, it is potentially criminal since the housing code does provide for criminal penalties. The general problem of lead poisoning, then, is more accurately analyzed as the result of a systematic program of lawbreaking by one interest group in the community, with the toleration and encouragement of the public authority charged with enforcing that law. To ignore these continued and repeated law violations, to ignore the fact that the supposed law enforcer actually cooperates in lawbreaking, and then to load a burden of guilt on the mother of a dead or dangerously-ill child is an egregious distortion of reality. And to do so under the guise of public-spirited and humanitarian service to the community is intolerable.

But this is how Blaming the Victim works. The righteous humanitarian concern displayed by the drug company, with its poster, and the health department, with its coloring book, is a genuine concern, and this is a typical feature of Blaming the Victim. Also typical is the swerving away from the central target that requires systematic change and, instead, focusing in on the individual affected. The ultimate effect is always to distract attention from the basic causes and to leave the primary social injustice untouched. And, most telling, the proposed remedy for the problem is, of course, to work on the victim himself. Prescriptions for cure, as written by the Savage Discovery set, are invariably conceived to revamp and revise the victim, never to change the surrounding circumstances. They want to change his attitudes, alter his values, fill up his cultural deficits, energize his apathetic soul, cure his character defects, train him and polish him and woo him from his savage ways.

Isn't all of this more subtle and sophisticated than such old-fashioned ideologies as Social Darwinism? Doesn't the change from brutal ideas about survival of the fit (and the expiration of the unfit) to kindly concern about characterological defects (brought about by stigmas of social origin) seem like a substantial step forward? Hardly. It is only a substitution of terms. The old, reactionary exceptionalistic formulations are replaced by new progressive, humanitarian exceptionalistic formulations. In education, the outmoded and unacceptable concept of racial or class differences in basic inherited intellectual ability simply gives way to the new notion of cultural deprivation: there is very little functional difference between these two ideas. In taking a look at the phenomenon of poverty, the old concept of unfitness or idleness or laziness is replaced by the newfangled theory of the culture of poverty. In race relations, plain Negro inferiority—which was good enough for old-fashioned conservatives—is pushed aside by fancy conceits about the crumbling Negro family. With regard to illegitimacy, we are not so crass as to concern ourselves with immorality and vice, as in the old days; we settle benignly on the explanation of the "lower-class pattern of sexual behavior," which no one condemns as evil, but which is, in fact, simply a variation of the old explanatory idea. Mental illness is no longer defined as the result of hereditary taint or congenital character flaw; now we have new causal hypotheses regarding the ego-damaging emotional experiences that are supposed to be the inevitable consequence of the deplorable child-rearing practices of the poor.

In each case, of course, we are persuaded to ignore the obvious: the continued blatant discrimination against the Negro, the gross deprivation of contraceptive and adoption services to the poor, the heavy stresses endemic in the life of the poor. And almost all our make-believe liberal programs aimed at correcting our urban problems are off target; they are designed either to change the poor man or to cool him out.

I V

We come finally to the question, Why? It is much easier to understand the process of Blaming the Victim as a way of thinking than it is to understand the motivation for it. Why do Victim Blamers, who are usually good people, blame the victim? The development and application of this ideology, and of all the mythologies associated with Savage Discovery, are readily exposed by careful analysis as hostile acts—one is almost tempted to say acts of war—directed against the disadvantaged, the distressed, the disinherited. It is class warfare in reverse. Yet those who are most fascinated and enchanted by this ideology tend to be progressive, humanitarian, and, in the best sense of the word, charitable persons. They would usually define themselves as moderates or liberals. Why do they pursue this dreadful war against the poor and the oppressed?

Put briefly, the answer can be formulated best in psychological terms—or, at least, I, as a psychologist, am more comfortable with such a formulation. The highly-charged psychological problem confronting this hypothetical progressive, charitable person I am talking about is that of reconciling his own self-interest with the promptings of his humanitarian impulses. This psychological process of reconciliation is not worked out in a logical, rational, conscious way; it is a process that takes place far below the level of sharp consciousness, and the solution—Blaming the Victim—is arrived at subconsciously as a compromise that apparently satisfies both his self-interest and his charitable concerns. Let me elaborate.

First, the question of self-interest or, more accurately, class interest. The typical Victim Blamer is a middle-class person who is doing reasonably well in a material way; he has a good job, a good income, a good house, a good car. Basically, he likes the social system pretty much the way it is, at least in broad outline. He likes the two-party political system, though he may be highly skilled in finding a thousand minor flaws in its functioning. He heartily approves of the profit motive as the propelling engine of the economic system despite his awareness that there are abuses of that system, negative side effects, and substantial residual inequalities.

On the other hand, he is acutely aware of poverty, racial discrimination, exploitation, and deprivation, and, moreover, he wants to do something concrete to ameliorate the condition of the poor, the black, and the disadvantaged. This is not an extraneous concern; it is central to his value system to insist on the worth of the individual, the equality of men, and the importance of justice.

What is to be done, then? What intellectual position can he take, and what line of action can he follow that will satisfy both of these important motivations? He quickly and self-consciously rejects two obvious alternatives, which he defines as "extremes." He cannot side with an openly reactionary, repressive position that accepts continued oppression and exploitation as the price of a privileged position for his own class. This is incompatible with his own morality and his basic political principles. He finds the extreme conservative position repugnant.

He is, if anything, more allergic to radicals, however, than he is to reactionaries. He rejects the "extreme" solution of radical social change, and this makes sense since such radical social change threatens his own well-being. A more equitable distribution of income might mean that he would have less —a smaller or older house, with fewer yews or no rhododendrons in the yard, a less enjoyable job, or, at the least, a somewhat smaller salary. If black children and poor children were, in fact, reasonably educated and began to get high S.A.T. scores, they would be competing with *his* children for the scarce places in the entering classes of Harvard, Columbia, Bennington, and Antioch.

So our potential Victim Blamers are in a dilemma. In the words of an old Yiddish proverb, they are trying to dance at two weddings. They are old friends of both brides and fond of both kinds of dancing, and they want to accept both invitations. They cannot bring themselves to attack the system that has been so good to them, but they want so badly to be helpful to the victims of racism and economic injustice.

Their solution is a brilliant compromise. They turn their

attention to the victim in his post-victimized state. They want to bind up wounds, inject penicillin, administer morphine, and evacuate the wounded for rehabilitation. They explain what's wrong with the victim in terms of social experiences *in the past,* experiences that have left wounds, defects, paralysis, and disability. And they take the cure of these wounds and the reduction of these disabilities as the first order of business. They want to make the victims less vulnerable, send them back into battle with better weapons, thicker armor, a higher level of morale.

In order to do so effectively, of course, they must analyze the victims carefully, dispassionately, objectively, scientifically, empathetically, mathematically, and hardheadedly, to see what made them so vulnerable in the first place.

What weapons, now, might they have lacked when they went into battle? Job skills? Education?

What armor was lacking that might have warded off their wounds? Better values? Habits of thrift and foresight?

And what might have ravaged their morale? Apathy? Ignorance? Deviant lower-class cultural patterns?

This is the solution of the dilemma, the solution of Blaming the Victim. And those who buy this solution with a sigh of relief are inevitably blinding themselves to the basic causes of the problems being addressed. They are, most crucially, rejecting the possibility of blaming, not the victims, but themselves. They are all unconsciously passing judgments on themselves and bringing in a unanimous verdict of Not Guilty.

If one comes to believe that the culture of poverty produces persons *fated* to be poor, who can find any fault with our corporation-dominated economy? And if the Negro family produces young men *incapable* of achieving equality, let's deal with that first before we go on to the task of changing the pervasive racism that informs and shapes and distorts our every social institution. And if unsatisfactory resolution of one's Oedipus complex accounts for all emotional distress and mental disorder, then by all means let us attend to that and postpone worrying about the pounding day-to-day stresses of life on the bottom rungs that drive so many to drink, dope, and madness.

That is the ideology of Blaming the Victim, the cunning Art of Savage Discovery. The tragic, frightening truth is that it is a mythology that is winning over the best people of our time, the very people who must resist this ideological temptation if we are to achieve nonviolent change in America.

2
Savage Discovery
in the Schools

The Folklore of
Cultural Deprivation

I

About five years ago, when the parents of Roxbury were struggling with Mrs. Louise Day Hicks over the quality of education in Boston schools, a friend of mine, a black woman, was concerned about how well her daughter could read. The girl seemed very bright, bright enough to read a good deal better than she was reading, so her mother went to the teacher to find out what might be wrong. The teacher was pleasant and affable and smiled reassuringly as she said, "Don't worry. Donna is doing very well, for this neighborhood." *For this neighborhood!* These three words sum up the central problem of public education. The teacher had been persuaded by her education professors, her supervisors, her fellow teachers, or all three, that children from "this neighborhood"—that is, poor children, black children—could not be expected to learn to read very well. If we were able to follow her to her classes in pedagogy or to look over her shoulder as she read an occasional article in a journal, we would discover further that she had been taught, not that Negro children are intellectually inferior (that one has gone out of style, at least in the North), but that they are "culturally deprived" as a result of their poverty and inadequate home background.

At that time, the favored solution for improving education for black children was school integration. Then Louise Day Hicks emerged on the scene and became chief of the forces in Boston battling against integration. She would say, over and over again, in her reasonable schoolgirl tones, "The culturally deprived children of Roxbury need education, not transportation." Assistant Superintendent of Schools Marguerite Sullivan, teaching the theory of cultural deprivation to a League of Women Voters audience, said, "These parents have no backgrounds. They're just a pair of hands." And the ineffable William O'Connor, Mrs. Hicks' kinsman and staunch supporter, on the occasion of his assuming chairmanship of the School Committee, fluted out the unbelievable statement, "We do not have inferior schools; we have been getting an inferior type of student."

Listening to these and similar maddening statements constituted my introduction to the political and ideological use of the cultural deprivation hypothesis, which is based on the formulation that the differences in educational achievement of poor as compared with middle class children—and, more specifically, differences between black and white children—are mediated by differences in home background. Uneducated parents, crowded living quarters, absence of books, family disinterest in education—all combine to handicap the poor black child as he enters the school system. There is a specific denial of any *innate* inferiority; rather there is perceived a *functional* inferiority that is attributable to the depressing and stultifying effects of living in poverty, which is, of course, condemned as bad and unjust.

It may be instructive to listen to the voice of the Boston Schools (the elegant prose is Miss Sullivan's) explaining what's wrong with poor children:

> Many of these children have low aspirational levels, lack those out-of-school experiences which are so richly provided when parents are in more favorable circumstances. . . . By virtue of their limited background (they) fail to meet the expected outcomes as defined in Curriculum Guides. . . . It is our hope to raise the achievement of these pupils closer to their potentials which have for too long been submerged by parental lack of values.[1]

The phrases carry a not-so-subtle prejudice—"limited background" and "parental lack of values." But this formulation is still well within the mainstream of cultural deprivationist rhetoric, as is the following description of a prekindergarten program in the same school system:

> The purpose of this program is to provide the youngsters with experiences which will make up for the deficiencies in their backgrounds which cause them to fail on the kindergarten and primary level. . . . Many youngsters come from homes where the necessary skills to cope with kindergarten curriculum have not been taught or developed. . . . (They) fall behind immediately and are likely to stay behind until they drop out of school. . . . Miss Catherine Maney, Coordinator of the program, states: "With most of these children we're starting off with a blank slate. Many of them don't really know who they are, or where they fit in. . . . Most of their parents don't talk to them. They lack the time—or the interest."[2]

Blank slates, silent, disinterested parents, and the dreadful inability to cope with the kindergarten *curriculum,* no less. Once again Nature imitates Art, and the old cartoon joke comes alive as Miss Maney prepares to flunk the youngsters in sand-box.

If this ideology were preached only by persons like Hicks and Sullivan, who are, in the long run, rather easily identified as racists, things would not be so bad. But in most formulations of cultural deprivationism there is genuine concern for the educational welfare of the ghetto child and a commitment to educational equality. A conscientious and committed superintendent has captured the essence of this point of view, with all its kindness and concern:

> A victim of his environment, the ghetto child begins his school career, psychologically, socially, and physically disadvantaged. He is oriented to the present rather than the future, to immediate needs rather than delayed gratification, to the concrete rather than the abstract. He is often handicapped by limited verbal skills, low self-esteem, and a stunted drive toward achievement.[3]

Upon moving from Boston to New Haven several years ago, we learned how pervasive and subtle the effect of this ideology is. Initially, New Haven's schools seemed to us far better than Boston's. The appointed school board was dominated by progressive, intelligent professional people, who had recently, we were told, integrated the junior and senior high schools. The new superintendent was coming fresh from his ennobling experience in a suburban system that had participated in a ghetto-to-suburb busing program. We were invited to a neighborhood meeting to become acquainted with this gentleman. On the subject of the difficulties in educating inner-city children, he said, with an ingratiating smile, "Your children" (meaning the children of you whites, you middle-class liberals, you professionals, you nice, neat, clean, ambitious, educated people) "could be locked up in a closet and they'd still learn. But these children . . ." What children? Inner-city children, poor children, then—of course—"culturally deprived" children. The tune was far more gentle and melodious than the harsh marching songs of Mrs. Hicks, but the message was the same, as we quickly learned when our daughter began to provide us with perceptive reports.

The schools were integrated? Up to a point—the point being the doorway of the classroom—because New Haven had fallen head over heels in love with the tracking system. "Culturally deprived" children were, of course, put in the low tracks; "our" children in the high. The top track might contain three or four middle class black kids, the bottom track one or two white faces. Racism and unequal treatment were abundant, teachers' expectations and performances in black classes were low (echoes of "in this neighborhood"!), the staff was crowded with people planning programs to shape up the inner-city children, and about one-third of high school sophomores were functionally illiterate. The New Haven schools turned out to be about as bad as Boston's, despite all the progressive polish and enlightened rhetoric, and the barbaric teachers from Kozol's Gibson School could transfer to Welch, or Day, or Winchester in New Haven and feel perfectly at home. If you've seen one culturally deprived child, as Vice-President Agnew might well have said, you've seen them all.

This is the folklore of cultural deprivation as it is used in an ideological fashion to preserve the core of the *status quo* in urban education—to forestall any questioning about the fundamental problems of recruiting and training teachers, achieving racial integration, and, in particular, governing the school system. Waving this banner, educationists can advocate Head Start, smaller classes, More Effective Schools, "scatteration" to the suburbs by one-way busing, teaching machines, or Swahili—almost anything that involves changing or manipulating or treating the *child*. They fight to the death any proposal that implies there might be anything at all wrong with the teacher or the teaching, and resist any exploration of, or intrusion into, the monopolistic control of public education by the teaching profession, particularly if it implies participation in decision-making by laymen from the community.

There are, of course, great discrepancies between the dogma of cultural deprivationism and the findings that have emerged from the ingenious, but rather scanty research from which it allegedly is derived.[4]

They found that lower class children, particularly lower class minority children, have had less exposure than middle class children to certain kinds of experiences that are helpful in the school situation. What kind of experiences? We are by no means sure, but they seem to be related to hearing, talking, and seeing. Middle class youngsters see and hear a greater variety of things that are important for school work. In the judgment of many observers, this qualifying clause—"that are important for school work"—is quite significant. Middle class kids are better able to distinguish between words that sound alike, are better able to perceive colors and shapes, and, in imitating their parents' speech, have learned to talk in a style similar to that of most teachers. Thus, the middle class child is somewhat better prepared for the school experience than is the lower class child. But it would not be unreasonable to present this proposition in its reversed form: The school is better prepared for the middle class child than for the lower class child. Indeed, we could be tempted to say further that the school experience is tailored for, and stacked in favor of, the middle class child. The cause-and-effect relationship between the lack of skills and experiences found among lower class children and the conditions of lower class life has yet to be delineated. So far, explanations of this relationship have been, at best, sketchy, and have been based on casual observation. We know poor and middle class children exhibit certain differences in styles of talking and thinking, but we do not know yet why or how these differences occur.

We do know, however, that these differences—really differences in *style* rather than ability—are not handicaps or disabilities (unlike such barriers to learning as poor vision, mild brain damage, emotional disturbance or orthopedic handicap). They do represent inadequate *preparation* for the reality of the modern urban school. They are, in no sense, cultural or intellectual deficits.

Finally, we can illustrate that these differences are relatively small by noting that a short pre-school experience goes a long way toward wiping out gaps in preparatory skills; in fact, nursery school or kindergarten attendance is one of the most significant predictors of whether or not a child—lower or middle class—will get off on the right foot in school. The pilot demonstrations of Deutsch and others have shown that a carefully-organized experience prior to entering kindergarten or first grade brought lower class children to a state of readiness approximately equal to that of middle class children and produced interesting side effects, such as marked improvement in performance on intelligence tests. Capitalizing on these demonstrations, the Head Start program applied this principle to poor children across the country and obtained generally good results.

But pre-school preparation, for all its popularity and usefulness, has not dealt with the central problem of inferior slum schools, particularly those in the Negro ghetto, and the gains of Head Start have been washed away when the children moved into the regular public school system. (The essential irrelevance of the cultural deprivation hypothesis to the basic problem of the urban schools is starting to become very clear.)

This is not to minimize either the dreadful, crippling effects of poverty and segregation or the important research done by Deutsch and others.[5] It is intended to point up that distortions of these rather narrow, preliminary, and highly technical research findings are used to blame the ghetto child for the failure of ghetto schools and to divert attention from the inadequacies of the ghetto schools and teachers. This is illustrated most dramatically (and expensively) in the conclusions to be found in the Coleman Report. But before turning to that document, we should say something about two additional elements of cultural deprivation folklore— Negroes are not interested in education, and Negro children are "nonverbal."

Attitude surveys have shown consistently that Negroes have an enormous commitment to learning, and census figures show tremendous leaps in educational achievement. Significantly, the *rate* at which Negroes are increasing their educational level is greater than that of whites. For example, in 1920 the median level of school grade completed by blacks over the age of twenty-five was 5.4. By 1960 this figure had *doubled* to 10.8. During the same period the increase for whites was from 8.5 to 12.3, only a 45% increase. In recent years, the rate of increase for whites has been slowing down while for blacks, it has remained quite rapid. This projection will be readily verifiable when the 1970 census figures are compiled. A continuation of past trends would result in a figure close to 12.0 for blacks and between 12.5 and 13.0 for whites.

There is more immediate evidence in the tutoring programs flourishing in the big-city ghettoes of the North. Thousands and thousands of Negro families arrange tutoring for their children because they despair of their children ever learning enough in school. And no matter how many hundreds of college students and others swarm into the ghetto to tutor children, the demand always exceeds the supply. Does this reflect an indifference to, or a hunger for, learning?

As another example, let me refer to the second school boycott in Boston, in February 1964. The boycott was called by the Massachusetts Freedom Movement led by James Breeden and Noel Day, as one of a series of actions protesting continued segregation and neglect in the schools of the black community. As part of the demonstration it was decided to establish one-day freedom schools in churches and settlements throughout the community to give the children a taste of relevant education, and to give the city an example of exciting education in the ghetto. We organized thirty-three schools and seven stand-by schools, including "principals" and "faculty" who prepared lesson plans and teaching materials carefully. We were hoping that most of the black children would participate in the boycott and, further, that at least three or four thousand of them would not only take the day off (no hardship for most kids), but would also come to Freedom School.

My assignment in this demonstration was to manage the deployment of children from several gathering-points to the thirty or forty freedom schools. We had rented a dozen buses and had a fair number of people working on the mechanics of moving the children. We were smugly confident of our ability to handle as many as five thousand freedom students (the most wildly optimistic prediction of attendance was four thousand).

On the day of the boycott, more than ninety per cent of black children stayed out of school. Ten thousand came to Freedom School. Ten thousand children—from first-graders to high school seniors—came, to learn something for a change. We were overwhelmed. New locations had to be found; surprised principals were drafted for duty as they walked in the door; what seemed like a plague of yellow buses was crisscrossing the streets of Roxbury. When things finally settled down, when all the schools were operating, materials and lesson plans had been delivered, extra lunches had been ordered, the itinerary of some of the touring faculty stars—including Bishop Stokes, Bill Russell, and the late Gordon Allport—had been rescheduled, and the pickup schedules to bring the kids back from Freedom School had been prepared, it was well into the afternoon. I trotted into one of the classrooms, wanting at least to see what it was like, even for the last five or ten minutes.

It was astonishing. The classroom might have held forty, even fifty children comfortably. There must have been a hundred there—sitting on the floor, on window sills, sitting two-to-a-seat—listening intently, questioning, debating, comparing, doubting. When two-thirty came and time for dismissal, they roared a protest. They wanted more. It was as if they were trying to gulp and chew a lifetime of learning in one day.

Since that day, no one has been able to tell me that black children are indifferent to education. To their schools and their teachers, perhaps—it must be hard for them to keep their anger at such a low level of visibility that it can be mistaken for apathy or indifference—but not to education.

Think how infuriating the accusation of indifference must be to members of the black community. It has been the Negro, after all, who has protested that his children are being deprived of education. Those to whom he complains reply by accusing him of not caring about the education of his children, and, so pervasive is the myth, such demagoguery passes unchallenged by society at large.

Examination of the question of "nonverbal" poor children reveals again that the truth is almost diametrically opposed to the myth. It is common for teachers and psychologists to report—sometimes quite petulantly—that slum children, particularly Negro slum children, don't talk, answer in monosyllables and are extremely inarticulate. They conclude, from their interactions with the slum child, that the child is nonverbal. Another observer, particularly one who has seen and heard the same child in the street or on the playground, might conclude that the child doesn't trust the psychologist. Away from the eyes of their middle class overseers, poor children are far from nonverbal.

Again, this is a misconception that is easily dismissed by the evidence presented directly to one's own eyes and ears, as well as by the results of formal research. Consider, for example, the many ways in which language is enriched by means of the verbal styles of the poor, by their ability to create fresh and vivid new words and new meanings for old ones. After all, slang—especially lower class speech—keeps language alive and growing.

Serious students of language (as it relates to social class) have dealt, not with simple-minded concepts like "verbal" and "nonverbal," but rather with issues of style and of differing ways of using and relating to language.

The middle class child can be labeled as more "verbal"

than the slum child, or he can be labeled more "word-bound." Both labels refer to the same phenomenon—the middle class child is more comfortable with, and skilled in using, words *as words;* the lower class child is more comfortable with words as they relate to actions, feelings. The middle class child says a rock is a stone; a lower class child says a rock is hard, and you throw it.

Often it has been found that middle class children can define more words than lower class children. They can define words like "kangaroo" and "harp" and "caboose." Lower class children don't usually know what those words mean. Is it important for children going to school to be able to define "caboose"? It is very important, not for functional reasons, but because teachers make simple-minded judgments about who is "verbal" and who is "nonverbal" and, more important, treat children accordingly.

It is amusing to speculate what would happen if the tables were turned and slum children were to test the verbal abilities of teachers and psychologists by choosing a list of words for *us* to define. A taste of the results of such a test is available to parents of teenage children. Teenagers are constantly exasperated by the inability of their nonverbal parents to understand the meaning of what are, to them, everyday words. In fact, the teenagers' concept of "square" (if the term is still in use), when they talk about their parents, is almost identical to the concept of "cultural deprivation" as it is used by educational bureaucrats. In both cases it reflects an extremely self-centered and rigid way of looking at their world. Fortunately, with teenagers, it's a phase they grow out of.

Let me present an example of naive interpretation of research. The test is this: the child is shown four pictures—a policeman, a doctor, a farmer, and a sailor. He is asked why the four pictures go together, what they have in common. This is what is known as a test of concept formation, a test of the ability to generalize, to form categories and concepts —skills that are very much related to verbal performance. The middle class first-grader tends to pass the test with flying colors; he comes up with a good, acceptable concept or category by saying that they are all men or they are all people. This gives great joy to the person who is giving the test, and he smiles approvingly at the little boy.

Now, when the lower class child sees the four pictures, he might say they go together because the doctor helps the other men and gives medicine to them; or, he might say something really silly—they go together because they *like* each other. That answer really makes the test-giver frown. It seems pretty dumb; it shows a failure to abstract, to form categories; it's just experiential.

Does this mean that the child doesn't *know* they're all men? Or all people? Of course he knows it; it's perfectly obvious. But he is not oriented to relating words to other *words*. He gets down to far more fundamental issues. He asks what these four men might do to each other. Do they like each other? Or hate each other? Will they help or harm each other? These are, after all, important questions in life. If they are largely irrelevant to the school situation, how relevant is the school situation to life?

II

We come now to the Coleman Report, the U.S. Office of Education document officially titled *Equality of Educational Opportunity*,[6] an impeccably liberal and scientific work, which quickly acquired the reputation of being comprehensive, incisive research upon which the solution to the problem of city schools must be based. It is, for example, the foundation upon which Nixon's new education program is built. The Coleman study is one of the largest single pieces of social science research ever conducted—at least in terms of money, the use of highly skilled manpower, and the quantity of data assembled. In over 4,000 different schools throughout the country, 645,000 students and 20,000 teachers answered questionnaires and tests that produced millions of pieces of information that had to be processed through computers and elaborate statistical procedures to produce this enormous volume. To plan, execute, analyze, and report on such a study in a mere two years was an astonishing feat, a masterpiece of logistical virtuosity in research administration fully justifying Professor Coleman's shining reputation as a methodological and statistical wizard.

Unfortunately, the report is also a triumph of sophisticated research design over common sense.

The study addressed four questions: Are schools segregated? Are schools that are attended by differing groups equal? Do students from differing groups achieve differently? What is the relationship between achievement and the nature of the schools attended? The first two questions are, in a sense, superfluous; the answers are well known and not in any sense in dispute. Nevertheless, Coleman spends chart after chart and table after table demonstrating that schools are indeed segregated, then more charts and tables showing that schools attended by whites and blacks are by no means equal in facilities, programs, or expenditures.

The answer to the third question—do differing ethnic groups differ in school achievement—is also well-known and well-documented; but it remains, in fact, the central phenomenon to be discussed. The stir about segregated schools, ghetto schools, compensatory education, integration, and now community control, swirls around the fact that black children learn less in school than white children do. Coleman nails this down with a barrage of statistics and notes what all other observers have noted: that the gap between white and black children—relatively small in the early grades— grows larger and larger in the later grades.

Despite all of Coleman's confirming evidence (which is spelled out in an inordinate number of pages, graphs and tables), he doesn't reach the heart of the problem. *Why* don't black children perform as well? On this question Coleman's report is most disappointing. First of all, his data are correlational; he reports only what characteristics of children and schools go along with, are found together with, differing levels of achievement. While his findings are instructive, they cast little light on the causes of differing levels of achievement.

For example, Coleman discloses that color and ethnicity have a major effect on learning. In other words, blackness and low achievement are highly correlated; or put in its most elegant form, black children learn less than white children since it is clear that white children learn more than black children. In Coleman's view, this relationship is so predominant that it must be *controlled for*. (I had hoped that he might investigate it, rather than control for it.) This means, difficult as it may be to believe, that in seeking for additional factors related to achievement, the researchers dealt with different racial groups *separately*. Coleman tries to explain why he adopted this strategy:

> . . . it is important to make clear why the racial groups were kept separate in the analysis. When achievement differs as

much as it does between these groups, then to analyze the groups together, without controlling for race or ethnicity of the student, would cause any school characteristics highly associated with race or ethnicity to show a spurious relation to achievement.[7]

What Coleman did is, in general, perfectly standard procedure. In research of this kind, when a number of factors are potentially related to the variable being studied—in this case achievement—it is absolutely sound to find the factor with the largest correlation and to control it, to take it out of the picture as you go on to examine additional factors. That is to say, it is statistically sound; however, from a practical point of view it is an outstanding example of methodological requirements overcoming the dictates of common sense.

For many years observers from all camps have agreed that black students achieve at lower levels than white students. This has been, not a matter of dispute, but, rather, the central burning fact that has engendered the series of policy controversies that have raged in the field of public education— first about desegregation and de facto integration, then about compensatory education, and now about community control and decentralization. The relevant outcome factor, the important variable to be explained—what is called the dependent variable—was *not* educational achievement in the abstract, but rather the black-white *gap* in educational achievement. This is what should have been studied, this is what had to be explained. Removing it from the equation, controlling for race, and analyzing black and white educational achievement *separately* made the report itself—no matter how elegant in the scientific sense—almost irrelevant politically. Its findings, then, are frustratingly ambiguous and unenlightening.

One of the findings—that "family background" is also correlated with school achievement—is also well-known, but in fact, it was taken as an assumption by the researchers. They say, for example, that "the larger part of school-to-school variation in achievement appears to be not a consequence of effects of school variations at all but of variations in family backgrounds of the entering student bodies."[8] They began with this finding as a previously established fact: "Studies of school achievement have consistently shown that variations in family background account for far more variation in school achievement than do variations in school characteristics. Because of these important family differences, the general approach to be taken will be to examine effects of school variation after taking account of the effects of background differences between children."[9]

Controlling for race and family background, the investigators find that "variations in school quality are not highly related to variations in achievement of pupils." The relatively small effect attributed to differences between schools is allocated to three factors, in descending order of importance: differences in the character of the student body, differences in teachers, and, of little significance, differences in facilities, programs, resources, and curriculum. On the last point, Coleman concludes, "Differences in school facilities and curriculum, which are the major variables by which attempts are made to improve schools, are so little related to differences in achievement level of students that, with few exceptions, their effects fail to appear even in a survey of this magnitude."[10]

Considering what he controlled, I must say that I am not surprised at this finding. What he did—if I may translate from methodologese—was to compare school expenditures among schools in white, upper-middle class areas—for example, schools in Scarsdale, Shaker Heights and Newton—to see if the variations in expenditures were reflected in differing levels of achievement among the children in that set of cities. Then he made a separate comparison of expenditures in poor black neighborhood schools—say, in Harlem, Hough, and Roxbury. He found that variations in expenditures made very little difference. However, he did not compare, in a direct and primary fashion, Scarsdale with Harlem, Hough with Shaker Heights, and Roxbury with Newton, on the grounds that the children in these schools were so markedly different in color and social class (factors which, in themselves, were already known to be highly related to achievement) that the results would be "spurious." So, according to this maddening logic, it only *seems* important that Newton students have perhaps twice as much money spent on their education as Roxbury students do—the real cause of the difference in achievement is the color and class of those students.

This massive exercise in statistical purism, in 737 pages of huge double-columns, has managed to disguise as *findings* what amounts to nothing more than an enormously inflated *restatement of the problem!*

One is reminded of a story about a patient with strange symptoms: his left eye was watering all the time, he had a subnormal temperature and the toes on his right foot cramped whenever he walked upstairs. It was a troublesome affliction for the patient so he visited a doctor. The doctor, who had never heard of such a collection of symptoms, found this strange disease a source of great curiosity and intellectual stimulation. He was scribbling the history and description of symptoms on the chart, leaping up every few minutes to pull medical texts down from his library shelves. He leafed through them rapidly, making notes as he did so, becoming more and more puzzled and intrigued at the same time. Finally he asked the patient, "Did you ever have this before?"

"Yes, in 1962 on my summer vacation." "Aha!" the doctor leaped up in triumph. "Aha! *You've got it again!*"

It was, of course, a flawlessly logical diagnosis.

The second major criticism I would offer is that the Coleman Report treats the *relationship* of family background to school achievement as, in fact, a cause-and-effect relationship.

In other words, when Coleman finds that lower class children do poorly and middle class children do well, and, further, that the general class level of the classroom and the school is related to level of achievement, he concludes that the class factor—attending a school that is largely for poor kids or largely for affluent kids—is a *cause* of good or poor achievement. This is faulty reasoning and not scientifically acceptable. Because the investigators approached the data with that particular orientation, this conclusion seemed so plausible as to be obvious. But it would have been exactly as plausible to conclude that the relationship between color and achievement is a cause-and-effect relationship, to decide that black children learn less because they are black. Coleman, of course, does not even consider such a conclusion, since it is obviously based on a racist assumption.[11] The point I am trying to make is that the nature of the available evidence for the two possible conclusions is exactly the same. The investigators, while implicitly rejecting the racist conclusion, explicitly accept what might be termed the cultural deprivation conclusion. This acceptance of the cultural deprivation hypothesis as a given—which has been suggested in several of the quotations cited above—is evident throughout the report in sentences like, "Obviously, a large part of this disadvantage arises from the background culture from which these groups come."[12] There is no question that children of low socio-economic background do less well in school; that they do less well *because* of that low socio-economic background is not at all clear, and the evidence in the Coleman Report on this point is scanty and equivocal, and doesn't really illuminate the problem at all.

A specific example of the kind of bias in evidence—which, doubtless, is not at all conscious and is guided largely by statistical requirements—can be cited as my third criticism. In speaking of the characteristics of the student body as the major *school* factor that influences achievement, the researchers have chosen two measures by which to judge these characteristics: what they call "educational background"—measured by whether there is an encyclopedia in the home, and "educational motivation"—measured by whether the student has concrete plans to attend college. As has been indicated, these two items are used as primary indices of the composition of the student body, which in turn is viewed as a major influence on achievement. For example, in analyzing the issue of integration, the report states, "The apparent beneficial effect of a student body with a high proportion of white students comes not from racial composition per se, but from the better educational background and higher educational aspirations that are, on the average, found among white students."[13] Keep in mind that "better educational background" means having an encyclopedia in the home, and "higher educational aspirations" means having plans made to attend college.

A first, minor point is the contrast between the fact that books and encyclopedias and libraries *in the school* supposedly have no effect on achievement, but encyclopedias on the bookshelves in the *homes* of one's *classmates* supposedly do influence achievement. This must be considered another example of methodology conquering common sense. Looking

49

at the data, however, raises more important questions. The researchers used a number of items to measure educational background, including: newspapers in the home, educational level of father and mother, books in the home and, of course, encyclopedia in the home—(on all of which whites did somewhat better than Negroes); in addition, they measured parents' interest in children's progress in school, parents' reading to children, parents' efforts to motivate children to do well, and parents' attendance at PTA meetings (on all of which Negroes did substantially better than whites). It is interesting that, of all these items, the research team chose the presence of an encyclopedia as their index—an item that favors whites, is a measure of economic ability, and is about the most static factor of all. It would seem that parent activity would be considered more relevant.

So much for "educational background." As to "educational motivation," again, a large number of items were used, on most of which there was little or no difference between whites and blacks. On a couple—such as having concrete plans to go to college—whites excelled. On quite a few others—including number of books read over the summer, desire to excel in classwork, *wish* to go to college and amount of homework done—Negroes scored better. Again the item selected as an index of motivation is one of the few that favors whites and is most influenced by economic status— going to college, after all, requires not only the desire for higher education, but the cash to pay the tuition.

The way Professor Coleman deals with the obvious paradoxes that necessarily arise from this kind of selection and manipulation of data constitutes the subject of my fourth criticism. He is, of course, soon confronted with the fact that, on the one hand, he counts the desire for education as a positive influence on achievement while, on the other hand, he notes that Negro parents and pupils demonstrate, if anything, more motivation and desire for schooling than do whites, but wind up with less. How does he treat this highly suggestive contradiction—a contradiction, incidentally, that has impressed almost every observer of the urban educational scene? I will quote Coleman, without comment, and let the reader judge:

> "These reports, *even if exaggerated,* [my emphasis] indicate that the Negro children, their parents, or both, are highly directed toward the school system as a means toward social mobility. The general pattern that the reports show of parents highly interested in their educational success, is probably correct. It is evident, however, that this interest often does not get translated into action which supports the child's work in school."[14]

> "[The data] gives a picture of students who report high interest in academic achievement, but whose reported interest is not translated through effective action into achievement."[15]

> "Most striking differences are the especially high level of motivation, interest, and aspirations reported by Negro students. These data are difficult to reconcile with the facts of Negroes' lower rates of completion of school, and lower college-going rate. They appear to show at least one thing: Negroes are especially strongly oriented toward the school as a path for mobility. This finding is consistent with other research that has shown greater aspirations for college among Negroes than among whites of comparable economic levels. But the results suggest as well a considerable *lack of realism* [emphasis added] in aspirations, especially among Negroes whose responses deviate most from actual rates of college-going and completion of high school."[16]

Is this, or is this not, a clear case of blaming the victim? My fifth criticism is that Coleman did not look at all for:

the way in which the system, the school and the classroom are organized; the atmosphere; the attitudes, prejudices and expectations of teachers and administrators; the interactions and relationships between teachers and pupils in the classroom. He obtained all information about a given school from questionnaire responses provided by that school's principal. The scanty information about teachers he obtained in like manner. In short, he spent most of his time counting the obvious and essentially no time researching what many observers and educators feel are the central issues.

I cannot refrain from a final criticism (even though the matter in question probably did not bias the results in any gross way). Although Coleman talks continually about "achievement," he used a criterion which is not a test of achievement at all, but rather is a highly biased and totally inadequate measure of intelligence—vocabulary knowledge.

That's the Coleman Report: millions of taxpayers' dollars spent, millions of correlations calculated, dozens of gratuitous speculations and preconceptions formulated, and virtually no light shed on the subject.

III

Fortunately, there has been some good research done on the problem of ghetto education.

Typically, a survey of the research related to these issues reveals (as the analysis of the Coleman Report in the previous section was designed to show) that the results are simply a restatement of the basic dimensions of the problem. Usually, too, the speculations and conclusions offered are not supported by the findings but give great comfort to the cultural deprivationists. Also, used in this way, the findings could be turned to the use of psychologists like Garrett,[17] Shuey,[18] and Jensen,[19] who still hold to the belief that Negroes have lower average intelligence levels than whites.

A great deal of the relevant research that goes beyond endlessly repeated descriptions of the surface aspects of the problem—that tries to analyze the causes of the black-white educational gap—can be tied together to support the following linked hypotheses: first, that the *effect* of poverty, race, and family background can be observed to a small extent in the minds of the children but to a much greater extent in the interactions in the classroom, which ultimately produces a falling off of academic performance; second, that the primary effect of poverty, race, and family background is not on the children, but on the teacher, who is led to *expect* poorer performance from black and poor children (when such children make up the great bulk of the class, the teacher's expectations are even more pessimistic); and finally, that the expectations of the teacher are a major determinant of the children's performances.

In the social sciences, crucial experiments are rare. It is not usually possible to exercise the kinds of controls or to develop an incisive research design that will permit one to ask of the data, "Is it 'Yes' or is it 'No'?" But such a study *has* been done on the topic of cultural deprivation. It has been rather widely read, but it has been heeded very little. I am referring to a study on the Harlem schools, designed and conducted by James Jones, Kenneth Clark and the staff of the Haryou Planning Project.[20] I replicated the study in the schools of Boston and achieved almost identical results.[21]

Most expositions of the cultural deprivation hypothesis have been somewhat euphemistic, in that those called culturally deprived are usually black and the supposedly nonculturally deprived are white. Jones and Clark reasoned that if the cultural deprivation theory were, in fact, valid, it should also apply *within* a population of all black or predominantly black schools. The obvious fact that there is great social, economic, educational and cultural variability within the Negro community itself is often forgotten or overlooked. Only a minority of black children can be identified as "culturally deprived," by whatever criterion may be used—income, quality of housing, intactness of family, educational level of parents, presence of books in the home, etc. The majority of black children—and all of poor children—live with both of their parents. The father works steadily and brings in an income that is above the poverty line. Substantial numbers of Negro families are quite affluent and are headed by well-educated fathers in the professions or in other middle class and upper class occupations. Of course in Harlem (and in the Roxbury section of Boston) there are schools where great numbers, even the majority, of the children can be counted as "culturally deprived"—they are very poor, they live in substandard housing and their families are headed only by the mother, who is often dependent on welfare. But there are schools in other neighborhoods where most of the children would be counted as lower-middle class. They are not poor, though only a few of them are affluent; their mothers and fathers are both at home; their housing is adequate; their parents are usually high school graduates, sometimes college graduates; they have access to books and encyclopedias in the home. In no meaningful sense could the children in these schools be called culturally deprived.

If the cultural deprivation theory were valid, a comparison between these two kinds of schools should show systematic differences despite the fact that both groups of schools are predominantly black. On such educational indices as reading achievement tests, the obvious mythical patterns should appear. In the "culturally deprived" schools, the children should be slower and less able in learning how to read; as they move along from grade to grade, the achievement gap between them and their better-off cousins up the hill should grow larger and larger. This is the pattern that would be predicted by the cultural deprivation theory. What, in fact, happens?

In both Harlem and Roxbury, the pattern is remarkably similar, and it does not follow the theoretical curve. In early grades—second, third and fourth—there are no significant differences between the presumably culturally deprived children and the others. In Boston, as a matter of fact, the so-called culturally deprived children in the second grade read slightly better than the middle class children, although the difference was not statistically significant.

In the fifth and sixth grades, however, the expectations start to come true—the culturally deprived children begin to fall behind. And by the eighth grade the differences are large and clear-cut. The performance of the children has finally been made to fit the theory.

This is a very puzzling, yet interesting, set of results. Let me recapitulate the paradoxes. In the early grades when, presumably, the effect of the home background—and the cultural deprivation or advantage—are greatest, there is little or no difference in reading performance between children in the two kinds of schools. But four or five years later, when the influence of the school has had a chance to take effect, the "culturally deprived" child shows his expected reading deficit. Clearly, whatever mechanism accounts for these strange findings is found primarily in the interaction of the school with the child.

On the basis of a large quantity of data on the expectations of the teachers in the Harlem schools—their estimates of the academic potentials of their pupils, how many children would be dropouts, how many would graduate from high school, how many would receive academic diplomas—the Haryou staff concluded that the main dynamic in the school situation was the teacher's attitude—the belief that the children sitting in the classroom were essentially uneducable "because of their backgrounds." The authors of *Youth in the Ghetto* conclude:

"Less is expected of such pupils; they are rewarded for poorer performance, and the result is a steadily increasing gap between what they accomplish and what pupils at their grade level should accomplish."

Estelle Fuchs[22] has conducted a careful study of how these expectations are actually implanted in the minds of new teachers. She asked the teachers going into poor schools to keep a diary of their experiences in school and then analyzed the entries in the diaries as they changed over time. The diaries mirrored how new teachers are influenced and socialized by the veteran teachers, how their initial high expectations and enthusiasm are damped and ultimately destroyed, how they learn to expect that the children will do poorly, how their enthusiasm is transformed into boredom and disgust.

Let me quote briefly from a diary kept by one of Professor Fuchs' students. First, read an entry from an early optimistic period, dated October 26:

> Mrs. Jones, the sixth-grade teacher, and I were discussing reading problems and I said, "I wonder about my children. They don't seem too slow; they seem average. Some of them even seem to be above average. I can't understand how they can grow up to fifth- and sixth-graders and still be reading on the second-grade level. It seems absolutely amazing."

Mrs. Jones explained about the environmental problems these children have. "Some of them never see a newspaper. Some of them have never been on the subway. The parents are so busy having parties and things that they have no time for their children. They can't even take them to a museum or anything. It's very important that the teacher stress books" . . . she said that the educational problem lies with the parents. They are the ones that have to be educated.[23]

Compare this with the last entry in this teacher's diary, at the end of the school year:

> I believe my school is a pretty good school. It isn't in the best neighborhood. There are many, many problems in my school but on the whole I think that the teachers and the administrators work together and I do believe that they are doing the best they can with the problems that are around.
>
> You have to remember that in a school such as ours the children are not as ready and willing to learn as in schools in middle-class neighborhoods.[24]

These and many other studies and descriptions demonstrate beyond doubt that teachers in ghetto schools are, in fact, imbued with these kinds of expectations and attitudes. They expect that the children will do poorly and, ultimately, their expectations are borne out. What does this prove? It proves nothing. It is only a relationship, a correlational finding. It is consistent with the hypothesis that low expectations *produce* poor performance; however, it is also consistent with the hypothesis that the teachers are good predictors of academic potential.

So the correlation is consistent with the hypothesis that I have advanced, but it does not support it unequivocally. It remained for Robert Rosenthal[25] to demonstrate once and for all that teachers' expectations do in fact have a dramatic effect on the classroom and the test performances of school children.

The design of this brilliant Rosenthal experiment was sneaky and elegant. The crucial element in it was to persuade the teachers that specified pupils in their classes could be expected to show a marked academic improvement during the course of the year. He did this by giving a new intelligence test to all children; he described it to the teachers as a test designed to predict and identify academic "bloomers" or "spurters." He randomly designated about one child out of five as a "spurter." He and his fellow experimenters casually passed on this information to the teachers and then sat back and waited. This was the total extent of their intervention in the schools; they told a white lie about the "blooming potential" of a group of pupils who were, in fact, not different in any way from their classmates. Tests were repeated several times during the course of the year to determine the effect of the false structuring of the teachers' expectations.

The results were eye-opening. The fake "bloomers" did, in fact, *bloom*. Depending on the grade they were in, they showed average gains of up to twenty-seven points in I.Q. scores. In comparison with the control group—those about whom nothing was said—the "spurters" showed significantly greater improvement. But the control group *also* showed gains that were considerable, though of nowhere near the proportions of the experimental group. Further, in the classrooms where the experimental group gained the most, the other children gained proportionately more. The effect of expectation apparently "radiates." There is an expectational fall-out, as it were. (This may be the key to the differential achievement of poor children and black children when they are in segregated settings as against when they are in heterogeneous settings. A few years ago, when the push for school integration was still strong, Negro parents who had no great desire to have their children mix socially with whites expressed the same idea in more earthy terms: "If my son is sitting in a classroom with white kids, there's no guarantee that he'll learn more, but I sure as hell know that he'll be *taught* more!")

Rosenthal and his associate, Lenore Jacobson, found other interesting attitudinal changes. The teachers rated the "spurters" as more curious, more interesting, more appealing, and better adjusted than the others. There was clearly a generalization of positive attitudes. On the other hand, control children ("non-spurters," as it were) who showed substantial but unexpected academic improvement and gains in I.Q. were rated more *negatively* by the teachers. They were seen as less curious, less appealing, more maladjusted. And if such children were in "slow-track" classes, these attitudes were more exaggerated. In other words, such children who do well—*in contradiction* to the teachers' expectations—are viewed as difficult and as likely adjustment problems. (Is it possible that we have here a germinal insight into the growing problem of what ghetto teachers call the "disruptive child?" Could the disruptive child be a modern version of the "uppity nigger"?)

The conclusion to be drawn from the Rosenthal experiment is that teacher expectations are, in fact, a major contributing factor to pupil performance. It takes no great leap of logic to conclude further that the pervasively low teacher expectations found in slum and ghetto schools must be a major cause of the poor achievement in those schools. The anecdotal and descriptive evidence offered by such writers as Fuchs, Kozol, Herbert Kohl, Edgar Friedenberg, and Jeremy Larner confirm this conclusion. The hypothesis developed by Clark, Jones, and the Haryou staff from the findings of their study seems to be confirmed by this additional data.

On this basis, we can refine and alter our understanding of

the problem of ghetto education. We are dealing, it would seem, not so much with culturally deprived children as with culturally depriving schools. And the task to be accomplished is not to revise, and amend, and repair deficient children but to alter and transform the atmosphere and operations of the schools to which we commit these children. Only by changing the nature of the educational experience can we change its product. To continue to define the difficulty as inherent in the raw material—the children—is plainly to blame the victim and to acquiesce in the continuation of educational inequality in America.

3
Mammy Observed
Fixing the Negro Family

I

The only time my name ever came up for discussion in the columns of *The New York Times* was during the weeks in the fall of 1965 when the controversy surrounding the document known as the *Moynihan Report,*[1] on the subject of the Negro Family, was at its height. It happened that I was one of the first to criticize the report publicly and became identified as one of the main opponents of Moynihan in the ensuing debate. Struck by the similarity between the cultural deprivation mythology and that being projected by Moynihan (and by what I then began to see as the more general ideology that I have now formulated as Blaming the Victim), I wrote a lengthy critique which was rather widely distributed in civil rights circles and which provided the basis for two magazine articles.[2] My memorandum and articles, along with articles by Benjamin Payton, James Farmer, and others,[3] together with the activities of these and other leaders of the movement, temporarily derailed the Moynihan Report. But an ideology like Moynihan's resonates so perfectly with the mood and purposes of the public and of its intellectual leaders, who perform the task of composing and conveying the official wisdom of the day, that it is as hard to slay as the Hydra. Moynihan's critics appeared to win the battle— the subject of the Negro Family was stricken from the agenda of the 1966 White House Conference and the chairman of the Planning Conference in November 1965 prefaced his remarks by saying, "I want you to know that I have been reliably informed that no such person as Daniel Patrick Moynihan exists." But Moynihan clearly won the war. Subsequent articles, reviews and columns in *Life, Look, The New York Times* and other influential publications supported and adopted the Moynihan thesis and swamped the opposition, which by that time had grown to be a substantial group of critics, most of them trained social scientists.[4]

Moynihan was able to take a subject that had previously been confined to the Sociology Department seminar room, filled with aromatic smoke from judiciously puffed pipes, and bring it into a central position in popular American thought, creating a whole new set of group stereotypes which support the notion that Negro culture produces a weak and disorganized form of family life, which in turn is a major factor in maintaining Negro inequality.

On its face, this seems to have a certain plausibility. The stereotypes appear to be, if not actually benign, at least lacking in malice, and, to a surprisingly large number of thoughtful and educated people, rather self-evident, requiring little in the way of proof or intellectual underpinning. Moreover, it is very easy to find expressions of what I have termed group stereotypes, both in journalistic and in essentially scientific (or at least arithmetical) contexts.

In August of 1965, for example, the still confidential report was heralded by an "inside dope" article in *Newsweek* that included the following paragraphs:

> A Negro child has a hazardous life. For one thing, his parents are likely to be divorced or living apart. . . . For another, the Negro child is fairly likely to be illegitimate. . . . In addition the Negro child is far more likely to be a relief recipient. . . . He is normally unsuccessful in school. . . . He has trouble getting a job . . . and he is so psychologically and educationally bankrupt he can't escape to the armed forces. These and other characteristics of lower class Negroes are symptomatic of an ailment that began with slavery. . . .
>
> Slavemasters began the process by denying Negroes the sacrament of marriage, by breaking up families on the auction block. . . . Thus scarred by history, the Negro family was already fragile by the eve of the great black Diaspora to the cities. The Negro came to the city for factory work . . . and found, instead, "catastrophic" unemployment rates. . . . Negro women . . . are forced to take jobs thus undermining the man's role as breadwinner. . . . The father stays on as an ineffectual dependent or he drifts off, perhaps to the few remaining places where a ravaged man can assert his manhood: In the bedroom or on the street. Either way the model he presents to his sons is one of futility, alienation, and despair. Family discipline breaks down—and so does performance.[5]

With so much journalistic attention focused on it, the report surfaced as a solid document, complete with a Government Printing Office number and a very modest price (forty-five cents). Those who had been alarmed and concerned by the advance reports were appalled by the emphasis in *The Negro Family* on the handicapping effect of the supposedly deviant Negro family and by the implication that efforts to end discrimination and to achieve the goals of the civil rights movement were futile in the face of a central weakness in the Negro community:

> At the heart of the deterioration of the fabric of Negro society is the deterioration of the Negro family. It is the fundamental source of weakness of the Negro community at the present time. . . . Unless this damage is repaired, all the effort to end discrimination and poverty and injustice will come to little.[6]

Some time later, in a remarkable apologia defending himself against his critics and restating his position, Moynihan said:

> . . . compassion for the suffering Christlike nonviolent Negro demonstrators of the South was a different thing from loving and understanding the frequently debased and disorderly slumdwellers of the North . . . mere equality of opportunity would not be sufficient, for in present terms Negroes were simply not competitive . . . even full employment would not provide the economic stability that was clearly the basis of family stability for this group. (There are other groups with different traditions . . . who can take a lot of punishment without much impact on the family structure. But urban Negroes cannot, and this is really all there is to it.)[7]

One can readily summarize and simplify the essential elements of this ideological position. First, the Negro family, as a major institution within a Negro subculture, is weak and unstable, tending toward a matriarchal form. Second, the present status of the Negro family is rooted in the experience of slavery. Third, the distortions in Negro family structure have been maintained by Negro unemployment that has continued at disastrously high levels for many decades. Fourth, the weakened Negro family produces children, particularly sons, who are so damaged by their family experience that they are unable to profit from educational and employment opportunities. Fifth, therefore efforts to achieve formal change in such social institutions as ghetto schools and discriminatory employment practices will have little effect on present patterns of inequality of status; the ending of Negro inequality and poverty will not, and cannot, be achieved until something is done to strengthen and stabilize the Negro family.

I I

That the Negro family is unstable and matriarchal seems, at first glance, unarguable. One-fourth of Negro families are, in fact, already broken, and headed by a woman. Perhaps as few as one-half of all Negro children reach the age of eighteen having lived continuously with both parents. These and similar statistics are splashed on the canvas with broad strokes to paint a grim picture indeed, grim enough to convince most readers that the "Negro family" is undoubtedly "crumbling" and that "national action" is indispensable.

However, as Whitney Young, Bayard Rustin and others have pointed out, one runs extreme intellectual risks in presenting data of this sort in terms of minority proportions. It is like looking through the wrong end of a telescope. Using the complementary figures, one can say that three out of four Negro families are intact and headed by a man, that seven out of ten Negro children are living with both parents, and that, according to records, the overwhelming majority of Negro babies are born to a man and wife who are legally married. So, we must first emphasize that statements about "family instability" are applicable to only a relatively small segment of the Negro community.

An additional issue stems from the fact that nearly half of

all Negro families can be counted as poor, contrasted to only ten to fifteen per cent of white families. Almost any comparison of racial groups that does not include a correction for economic status is automatically distorted; comparisons of white and Negro families are no exception to this rule.

The fact is that a very large number of poor *white* families —like poor Negro families—are "unstable" or "crumbling." Almost four million *white* families are headed by a woman, compared with slightly more than one million black female-based families. About 100,000 *white* girls are reported to produce illegitimate babies each year. There are close to five million *white* children under eighteen—along with perhaps two million black—who are not living in households with both parents. These gross indices of so-called deviant family status are highly correlated with economic status and economic stress. Controlling for income reduces the apparently huge Negro-white differences to relatively small differences on most of these measures, and on some, eliminates differences altogether.

This connection between poverty and family structure also counteracts another element of the mythology of the Negro family—that deviant family status is a *cultural* feature reflecting values and styles of life and transmitted from generation to generation. The fact that the majority of Negro families are intact—that these presumedly deviant forms occur with relative infrequency within the Negro community —argues persuasively that they do not reflect a Negro *culture*. And a closer look at the families themselves reveals that we are not even confronted with some kind of deviant *subculture*. An examination of "cultural" details—such as child-rearing practices, values, and family roles—shows wide variations among poor Negro families, and even among poor one-parent Negro families. Hylan Lewis[8] has found that

Negro mothers, raising families without a partner to share in the parenting, differ among themselves to at least as great an extent as contrasting groups of parents—white-Negro, rich-poor, rural-urban—differ from one another. Some are strict disciplinarians, some are easy-going and permissive, others are downright neglectful of their children. Many go to church twice a week, a few to the tavern twice a day; but most are not faithful attenders of either institution. Most of these mothers are grimly determined that their children will get a better education, a better job, a better life than they did; but many show little concern about education, and others bitterly reject any possibility of a better life. In some of these families the son is king, in others the crown is worn by the daughter; but again, in most the imbalance between the sexes is not very great. So, although it is true that there is a larger proportion of broken families among Negroes than among whites, this subset of families cannot, by any stretch of imagination, be considered members of a homogeneous subculture.

In particular, it is a risky assumption to move from noting the physical absence of a father in one-fourth of Negro families to a conclusion that the Negro family is subject to "matriarchy." While there may well be ethnic or subcultural variations in the prevalence of matriarchy (Irish families are also supposed to be matriarchal), the *facts* of the situation are that all families of all ethnic groups demonstrate a variety of power-authority patterns. Andrew Billingsley, whose splendid work on black families will be discussed in more detail later, has studied this matter by examining actual families rather than extrapolating from gross census statistics. He found that among lower class Negro families the equalitarian form of father-mother power distribution was clearly predominant, with matriarchal and patriarchal family structures following in that order.[9]

The prevalence of broken families and the relatively greater importance of the mother are primarily characteristics of poor families. But these characteristics result from their poverty rather than their "culture," and the fact that many Negro families—which are about four times more likely to be poor than are white families—demonstrate this pattern should be neither a surprise nor a special occasion for handwringing by white politicians.

The idea of the broken family as a component of a special Negro culture is most evident in the second element of the stereotyped wisdom about the Negro family: the concept of the "heritage of slavery." The notion that a weak and unstable Negro family is culturally transmitted is based on a historical rather than an observational approach to the question. That is, there is no available evidence tracing, within a group of specific families, the transmission of a specific family structure from one generation to another. Rather, a historical relationship is noted—a similarity in phenomena in different periods of time—and the idea of cultural transmission is put forth as a plausible explanation of the relationship. (There *is* evidence of continuity in family stability, status, and achievement among a small group of *upper* class black families;[10] this is, of course, consonant with the white upper class family's ability to preserve and pass on resources and access to privilege and position.)

To challenge the idea that the present form of the Negro family was inherited from slavery days is not, of course, to deny the unique horror that was American slavery and the inhuman practice of preventing and destroying family life among the slaves. Under such conditions, in most cases the mother-child unit was the functional family. Today there also are a substantial number of Negro families made up of mother-child units. "Obviously," this is a historical phenomenon. Perhaps "obviously," perhaps not. In scientific discourse "obviously's" win no Brownie points. Let us look a little closer.

Of course, the argument has a certain dramatic credibility. To proclaim that *the* "Negro family" was destroyed by the villainous slavemaster and that subsequent generations of Negroes have learned (from their fat, doughty mammies and a succession of shifty, irresponsible pappies) precisely how to have a disorganized family can be satisfying, particularly for the concerned white citizen. First, it at least allows the partial incorporation and perpetuation of the racial stereotypes that we have all had drilled into us since infancy, while at the same time it substitutes liberal, quasi-sociological rationales for unacceptable and crude racist explanations. Second, it loads the greater part of the blame and guilt onto the shoulders of that long-dead ancestor of ours, the villainous slavemaster.

A more accurate historical approach, such as E. Franklin Frazier's,[11] shows that each generation of Negro families—including the present generation—has been subjected to economic and social stresses, beginning with enslavement and continuing through ghettoization and exclusion from employment and other economic resources, and that a variety of family forms and functions have emerged as a flexible adaptation to these stresses. A scholar like Frazier does not fall into the trap of assuming that because a family on a slave plantation has a superficial similarity in *form* to that of an AFDC family in a ghetto tenement, that there is also a detailed and *transmitted* similarity in *function;* nor does he equate a stable two-parent family of a sharecropper in the rural South with a similar family of a factory worker in a northern metropolis. Clearly, "culture" and what Frazier calls "folkways" are an important factor in understanding the historical development of the family in any subsection of the population—including the many *different* subsections of the Negro population—but this is only one factor constantly interplaying with more potent social and economic factors. Simplistic talk about the unstable Negro family and its "heritage of slavery" is essentially an ingenious way of "copping a plea." As the murderer pleads guilty to manslaughter to avoid a conviction that might lead to his being electrocuted, liberal America today is pleading guilty to savagery and oppression against the Negro of one hundred years ago in order to escape trial for the crimes of today.

The final argument against the "heritage of slavery" myth is provided by the next element in the new ideology of the Negro family, the only element that is essentially correct—that differences in family structure can be most adequately related to contemporary issues such as employment.

The relationship between poverty and broken families can be found throughout the slums of the world's great cities, and descriptions of these relationships can be found in all kinds of literature and scientific monographs. The unstable, matriarchal family described in the plays of Sean O'Casey and in the books of Oscar Lewis reflect the poverty of the slums of Dublin, Mexico City, and San Juan, just as those described by the U.S. Census Bureau reflect the poverty of Harlem, Roxbury, or Hough. So there is no need to call on the "heritage of slavery" as a causative explanation (though it remains useful in understanding historical context). The existence of large numbers of broken Negro families is fully explained by *contemporaneous* poverty and discrimination.

Consider the striking relationship between marital separations and unemployment among the Negro population—this is documented vividly in the Moynihan Report itself. It shows that a rise in Negro unemployment one year is followed the next year by a rise in the proportion of separated Negro couples, a drop in unemployment is followed by a drop in separations. The parallel rising and falling of these two curves demonstrates the immediate and highly significant impact of economic status on family status. How much more contemporary can you get? When people lose their jobs, their marriages are in danger, and that danger is especially dramatic for men expected to support families. That is the condition of today; the status of a person's great-grandfather—as a plantation field hand, or a house slave, or even as a free Negro boot-maker—is largely irrelevant.

Family breakup, through divorce or separation, is the major cause of fatherless families, but two other causes are numerically also significant: death and birth; premature death and illegitimate birth. Both of these are closely linked to economic factors.

The death of a father of young children is a tragedy that occurs far more frequently to Negro than to white families. Among non-white families with female heads and with children under eighteen—that is, among so-called "disorganized" Negro families—one-fourth of the women are widows. Contrasted to whites, young Negro men in the prime of life (between the ages of twenty and forty) have twice as great a chance of dying. Out of every twelve young Negro men aged twenty, one will die before he is forty. One out of twelve. And in this age range, most of those who die leave orphans behind. This is a fact that cannot be readily attributed to cultural factors, either of class or race. It is hardly a matter of a Negro cultural tendency to develop matriarchal family forms. It is, very simply, the end result of discrimination in the provision of health services. In this country, to be poor is to be deprived of medical care. The rich, and particularly the white rich, are permitted to buy an additional decade of life. (The subject of health care will be discussed in more detail in Chapter Six.)

Another major factor to be considered is that illegitimate birth leads to the formation of a mother-child family unit. One-fourth of Negro births are illegitimate—the ratio is about eight times greater than among whites—and relatively few illegitimate Negro children are adopted. So in a very large number of cases Negro children grow up in fatherless families. How is this related to economic status? Why are poor women, Negro women, and particularly poor Negro women so much more likely to have illegitimate children? The popular answer is a variation on the cultural explanation: by virtue of their "background," poor girls and Negro girls grow up to be immoral and promiscuous. This is one more "obvious," well-known fact that is plausible and dramatic but simply not true. Young black women do not engage in premarital intercourse eight times more frequently than white women. All the evidence points to the conclusion that differences in the amount of premarital sexual activity between lower class and middle class females, or between white and Negro ones, is relatively small. Vast differences in recorded illegitimate births—and consequently the formation of mother-child family units—are accounted for by: poor access to contraception and abortion, few forced marriages, little concealment, and low availability of adoption services. White middle class women are no more committed to virginity, in practice or in theory, than poor women and Negro women are. It is simply that they can get and can afford Enovid; if they get pregnant, they are more able to obtain an abortion; if they have a baby, they are more able to conceal the absence of a husband, and they have a much greater chance to give up a baby for adoption. The differences are due, then, not to culture, or values or a racial habit of promiscuity cultivated on the old plantation; the differences are due to the effect of social and economic forces, and to the discriminatory withholding of information, resources and services *today*. (The subject of illegitimacy is dealt with in the next chapter.)

Elizabeth Herzog has summarized the arguments against the "heritage of slavery" theory very succinctly:

> It is difficult to be sure how much—if any—difference would remain in proportions of female-headed families if really sensitive comparisons were made between Negroes and whites on the same income level. . . . It seems reasonable to assume that some differences between white and nonwhite would remain even with a more sensitive income classification. Yet it does not follow that they might be ascribed primarily to the legacy of slavery rather than the hundred years since slavery. It seems more likely that differences between low-income white and Negro families, beyond that explained by income alone, may be attributed primarily to postslavery factors of deprivation and discrimination affecting every facet of life: occupation, education, income, housing, nutrition, health and mortality, social status, self-respect—the documented list is long and the documenting references myriad.[12]

I I I

We are left, nevertheless, with the undisputed central fact: one-fourth of American Negro families are broken; one-third of American Negro children are growing up fatherless. Even if we eliminate a good deal of misinformation about the prevalence and causes of this condition, is it not still true that one-third of the Negro child population, particularly the boys, constitutes a high risk—a damaged population whose family experiences so handicap them that they cannot take advantage of educational and employment opportunities? No matter how it came about, is it not true that, in this sense, the "deterioration of the Negro family" is the "fundamental source of weakness of the Negro community at the present time"? It seems like a reasonable conclusion. Is it true? Let us look at some of the evidence.

These questions emerge with a weight of face validity that reflects how thoroughly the thinking of educated Americans has been channeled into psychological forms; it is a line of reasoning and questioning which is intensely psychodynamic, if not downright Freudian. Writers about the Negro family dwell on the issue of sexual identification as if they had just stepped off the boat from Vienna forty years ago. They are more kosher than a rabbi, holier than a pope, more psychoanalytic than Freud himself. It sometimes appears that they worry more about the resolution of Negro Oedipus complexes than they do about black men getting decent jobs, black babies being bitten by rats, black teenagers being pushed out of school with the equivalent of fifth-grade education. In discussing the Negro family, they see psychological functions, particularly sex-role induction, as far more prominent than other more important functions of the family. In considering these questions, then, it is necessary first to step back and gain some perspective on the general functions of the family, an institution which is virtually universal in human cultures.

Teaching male and female roles is, after all, only one family function among many, and not the most important one at that. In fact, there are no cultures in which this function is assigned exclusively to the family, and in many cultures sex-role induction takes place largely outside the family. The primary business of the family is economic, arranging for appropriate division of labor among adults and for physical maintenance and care of children—providing food, shelter, and hygiene. The second order of business in relation to children is that of broad socialization: teaching language, transmitting customs, passing on values held by the surrounding society. Teaching sex-roles is one part of this second group of functions. In addition, however, sex-roles are taught and supported by many other institutions and practices in the community: in schools, in books, in occupational situations; and the child in American society is drenched with role expectations from all sides. Therefore, the Negro child being raised without a father is really not deprived of the basic information that boys play baseball and girls jump rope. He gets this message from his mother, relatives, friends, teachers, newspapers, television, schools and every institution he encounters. He doesn't need to see Willie Mays to know that this also applies to Negro boys. Willie Mays, after all, must have gotten the message from Joe DiMaggio and Ted Williams. (There is a separate issue—the problem of the Negro boy becoming not only a man, but a *black* man; but this identity struggle takes place primarily within the large community, not the family.)

This is *not* to say that a fatherless family represents the best of all possible worlds. Two parents are almost always better than one, and the psychological task of raising a reasonably effective child—son or daughter—is a difficult one for a mother going it alone. (The economic task is even more overwhelming, draining energy required for the psychological task.) It is difficult but it is possible, and the absence of a father is really not quite the disaster it is sometimes made out to be. Growing up in a broken family does not unfailingly doom a child to neurosis and failure.

One of the most thorough studies of the psychological effect of the broken home was the Midtown Manhattan Study, a monumental landmark of research in the epidemiology of mental health.[13] This study related a number of social variables to mental health status; obviously, from a psychiatric or mental health point of view, broken homes were considered a very important social variable indeed. Prior studies had shown, for example, that a very high proportion of adult psychiatric patients come from homes broken by death, divorce, and separation. In the Midtown Manhattan Study, this observation was confirmed: among psychiatric outpatients studied, a full twenty per cent—one in five—reported a history of a childhood broken home. But the next finding was a real surprise: of the non-patients in the general population sample, thirty-five per cent—more than one in three—reported that their home was broken by death, divorce, or separation before they reached the age of sixteen. In other words, a broken home is a fairly common event. The fact that, at any one time, almost ninety per cent of all children are living with two parents is misleading; in many instances, one of these is a stepparent who appeared on the scene after a prior family unit was broken.

Moreover, they found no overriding effect of broken homes on mental health; the effect varied markedly depending upon which parent was lost, the age of the child, and the social class of the family. Their study indicated that there is very little effect if the home is broken after the age of six, and that there is a substantially greater risk of emotional pathology if the *mother* is lost. A five-year-old child in a poor family who loses his mother is very clearly running a high risk of psychological damage; a twelve-year-old in a middle class family who loses his father is not.

These data from the Midtown Study require us to rethink the stereotype-filled, simplistic logic about these matters that we were so glibly taught in Abnormal Psychology 205 and which has now become part of our overly-abundant national treasury of facts that are not facts. Those of us immersed in some of the newer problems of community mental health have been constantly confronted by these and similar facts; they have required us to expand our theoretical base far beyond the traditional Freudian psychodynamic rule books. And we should have known better.

Consider the kind of built-in, rather predictable relationships that can be observed. While the death of the mother of a four-year-old, for example, is a stressful event in any family, it is usually only part of a chain of disastrous events in a very low income family. It is often preceded by long expensive illness; it is followed by problems of child care that add to economic distress and disrupt the basic family functions of providing food, clothing, shelter, and hygiene. Sooner or later it usually means separation from the father also, followed by an unpredictable pattern of moving from place to place, either to relatives or to foster homes. When the poor four-year-old's mother dies, his whole world often collapses. The chain of events for him is longer and more disruptive than it would be for either a middle class child or a child twelve or fourteen years old. And this stress chain is usually much different and less disruptive when the remaining parent is the mother rather than the father. The view that a female-headed broken family is especially pathological, then, is simply not consonant with the available evidence (although it is true, of course, that the fatherless poor family is that much more vulnerable to economic stresses).

These facts go against all the assumptions and beliefs about mental health and the Negro family. But they appear to be true. As Hylan Lewis has summarized in his writings, "the broken home has been reported as associated with emotional maladjustment, poor school achievement, juvenile delinquency, and illegitimacy. Yet, when data are controlled for socio-economic status, correlations such as these often fade out.[14]

The introduction of the variable of socio-economic status provides a basis for answering the underlying question: "If it is not the deterioration of the family that is the fundamental weakness of the Negro community, what is it?" Correlations between broken homes and social pathology are used to support the conclusion that Negro family structure is a cause as well as a result, a major—indeed *the* major—barrier to the achievement of Negro equality. The correlations are accurate, but, as Lewis points out, they are incomplete. The pattern of correlations is, in fact, triangular: poverty with pathology, poverty with broken homes, and broken homes with pathology. But analysis of the causal directions—what causes what—shows rather convincingly that economic stress —and for the Negro and other minorities, discrimination—is the basic cause; social pathology and broken homes are twin results.

The appeal and apparent plausibility of the new ideology on the Negro family are essentially emotional rather than rational; we can demonstrate this quickly by drawing an analogy. If we seek other results of poverty and discrimination that are similar to broken families in that they represent an additional burden and handicap, we can find many—functional illiteracy, emotional problems and, in particular, poor health. Disabilities are far more prevalent among Negroes than among whites. This is reflected in every kind of measure from infant mortality—with Negro rates two and three times higher than white rates—to life expectancy—whites live six to eight years longer than Negroes. Infections and chronic diseases assault and disable the Negro far more frequently than the white. So, at least as plausible a case could be made that "deterioration of Negro health" is the "fundamental cause of weakness in the Negro community," and pages of tables and charts could be put together into a dramatic document entitled "Negro Health: The Case for National Action." But it is doubtful that such a document would seize the imagination of America's concerned liberals.

This is but one example. Anyone with a tolerable command of social statistics could add an almost boundless set of additional correlations: unemployment and infant mortality; income level and narcotics addiction; dilapidated housing and number of tuberculosis cases; reading achievement and mental hospital admission rates, etc.

Social pathology (or human distress—they are the same thing defined from different standpoints) comes in packages. Everything goes together because each thing is a result of the same cause—poverty, oppression, exclusion. It is analogous to a syndrome—a collection of symptoms—that accompanies a specific disease. When a physician notes that the patient has a sharp pain in his side, nausea, a high fever, and an elevated white blood cell count, he starts thinking about the cause. He doesn't sit in his office and speculate whether the fever causes the pain, whether the white count produces the nausea. He diagnoses appendicitis and gets on to the business of treating the disease.

Similarly, what these endless correlations mean (when translated from statistics to the lives of human beings) is that poor people tend to live in slums, to be oppressed and exploited and mistreated, and to experience enormous amounts of social, economic, mental and physical suffering as a result. And Negroes experience a vastly disproportionate share of this suffering. It is much more reasonable to conclude, not that "family instability" leads to a "tangle of pathology," but that poor Negro families—that is, close to half of all Negro families—are bitterly discriminated against and exploited, with the result that the individual, the family, and the community are all deeply injured.

At this point let us return more specifically to the *Moynihan Report* itself, not only because it is such a classic illustration of Savage Discovery and the ideology of Blaming the Victim, but also because it demonstrates so clearly the dangerous consequences of this ideology. The line of argumentation taken by Moynihan and the other authors of his report is clear and simple (despite the fact that, in the subsequent controversy, the thrust of the report and the clear, often hysterical statements contained in it were obscured, and often denied). They say that "conventional remedies" (ending discrimination, etc.) are, because of the breakdown in the Negro family, insufficient to achieve equality; that the supposed weakness of the Negro family is a *cause* of inequality, a barrier to achievement. Although Moynihan has subsequently equivocated on this point and has even denied making such a point, there can be little doubt, upon reading the report, that a causal role was being attributed to the "breakdown" of the Negro family. Consider the following series of quotations from the Moynihan Report as evidence:

> The harsh fact is that as a group, at the present time, in terms of ability to win out in the competitions of American life, they are not equal to most of those groups with which they will be competing . . . collectively, in the spectrum of American ethnic and religious and regional groups . . . Negroes are among the weakest.

> The fundamental problem, in which this is most clearly the case is that of family structure. The evidence—not final, but powerfully persuasive—is that the Negro family in the urban ghettos is crumbling. . . . So long as this situation persists,

the cycle of poverty and disadvantage will continue to repeat itself.

Measures that have worked in the past, or would work for most groups in the present will not work here.

At the center of the tangle of pathology is the weakness of the family structure. Once or twice removed, it will be found to be the principal source of most of the aberrant, inadequate or anti-social behavior that did not establish, but now serves to perpetuate the cycle of poverty and deprivation.

Three centuries of injustice have brought about deep-seated structural distortions in the life of the Negro American. At this point, the present tangle of pathology is capable of perpetuating itself without assistance from the white world. The cycle can be broken only if these distortions are set right.[15]

The fifth element of the ideology emerges unequivocally: the idea that efforts to achieve formal change in social institutions of education, employment, and housing will not achieve racial equality unless, and until, there is a change in the victim of the inequities in those institutions. The customary cry of the Savage Discoverer emerges: change the victim! He is at fault, although through no fault of his own.

I V

One might hope that the Gresham's law of ideologies—that bad theories seem to drive out good—will not work against an excellent and very persuasive book by Andrew Billingsley, *Black Families in White America,* which is extremely well documented, highly informative, and most important, organized around a sound conceptual model. Billingsley treats the black family as a social system set within a larger social system, the Negro community, which in turn is articulated into another, larger system, the wider community, and so forth. These connections form a network of mutually interdependent relationships. He also emphasizes, within the total set of Negro families, the enormous variety of structures, as determined by historical, social, and class influences. In particular, he demonstrates that the Negro family is primarily subject to, and must adapt to, the pervasive racism of white America and the consequent oppression of the black community; and also, that improving the status and stability of the one-parent Negro families will have to be achieved through social change and redistribution of resources and of power, not through any process of change internal to the family itself.

Billingsley shows—as I and so many others have tried to show—that those who emphasize Negro family pathology have crucial defects in their position: they leave out of the equation for current action two important elements—racism and conflict. They do not incorporate an attack on racism as a necessary element in the achievement of Negro equality, and they do not seem to perceive that an equalization of status will necessarily be accompanied by conflict. They piously hope that a straight-forward income strategy will sufficiently strengthen the Negro family, and that Negroes will then be able to follow the traditional paths trodden by other minorities. (This is not to deny the value of such moves: if you break your leg in an automobile accident, it is obviously necessary that your injury be given prompt and adequate medical treatment. But the doctor who fixes your leg should not deceive himself into thinking that he is thereby making a contribution to the cause of automotive safety.)

Those who are concerned about what they perceive as Negro family pathology do *not*—thank God—advocate family counseling programs or any other direct intervention in family functioning. Their remedy is increased incomes, and they advocate a strategy of full employment coupled with a family allowance program (with usually about a $10 or $12 a month allowance per child to all families). For example, Dr. Moynihan himself proposed (as a remedy for family pathology) the resumption of twice-a-day mail deliveries to create 50,000 new jobs, a great bulk of which could be filled by Negro men with families. "For $5,800 a year, we get a man who can take pride in being a uniformed officer of the United States Government, who raises a family, pays taxes, votes Democratic *and* delivers the mail."[16]

This presents a sharp contrast to the kind of economic strategy supported by most civil rights leaders which is embodied in the A. Philip Randolph Freedom Budget, and Whitney Young's proposed "Marshall Plan for the Poor"; both propose broad public investment in housing, health, education, public works, and community development aiming for a decisive breakthrough: victory over the linked barriers of poverty and inequality. This strategy is based on a realistic and sober diagnosis of the *racist,* as well as the economic, factors that burden the Negro with poverty and exclusion; and it assumes the necessity for major social and institutional changes—not simply tidying up, picking up pieces, and fixing up the victims of defective cultural institutions.

We come, at last, to the core of the disagreement, the issue of what it means to be a human being. Can we deal only with man's stomach and his pocketbook, or do we also have to consider his soul and his dignity? Will a family allowance and a mailbag on his shoulder turn the trick? Is that the end of the "Negro problem"? Can we so easily avoid the basic issues of resources and power, status and hatred? It seems unlikely.

To the social engineer, who perceives a problem in census

tables about fatherless Negro families and a solution in government action to create $5,800 a year jobs (jobs that may not be necessary or meaningful), the estate of being human does not appear to be either complex or exalted. It should not be surprising, perhaps, that such a mind can attribute the effects of bigotry, racism and inhumanity to an oversimplified, naive version of the unresolved Oedipus complex.

So it is clear that the controversy, between the family pathologists and those who see such an emphasis as dangerous and diverting, goes far beyond the scope of academic quibbling about the interpretation of statistics. The controversy is more ideological than scientific. We have, after all, no comparative information on what happens to American Negroes and their families in a racist compared with a non-racist society; the experimental data are available in huge quantities but the control data are yet to be gathered. Participants in the dialogue, then, are distinguishable not by the statistics they quote, but by their viewpoint on such basic questions as:

—Is Negro inequality explainable by external events in society or by internal characteristics of the Negro, his family, and his community?

—Is it primarily a problem of the larger white society or of the Negro minority?

—Is it mainly an issue of power or money?

—Is the Negro oppressed or disadvantaged?

—Is he burdened or a burden?

—Must he achieve change in social relationships or only an increment in his own resources?

—Should he look to his strengths and actively influence his own condition, or to his weaknesses and be content to be the passive beneficiary of clever social engineering?

—Is he, finally, a victim of brutal racism, or just another peasant immigrant, but with a black skin?

Most of the family pathologists lean toward the second part of these alternatives; we who are dissenters lean toward the first part and believe that the basic problem is still centered in the white racist society that oppresses the Negro and that the solution lies in action to change the balance of power, to change the nature of black-white relationships. Achieving equality is an action to be taken, not a condition to be received.

Finally, it is not that Negro inequality cannot be eliminated until the Negro family is strengthened, but rather that the achievement of equality will strengthen the family, the community and the nation, black and white together.

4
The Prevalence of Bastards

Illegitimate Views of

Illegitimacy

I

Several years ago, I was asked to be a consultant to a group-
work program for unmarried mothers that was staffed by
women who spent fifteen or twenty hours a week as volun-
teers. The purpose was to provide recreational and socialization experiences for the young mothers, most of whom were
under twenty and had one child, usually an infant. The staff
workers were middle class and white; the clients, poor and
black. I was expected to help the staff understand the clients
better and work with them more effectively.

The typical client was an overwhelmed teenager who had
dropped out of high school as one result of her pregnancy;
she lived in a substandard slum tenement apartment on the
third floor on the typically stingy budget of a welfare recip-

ient. She was faced with the pressing task of constructing for herself crash programs in: how to be a mother; how to manage a household on a budget far below the poverty line; how to control rats and cockroaches in her apartment; how to live—often for stretches of 24 to 72 hours—all alone with an infant, without a husband, without relief of any kind, completely on her own; and finally, most important, how to negotiate hastily with her harried, overloaded welfare worker. (For an understanding of the desperation of living poor and powerless, I recommend acquaintance with a black, teenage, unmarried mother living on public assistance.)

The white staff workers were very devoted to the young women; they worried and fretted, became very involved and sympathetic, and spent endless hours helping them—finding extra clothing through some church or charity, locating volunteer babysitters for them and then taking them to the movies or bowling, looking for a slightly less dilapidated apartment, trying to mediate with the schools and arrange for the girls to finish their high school work.

A basic goal of the program was for the clients to complete their education and get a job.

I expected that the major topics of discussion in the hours I spent with staff members would revolve around such obvious pressing problems as how to cope with neglectful slum landlords and the penurious Welfare Department. On my own agenda I had the idea of developing a preventive program centering on sex education and contraceptive services for the unmarried *un*mothers in the neighborhood. But my first sessions with the staff were taken up with discussions of the strange sexual mores of the lower class black girl, and how to "motivate" clients to get themselves educated, employed, and "off welfare." These extremely kind, sympathetic, and endlessly helpful women were absorbed with the ways in which their clients were different, vulnerable and problematic, and they were dedicated to helping them adjust to their impossible life circumstances rather than changing the circumstances. They were, in a word, Blaming the Victim.

This is not at all surprising, of course. As is true of most middle class educated persons in America, this ideology was second nature to them. Most of what they had learned and read and heard in college, in church, and at home had taught them to view social problems in this way. Their good will, their kindness, and their altruism almost always flowed in exceptionalistic channels.

Of course, liberal social scientists and social welfare professionals have been gossiping for years about the sex lives of poor girls and Negro girls. They have been exchanging hard-won confidences about the promiscuity of these girls, how their sexual values are different from ours, and, in particular, about the unfortunate consequences of these deviant values and behavior patterns—the prevalence of bastards among the poor and the black. The very same professionals were appalled, and shocked, and outraged to hear a distorted echo of their own gossip coming from the mouths of senators and congressmen debating the 1967 Social Security amendments.

These 1967 amendments purported to halt the "welfare spiral" principally by establishing a ceiling on Federal support to state welfare programs for dependent children, by proposing programs to reduce illegitimacy, and by setting requirements that states begin programs that would presumably move people "off the welfare rolls and onto payrolls." The central image projected by the oratory of the proponents of this destructive legislation—Representative Wilbur Mills and Senator Russell Long—was of a sluttish, promiscuous, conniving welfare mother ("brood mares" in the words of

Senator Long) conceiving one illegitimate child after another in order to reap the munificent benefits of AFDC paychecks.

The strategy proposed was coercive and repressive. It rested on several unchallenged assumptions: that most welfare mothers had illegitimate children and that most illegitimate children were on welfare; that illegitimacy resulted from wanton sexuality and willful reproduction; and that spiraling welfare costs were directly linked to spiraling illegitimacy rates.

The conventional wisdom about illegitimacy, its causes, and consequences, the set of beliefs held by the white middle class staff members in the program with which I served as a consultant, the accepted ideology in professional and academic circles, is not all that different from the ideology that produced the restrictive and insulting 1967 amendments. Of course, the enlightened academics talk about "lower class standards of sexual behavior" or "sexual norms in the Negro ghetto." Unlike congressmen, they don't view restrictions on welfare as a way to "solve the maid problem," and they don't growl "let's get those welfare whores off their asses and into factories," as a congressman was quoted in the newsletter of the National Welfare Rights movement.

But in the literature of social stratification and race relations there has been a consistent emphasis on the marked differences in sexual patterns between black and white, and between lower and middle class. Consider (as one among a potential thousand examples) this quotation from the Kinsey group, who have studied sexual behavior more thoroughly than any other researchers in the United States:

> Insofar as reproductive behavior is concerned, the lower social level Negro pattern may be simply described: coitus is regarded as an inevitable, natural, and desirable activity to be enjoyed both in and out of marriage, contraception is

little known and considered at best a nuisance and at worst dangerous or unnatural; and pregnancy is accepted as an inevitable part of life; whether it occurs in or out of wedlock is a secondary issue.[1]

This comment is striking because they offer no data whatsoever to support it. As I will attempt to show at a later point, their data can, in fact, be used to argue against such a formulation.

Such formulations—and there are, as I suggested, many others that might have been quoted—find their way (in rather simplified form) into introductory textbooks that provide the great bulk of middle class liberals with their total fund of social science information. In addition, the ideas thus formulated are taken up by liberal journalists and given extended currency. In one of the most blatant examples of journalistic rape of sociology, Theodore White describes the sexual life of the ghetto Negro in vivid and stereotyped language, concluding with a memorably distasteful summary of life in Harlem as "biological anarchy in zoological tenements."[2]

The final linkage between illegitimacy and what is called the "welfare problem" comes from reputedly liberal scientists. Daniel P. Moynihan, the favorite "urbanologist" of both *Time* Magazine and President Nixon, has claimed that, "the issue of illegitimacy has nothing to do with whether black women are more or less promiscuous than white women; it has to do with the number of children on the welfare rolls. This is a legitimate concern of public policy."[3]

The whole ideology, the way in which the topic of illegitimacy is formulated in victim-blaming terms, consists of five beliefs. The first article of faith is that the poor, and particularly the Negro poor, lead incredibly active sex lives. Some say that the poor take sex too lightly—and are therefore promiscuous. Others say that they take it too seriously—and are therefore promiscuous. But all agree on the prevalence of promiscuity, particularly premarital promiscuity.

The second component of the ideology is the belief that poor girls are not at all concerned about the consequences of sexual activity, only the immediate pleasure it brings. Though perhaps dimly aware of the mechanics of reproduction, they pay little heed to the future and are blithely careless about contraception. (A hasty postscript is usually added: that this is characteristic of their "culture" rather than the result of individual traits of character.)

The third assumption follows naturally from the first two and is as profoundly plausible as "one and one are two." As a result of (one) excessive sexual activity prior to marriage and (one) lack of care about diaphragms and such, the black and the poor (two) get caught—that is, they have a lot of illegitimate babies. The proof of this is to be found in the computer printouts of illegitimate births: astronomically high in poor neighborhoods, low in rich; one in four among black newborns; one in thirty among whites. Here we find the core of the logical problem at issue, the tautological linking and blurring together of cause and effect, the hidden and defective syllogism that provides the central support for the whole ideology. The apparently unimpeded reasoning (that jumps with certainty from one to one to two) is difficult to impeach because it has the taste of truth about it. But to impeach it— to show that one and one are neither two, nor, indeed, one and one—will be the central task of this chapter.

The next point, the fourth, is somewhat tangential but is clearly attached inextricably to the whole tangle and must be dealt with. This is the belief in the acceptability of illegitimacy among Negroes and the poor, the belief that the average Negro mother is more philosophical, less upset by the news that her daughter is "in trouble." This places the birth of an illegitimate child in the category of events that, though not precisely welcome, are nevertheless inevitable and part of the human condition (falling, perhaps, somewhere between a bad year for crops and a flat tire on a country road). Such events are simply to be expected (with dry humor perhaps) just as are the passing distress and inconvenience that they carry with them.

According to the fifth element in this set of beliefs, these women are accepting ánd philosophical about bearing out-of-wedlock babies because welfare provides such a simple and practical economic solution to the problem. Thus, there is supposed to be a direct relation between the prevalence of bastards and the expanding rolls of Aid to Families with Dependent Children.

Presented in this bald way—one, two, three, four, five—the ideology may seem too stark and simple. It is rarely presented this way. Rather, pieces and bits of it are explicated fuzzily, gently, sympathetically. But that really is it—the core of standard American thought on the topic of illegitimacy. This, liberal social scientists and politicians and laymen alike tell us, is the way Negro girls and poor girls are.

II

Now, in fact, this is *not* the way poor girls and Negro girls are, either absolutely or in comparison with white girls and middle class girls. No puritanical denial of the exuberant sexuality of the young—rich and poor alike—is needed to refute this ideology. A quick review of readily available facts will show that these solemn truths are not, in truth, so.

Let us start with the data that provide so many scare headlines and eye-popping statistical charts: racial and social class differences in illegitimacy rates.

It is important to begin with an examination and acknowledgment of a widely reported and absolutely accurate fact: racial differences in the incidence of recorded illegitimate births are extraordinarily large. Among Negro girls, almost twenty-five per cent of births are recorded as illegitimate; among whites, the proportion is only three or four per cent. An eight-to-one ratio. (There are very similar levels of difference in the incidence of illegitimacy when one compares social classes, but it is easier to trace and analyze the differences by color. In a similar analysis of lower class-middle class differences, approximately the same patterns appear, and approximately the same explanations could be used to account for the differences. To avoid repetition, only the white-nonwhite analysis will be presented.)

Why, then, the eight-to-one ratio in illegitimacy? Why the welfare spiral? If the accepted ideology is false, what is true?

We must begin, as in the study of any social phenomenon, with the process of definition and identification. Who is counted as illegitimate, what criteria are used? Consider two contrasting events: A young black woman, frightened, enters a county or city hospital. She whispers her name. ("Miss?" asks the admission worker, noting the bare spot on the third finger of the left hand.) She is whisked into the impersonal machinery of the obstetrics ward, is delivered more or less uneventfully by a sleepy resident, and only a day or two later is sent home. As she may or may not know, the space on her child's birth certificate that calls for the name of the baby's father is blank. That is the basic clue and index to illegitimacy.

A white girl in the same situation is admitted to a maternity ward as a private patient, possibly with the help of a child welfare agency or a maternity home. Her physician, or even her social worker, may well conspire with her to conceal the embarrassing lack of a husband. The birth certificate may even be filled in with the name of a fictitious father, and the chances are fair that the baby will not be included in the count of illegitimate births.

These are not, of course, completely predictable events. The illegitimacy of a black infant is frequently not noted; the illegitimate status of the white girl's child is noted a good deal more often than not. The differences are only relative, but they do show that the statistics are distorted by the simple fact of concealment. There are no statistics on this factor of concealment, but there is good reason to believe that location of birth is one of its major contributing characteristics. It is much easier to conceal illegitimate status on the private service in a private hospital than on the ward in a public hospital. Numerous studies have shown that, in general, white women tend to have babies on the private service, black women on the ward. For example, a New York study[4] showed that, among married mothers, 86 per cent of the white births but only 18 per cent of the black births were on the private service. But among those identified as unmarried, delivering illegitimate children, 81 per cent of the whites as well as 97 per cent of the black mothers were on the ward.

One quick piece of arithmetic is sufficient to show conclusively that white illegitimacy is under-reported. There were approximately 100,000 recorded white illegitimate births in 1964 and approximately 60,000 adoptions of illegitimate children by persons other than relatives—and of those children more than 50,000 were white. Now it repeatedly has been shown (two recent independent studies in Boston, one of which I directed,[5] agreed on this finding) that only a minority of illegitimate children enter the channels of public and private adoption agencies (an even smaller number enter the channels of independent adoption). This minority includes few black children, but—and this is the significant point—it also excludes a very large fraction of white children. Furthermore, it is rare that more than half of illegitimate children initially accepted by an agency ever complete the long process that culminates in legal adoption. Among *white* illegitimate children, then, it is safe to conclude that the proportion who finally complete nonrelative adoptions cannot be more than about one-fourth. The official statistics that indicate that over one-half of the illegitimate white children complete such adoption, then, are grossly inaccurate, reflecting a case of extreme under-reporting. (It is hard to imagine a more inaccurate counting procedure than this one, which misses and leaves out of its tabulations about as many cases as it finds and includes.) This is consistent with the conclusions of the Kinsey group, who estimate that actual illegitimacy rates among their (almost exclusively white) subject population are at least twice as high as the official statistics would indicate.[6]

We come next to the logical leap back, from illegitimacy to promiscuity. Differences in illegitimacy rates, one might suppose, must surely reflect differences in rates of premarital sexual activity. (Backward leaps, in general, tend to be dangerous, leaving one in a very unstable position. This is no exception.) Let us trace the process backwards as well as we can (the scientific data are surprisingly scanty) with small cautious steps rather than bold leaps.

Illegitimate birth is necessarily preceded—let us be logical before we leap—by what we might term illegitimate pregnancy. To limit the discussion, we can first focus on premarital illegitimate pregnancy. Continuing our logical way however, we have to realize that illegitimate birth is only *one* possible outcome of a premarital pregnancy. It is, in fact, one of the *least common* outcomes of such a situation. The Kinsey group's data show that only about five per cent of out-of-wedlock pregnancies terminate in illegitimate birth. So that, while about one in ten of Kinsey's women had a premarital pregnancy, only a fraction of one per cent experienced an illegitimate birth.[7]

The most common outcomes of premarital pregnancy are first, abortion, and second, marriage during pregnancy, followed by a technically legitimate birth. Therefore, in order to understand the very tenuous relationship, between premarital pregnancy and illegitimate birth, we have to know about induced abortions and pregnant brides.

Estimates of the annual number of illegal abortions in the U.S. range from about 600,000 to two million. The most commonly quoted estimates range between one million and one and a half million. The Kinsey group, once again, has provided us with the most systematic information about abortion, particularly as it relates to out-of-wedlock pregnancy. In their sample of women (and it must be remembered that it is a highly unrepresentative volunteer sample, predominately white and college-educated) the outcomes, in terms of frequency, are: abortion the winner by many lengths; marriage-while-pregnant and illegitimate birth far behind, in the place and show positions. Among white, college-educated women (the bulk of the sample), of those who became illegitimately pregnant, eighty-three per cent obtained abortions, while only two per cent continued through to an actual illegitimate birth.

This pattern, however, varies very much according to color and social class. For example, among the small sample of Negro women who had only a high school education, forty-three out of every one hundred premarital conceptions—that is, close to half—resulted in a technically illegitimate birth, whereas only twenty-five—one-fourth—of the cases terminated with an induced abortion.

It is worthwhile, perhaps, to linger for a moment over these figures, reflecting the drastically different outcomes of premarital pregnancy when one compares the well-to-do girl's experience with that of the working class and the Negro girl. Given two groups, let us say one hundred girls each, one group white and well-to-do, the other lower class and black —all two hundred of whom are pregnant out-of-wedlock— what will be the ultimate yield in terms of illegitimate infants? Two whites, forty-three blacks! A twenty-to-one differential.

A word of warning. We cannot take these numbers exactly as they appear. The built-in biases of the sampling and other sources of error that affect the Kinsey data are well known. The precise numbers then may not be exact, but surely we can rely on the relative magnitude. So even if there is not as much as a twenty-to-one difference, the discrepancies linked to class and race are clearly enormous. And the major factor that differentiates the patterns of outcome is abortion, which is a predominantly white, predominantly middle class activity.

But there is much more to the story than abortion. The second most common outcome of illegitimate pregnancy is marriage before the birth, which is then counted as legitimate. A recent study[8] comparing marriage certificates and birth certificates shows that, at the most conservative estimate, one out of every eight Connecticut girls gives birth to an illegitimately conceived baby before she reaches the age of twenty-one. However, three-fourths of these births take place *after* marriage. These marriages are usually thought of as forced or "shotgun" marriages, but they are very often marriages that had been planned already, and the couple had been engaged at the time of conception.

In Detroit,[9] an even more careful study comparing marriage and birth certificates showed similar findings but added the information that forced marriages—or at least marriages of pregnant brides—were far more common among whites than among blacks. The Kinsey data, incidentally, are in agreement with this finding, although, as has been mentioned, that sample contained a very scanty showing of Negroes and of non-college-educated whites. No such comparison was directly reported, but a recalculation of their data on the basis of births that were "illegitimately conceived"—whether out of wedlock or in wedlock—shows the following patterns: For non-college whites, 70 per cent of such births occur *after marriage;* 30 per cent are out of wedlock (almost identical with the Connecticut data cited above); and for college whites the proportions are 83 per cent after marriage, and only 17 per cent out of wedlock. For blacks the comparable figures are: for non-college women, 39 per cent in marriage, 61 per cent out; for college women, 50 per cent in, 50 per cent out.

The evidence is clear, then, regarding a correlation between forced marriages and class and color. The correlation to class is particularly understandable on the basis of common sense and day-to-day experience; the better off a young man is economically, the more likely it is that he can afford to marry the girl he impregnates; and even more important, the more secure the girl will be in agreeing to marriage.

So, statistics on recorded illegitimate births give us only a slight clue to the occurrence of premarital pregnancy in the population. Outcomes of such pregnancies among girls of different color and different class positions are so drastically different that the relationship is severely attenuated. And we have to consider one more factor, the availability and access to contraceptive material and information.

A series of studies have demonstrated that the poorer a girl is, the less likely she is to have access to the knowledge and resources required for adequate family planning. Because of the high correlation between color and economic conditions this means also that Negro girls in general have considerably less access to this information than do whites. This would explain, for example, the fact that the Kinsey data for high school educated women (which represent a very small part of the total group) show that 47 percent of the black women had premarital intercourse as compared with 42 per cent of the whites. However, about 40 per cent of the black women became pregnant as compared with only 13 per cent of the white. This may be partly explainable by some quantitative differences in frequency of premarital intercourse, but obviously the major differences must be due to incidence of contraception.

What do we know about the willingness of the poor to *use* contraceptives if they are available?

Recent programs, many of them financed or administered by the Planned Parenthood Federation, have demonstrated beyond any doubt that the poor are eager to have, and to use family planning services. For example, in one program in Chicago, of 14,000 clients, approximately four out of five continued to take contraceptive pills regularly for thirty consecutive months. Of these 14,000, eighty-three per cent were black, half had not completed high school and one-sixth were welfare recipients.[10] Similar results have been reported from Washington, D.C., Atlanta, New York, and other cities. The readiness and willingness is *always* evident, whenever the problem of ability and access is dealt with. It should have been possible to predict this finding, one would suppose, from two facts; first: middle- and upper-income Negroes have consistently demonstrated *lower* fertility rates than whites of comparable class status; second: intelligence is distributed essentially randomly throughout the population. If middle class whites are smart enough to recognize the importance of family planning as a way of controlling what happens to their lives, as a way of introducing effective *choice* into the reproductive process, it would seem logical that the poor, and particularly the Negro poor, are just as smart and just as able to recognize the value of this procedure. Only a prejudiced observer would tend to make the assumption that the poor and the black are simply dumb and wanton.

Adelaide Hill and Frederick Jaffe, after an extensive review of the issues and data about Negro fertility, draw some cogent conclusions:

> Negro parents in all socio-economic groups (except the few now living on Southern farms) express a consistent desire for smaller families than do whites. In those few communities where skillful and sympathetic birth control services have been made available to impoverished Negroes, the response has been considerable. Adequate instruction in fertility control, however, is still beyond the reach of the poor because tax supported and charity medical agencies do not yet generally offer these services. The Planned Parenthood Federation of America estimates that there are some five million American women in impoverished families—about one-fourth Negro—who are in their child-bearing years, fertile, and not pregnant or seeking pregnancy at any given time, and who thus may be considered the minimum patient load for subsidized contraceptive services in the United States. Approximately 500,000 of these women are estimated to receive contraceptive services either from Planned Parenthood Centers or public agencies, leaving 4.5 million women not now being served. . . .
>
> This does not mean that *any* kind of program will work automatically, if the program is proffered with racist overtones, if it is coupled with constant threats to sterilize unmarried mothers on welfare, if it is presented as a punitive

means of reducing relief costs, and if the mere request for birth control is taken as *prima facie* evidence that there's a "man in the house," thus jeopardizing the women's eligibility for public assistance, the response is likely to be negligible.[11]

After all this, however, are poor families and Negro families actually more *accepting* of illegitimacy? And if they are, does not this willingness to accept illegitimacy necessarily influence a girl's readiness to come home with a little bastard in her arms?

The answer is partially dependent on one's definition of the term acceptance. One is reminded of Carlyle, upon hearing that Margaret Fuller had announced that she accepted the universe, snorting, "She damned well better!" Human beings can endure and live through a great deal, but this does not mean that they accept it in the sense that they are tolerant of it. What choice, after all, does a poor Negro girl with an illegitimate child have other than to accept it? And what choice do her mother and father have? Are they to imitate the old-time melodramatic scene of throwing the daughter out in the snowy night? What does their acceptance mean? They shrug and say, "Come in," and start looking around to borrow a crib and some baby clothes. What would any parents do who loved their daughter?

The best evidence I know of about attitudes of low income families, black and white, toward illegitimacy is to be found in the detailed and careful studies of Hylan Lewis.[12] By and large, the mothers in Lewis' families seem rather afraid of sex and afraid of its consequences (it may be that they are realistic rather than puritanical), and they worry about their daughters. If it happens that daughters have babies out-of-wedlock, their parents get upset, and angry, and ashamed. Many of them doubtless rant and rave, and scream and cry. But basically they are loving, supporting, and sympathetic.

These mothers accept their daughters, for better or worse, because they love them; and they love and accept their grandchildren. They do not value legitimacy any the less; perhaps they value it more because they have more practical and realistic knowledge of the consequences of illegitimacy. To dismiss events of this order with phrases about cultural tolerance of illegitimacy is both false and insulting.

The context of acceptance, after all, is choice. It has been shown that the highway from getting into bed with a boyfriend to standing on the doorstep with an illegitimate child is a road forked with a number of choice points—contraception, abortion, forced marriage, and finally adoption. The poor and the Negroes are, to put it simply, denied equality of choice at each of these points. Being forced to rely on public medical care, they are far less likely to receive accurate and effective contraceptive information; lacking money, they are usually unable to afford an abortion; lacking a job, the man is less able to offer the refuge of marriage; and finally, their babies are viewed, in terms of adoption, as "hard to place." Black babies and babies of mixed racial parentage, who are classified as black, are a less readily marketed product in the adoption exchange; they are lumped together with those having genuine defects. In the adoption market, the best-seller is the infant who is fair, structurally intact, and mechanically sound. If it carries a luxury brand name (mother: Radcliffe; father: Harvard Medical School), the bidding will go very high indeed. As a result, poor unmarried mothers are not encouraged to enter the competition, and black unmarried mothers rarely get in at all.

In our Boston study which I mentioned above, the unmarried mother who was from a white collar suburban family was much more likely to be accepted by an adoption agency than a girl from a blue collar inner-city area. (Young women who reach an adoption agency in the first place are over-whelmingly white, since black unmarried mothers are rarely referred.)

So the poor girl or the Negro girl who becomes pregnant out-of-wedlock is usually committed to single motherhood. In the rhetoric of Puritan morality, in the terms of Victorian melodrama, this represents the myth of "paying the price of folly." But once again reality deviates substantially from mythology. Motherhood, after all is said and done, is still a pretty good thing; who, indeed, dares knock it in America? Having a baby, legitimate or illegitimate, is still a joyful experience; and a two-person family, though statistically deviant and economically difficult, is still familial. This fact has recently been recognized in the experimental beginnings of one-parent adoptions. Somehow, most unmarried mothers manage. They make do and make a life for themselves. Many, perhaps most, marry at a later point. Others find jobs, go to school, pick up the pieces.

Surprising as it seems to devotees of the mythology of illegitimacy, only a minority of unmarried mothers depend on public assistance. There are about 3.5 million children under the age of eighteen who are illegitimate. And about an equal number—3.5 to 4 million—receive public assistance under the AFDC program. But these are *not* the same children! The group of illegitimate children and the group of AFDC children are two separate populations that overlap to only a small degree. Only about one AFDC child in six is illegitimate; fewer than one out of five illegitimate children receives AFDC support.

These facts illustrate the complete lack of logic in any program that proposes to reduce the welfare loads by reducing illegitimacy. Such a program proposal may make for effective political oratory and may produce some juicy head-lines, but it lacks any solid foundation in fact. It is true that in recent years there has been a rapid rise in the size of AFDC caseloads and there has also been a rise in the ab-solute number of illegitimate births and in the proportion of births that are illegitimate. However, there has *not* been any significant rise in illegitimacy *rate,* which is the crucial in-dicator. The illegitimacy rate (as distinguished from the ratio of illegitimate to total births) is measured by the total in-cidence of out-of-wedlock births among all women of child-bearing age. The relationships among these data and their interpretive significance recently have been analyzed and ex-plicated in great detail and clarity by Elizabeth Herzog.[13] The increase in welfare loads has been accounted for largely by other significant changes, notably the general increase in the child population and the increased use by the poor of their *rights* to receive public assistance.

One of the major defects of our welfare system—one of the characteristics that serves as a focal point for criticism—is its failure to provide help to the majority of the poor. A recent nationwide study has shown that, among the very poor families studied, only one in four had *ever* received public assistance. Richard Cloward and his collaborators have re-viewed a number of studies and have concluded that fewer than *half* of all persons entitled to, and legally eligible for, welfare help ever actually receive it.[14] In New York, which provides for supplemental grants to low-income families with employed fathers, only a very small proportion of those who are eligible are even aware of it. Recent changes in the ac-ceptance rates of applicants have accounted for much of the increase in the welfare caseloads[15]—the intake workers in local welfare departments are being less arbitrary and exclu-sive in establishing the eligibility of clients. This change in practice (which is usually a change in the direction of greater conformity to legislative and regulatory provisions, rather than in the direction of laxity) has come about, in turn, mostly as a result of the pressure brought from organized consumers of welfare; they have become much more aware and sophisticated about their own rights and also the rights of friends and neighbors who should, but do not, receive assistance. The National Welfare Rights movement, led by Dr. George Wiley, now has tens of thousands of members in cities all over the country. Mothers have energized and activated themselves and their co-recipients to fight for the standards of "health and decency" that are, in the abstract, due their children according to most state welfare legislation. The rise in caseloads and budgets of welfare departments all over the country reflects this new movement and results from this exercise of new power.

Let me cite an example from personal experience. At the Connecticut Mental Health Center in New Haven, we finally succeeded in persuading the administration to permit us to train and deploy a small team of community organizers to work with welfare mothers. Our workers contacted recipient families, brought them together to talk about common problems, and assisted them to form an organization, the Hill-Dwight Moms. There were a number of common complaints —insufficient allowances for heat and utilities, scanty food budgets, unwillingness to replace necessities such as irons; but at that time of the year, August, the greatest source of worry was lack of clothing for children going back to school. That the mothers had a right to expect additional grants to bring the clothing supply of the children up to standard was not in question. (The nature of the standards was something else though: Boys are supposed to get along with two sets of underwear, two dungarees, two slacks, one suit, one pair of shoes. Girls can have two bras, two underpants, one slip, two dresses, two skirts, two jerseys, and one pair of shoes. The *complete wardrobe* of any child between the ages of seven and thirteen can be purchased, according to these standards, for $144.80.)

The Moms wrote to the district welfare office supervisor, visited her, discussed the problem several times, and received reassuring promises that all the families were to be brought up to the clothing standards. Very little happened after this. They visited again, in force, determined to demand what the law and the regulations of the department said they were entitled to. This visit turned into a prolonged, somewhat ragged and anarchistic, but quite effective, sit-in. About two dozen Moms (and two of our workers) were arrested and carted off to jail on the standard New Haven charge of disorderly conduct; but after this demonstration, which was followed by more letters and several negotiating sessions, the clothing orders and extra allowance checks started to trickle out of the welfare office. As a result of this direct action (in the course of which a number of families eligible for state aid were discovered and enrolled) there was a significant rise in the welfare costs for this district. Multiply this effect by the number of such welfare rights groups operating all over the country—now numbering in the hundreds—and one begins to understand that the "welfare spiral" is due, not to the rise in illegitimacy, or "chiseling" or laziness, but to the plain old-fashioned American practice of demanding and getting one's rights.

To suggest that anyone—or at least more than a tiny handful of errratic or disturbed persons—would choose the bitter existence of AFDC as a way of life except as a last resort, is to demonstrate ignorance either of the basic nature of humanity, or of what life is like on AFDC. First, it must be recognized that public assistance, as it is administered by the states, *insures* poverty. Two-thirds of the states have a policy of giving recipients grants smaller than the state's own definition of *minimum* basic needs. One-fourth of the states pay less than sixty per cent of their own definition of minimum basic needs. And only a handful of states set their standard of minimum basic needs at a level that approaches the poverty line—the average standard is approximately forty per cent below the poverty level, the average grant is roughly fifty per cent below that level. In other words, the average AFDC family could have its public assistance grant almost *doubled* and still not quite rise above the poverty line. There are a number of states that provide monthly allotments to AFDC families of less than $20 a person. It is hard to believe that anyone could perceive this income as a desirable goal to strive for, or even as a standard of living to be moderately contented with.

In order to understand the conditions of life on AFDC, one can compare average income with the income of an AFDC family. As of April, 1968, the average per-person monthly grant throughout the country was $40.45. This balanced out the few states that had relatively high levels of grants—New York: $65.05, New Jersey: $58.45, Connecticut: $56.80, Massachusetts: $55.20—with a large number of states that gave very low grants—Mississippi: $8.45, Alabama: $15.10, Florida: $15.15, South Carolina: $18.50. The typical mother with three small children then, was enjoying a magnificent monthly income from AFDC of about $160. In the more niggardly states, this income amounted to an unbelievable $35 or $60 or $75 a month; but even in the most generous states, the monthly income was only $225 or $250 a month, which is *below* the established poverty line. How many women reading this page would be willing to undertake to raise three children in New York City on $260 a month? How many would be willing to try it at *double* that income?

Charles Lebeaux has reported precisely what life is like on AFDC for families living on what he calls "budgets of despair."[16] While this study is somewhat out of date, and related to particular problems in a particular city—Detroit in 1962—it is possible to generalize from it. With a maximum of $180 a month, a mother of three children might have to pay rent of $70 or $80 or even more (five of the 92 families studied were paying $100 or more) and then stretch the remaining $100 or $110 to cover food, clothing, transportation, recreation, school costs, and "incidentals." The result, of course, was that most families were constantly on the edge of disaster. If they ate enough, they couldn't pay rent or utilities; if shoes were bought for a child in school, there wasn't enough money for food. "No fruit, no vegetables" was the standard response to a question about diet; cheap cuts of meat, canned meat, and starchy foods made up the bulk of the diet of AFDC families. Children normally had one pair of shoes, and the replacement of a pair of shoes was a family crisis. Most children had no rubbers or raincoats. These families could manage only by running out or running behind. One family scavenged for pop bottles to cash in for a few pennies for a quart of milk; another mother was ashamed to admit that the lady downstairs gave her food; a third said bitterly, "A woman could always get $10 if she had to"; a fourth "borrowed" from the funds of a club of which she is treasurer and was so half-crazed with worry about exposure that the hospital she went to referred her to a psychiatrist. This is our welfare system that is supposed to be such a temptation to the lazy and promiscuous poor. Lebeaux sums it up well:

Consider our affluent society: in an economy generating wealth sufficient to supply every family of four with nearly

$10,000 per year income, we reduce a family to cashing in pop bottles to get food, we push a woman to thoughts of prostitution to feed her children, we force an honest woman into theft and then provide her with $25 an hour psychiatric treatment.[17]

Add to this the other difficulties and indignities of AFDC life—humiliation and shame, being subject to midnight raids to check on the presence of a man in the house, constant supervision and investigation, the need to almost beg for ordinary amenities of living like an iron or overshoes for the children—and it should be clear that almost no sane person chooses that life voluntarily. It should not be surprising that a recent survey in New York showed that, among AFDC mothers, over seventy per cent (and over eighty per cent of black mothers) would choose to work if suitable employment could be found for them.

The welfare problem is something far more grievous than an adjunct to illegitimacy. And, despite the views of Urbanologist Moynihan, illegitimacy has only a minor relationship to welfare. The real problem is not to get families *off* the welfare rolls, it is to make welfare—or its successor—dignified enough and sufficiently humanitarian to attract those lone mothers who now prefer to work and raise their children as best they can rather than endure the humiliation of a welfare life. Most middle class mothers with, say, an eight-year-old, a five-year-old, and a two-year-old, do not and would not work full time; to do so would be to risk the judgment of one's neighbors as a neglectful mother. The standards of maternal care for suburban affluent families are surely equally applicable to poverty-stricken one-parent families in the poor neighborhoods of the inner-city. Of course, if effective, high-quality day care centers were widely available, the nature of the problem would be altered. In such a case, a mother would not have to face the impossible choice between work and decent child care. She could work secure in the knowledge that her children were not suffering as a result of her working.

But the truth is that day care is not widely available and is not likely to be for some time to come. For the foreseeable future, the preferred system of child-rearing in America is likely to be care in the home by the mother. The most obvious and pressing task, then, is to develop a method of income maintenance that would permit fatherless families to subsist at a reasonable level of "health and decency" without forcing the mother into the labor market. That is the welfare problem, plain and simple.

I I I

In summary, it seems fair to say that unmarried motherhood is the mark, not of deviancy and degeneracy, but of victimization. The "problem" of illegitimacy is not due to promiscuity, immorality, or culturally-based variations in sexual habits; it is due to discrimination and gross inequities between rich and poor, and more particularly, between white and black. It is the visible sign and outcome of a total pattern of inequality in the distribution of, and access to, significant resources, and reflects the intent of the dominant majority to keep the poor in their place, insuring that the life of the poor is hard and precarious.

Our spiteful attitudes are very similar to those in the old joke about the attitude of English nobility: A duke and his new bride spent their wedding night in joyful encounter, and the newly deflowered duchess asked, in pleasureful wonderment, "Is this what they call sex"? "Yes, my dear." "And the lower classes, do they do it too"? "Of course, my darling." "Much too good for them."

We complain about the sex lives of the poor in much the same way we complain about their having television sets. We no longer require of the poor that they starve to death on the public streets, but we do believe that it's good for them to be a little hungry. We certainly won't stand for them enjoying life in any way at all, else what would motivate them to overcome their somewhat shameful state of poverty?

Of course, as I have hinted, illegitimacy is functionally useful to society. To eliminate it would be to eliminate the raw material of the adoption process, whose products are sought after by childless middle class couples. The great surplus of unadopted illegitimate children is, by these standards, an untidy by-product of the process, substandard material that is to be thrown back onto the resources of the hopelessly inadequate child welfare and public assistance system.

Society encourages illegitimacy not, as is generally thought, by encouraging premarital sex, but by discouraging responsible parenthood through making it impossible for the black and the poor to make responsible *choices* about parenthood.

Until we make such responsible choices as possible for the poor girl as for middle class daughters, we can only preserve our sense of righteousness by denying our own acts of oppression, and deprivation, and blaming the victim.

5
Learning to Be Poor

The Culture of

Poverty Cheesecake

I

"Do you want your prize to be one Hershey bar today, or two Hershey bars next Wednesday?"

A social scientist asks the question solemnly. He is conducting an experiment in an elementary classroom, and his subjects and listeners are the school children who have just been playing the simple game he has presented to them—perhaps a silly, or even boring game, but a considerable relief from the task of memorizing the capitals and principal products of Ecuador and Peru. The experimenter is no more interested in the game than the children are; he is eager to hear what the prize-winner will choose: one if he takes it now, two if he can contain himself and wait until next week.

"If you unexpectedly got a windfall of two thousand dollars, what would you do with it?"

The young lady asking the question holds her clipboard in standard fashion, casually, planted in the crook of her left arm. She is a pretty cog in the public opinion industry doing her part in the intricate business of conducting an attitude poll. After she conscientiously writes down the response, it will be coded, and processed, and fed into a computer, and the information will be transformed into one of two simple answers to a question that intrigues her employers—that two grand that just fell into your lap, will you save it or will you spend it?

These are two examples of the ways that behavioral scientists try to find out how much ability different persons have to *wait* to have their needs gratified. Like most human characteristics, this trait is presumed to be variably distributed throughout the population: some people can wait, others must have their reward immediately.

Academic and political experts on poverty and the poor have given wide currency to the proposition that this distribution is highly related to social class position. The pattern of behavior characterized by ability to delay need-gratification—what has been called the Deferred Gratification Pattern (D.G.P.)—is supposedly characteristic of the middle classes. Members of the lower classes, in contrast, are usually rumored to display the Non-deferred Gratification Pattern (N.G.P.). The formula has all the force and simplicity of a classical cigarette advertising commercial: M.C./D.G.P.; L.C./N.G.P. All it lacks is a catchy tune.

The consumer of tobacco is deliberately assaulted with such a message to create in his mind a preference for one brand of cigarettes. Now, no one accuses the academic and political intellectuals who transmit the slogans about deferred

113

need-gratification of having such a deliberate intent. They would be outraged—and properly so—at such an accusation. The fact is, however, that the effect is really very similar. The consumer of popularized social science is no more immune to brainwashing than is the consumer of tobacco; he can hardly resist developing a preference for the behavior patterns attributed to the middle class person, who is pictured as a mature man of prudence and foresight, able to plan ahead and reap the long-term rewards of virtue. He looks particularly good in contrast to the portrait of the lower classes—feckless folk indeed, thoughtless and impulsive, with a childish, if not immoral insistence on gratification now.

There is vast sociological literature detailing the supposed differences between the poor and the middle class on such variables—including values, child-rearing practices, level of aspiration, sexual behavior, and so forth. As in the case of ability to defer gratification, it is found that the middle class come out on top every time—they are said to have greater commitment to education, achievement, orderly family lives, sexual regularity, and to rear their children in such a way as to impel them to do likewise.[1] More recently, these ideas have been pulled together into such packages as the "culture of poverty"[2] and the "lower class culture."[3] And here is where we start to run into ideological trouble. Viewed simply as descriptions, all these different portraits of poor people might simply be dismissed as stereotypes or exaggerations. They might be left to the ministrations of a Poor People's Anti-Defamation League, if there were one. But aficionados of the culture of poverty go several steps further into very dangerous territory. They identify the culture of poverty and lower class culture and the presumed life styles of the poor as themselves *causes* of continued poverty. This theme in the writing of

Oscar Lewis—otherwise exciting and insightful when viewed as highly sensitive descriptions of some families living in poverty—is, to me, very disturbing. He makes such statements as:

> Once the culture of poverty has come into existence it tends to perpetuate itself. By the time slum children are six or seven they have usually absorbed the basic attitudes and values of their subculture. Thereafter they are psychologically unready to take full advantage of changing conditions or improving opportunities that may develop in their lifetime.[4]

In fairness, it should be stressed that Lewis' thinking along these lines is quite cautious. He states that by no means all of the world's poor live in the culture of poverty (and is inclined to think it may be essentially absent in some of the socialist countries), and that, in the United States, only a small minority of the poor—no more than one in five—can be placed within it. Those who quote Lewis so freely and simplify his ideas so readily are much less cautious. In my judgment, this is because they share neither his genuine empathy for the poor nor his conviction that social changes of a structural nature are necessary to deal with the problem of poverty.

The extent to which these ideas have penetrated the thinking of the social welfare establishment and that of its pet academics can be grasped rather well by reading a revolting government publication, a little pamphlet called *Growing Up Poor*[5] (which might well have been subtitled *Dick and Jane Go Slumming*). In its 108 pages, Catherine Chilman has managed to pack every nefarious idea about the poor that has ever been dreamed up in the past thirty years, up to and including, incredible as it may seem, the question of the poor's "social acceptability." It is a downright emetic book, yet every person concerned about these questions should read it in order to understand what social workers and social scientists are whispering to each other behind their cupped hands. Let me provide a preview with a few choice quotations:

> With all its faults, the middle class way, compared to that more typical of the very poor, seems to be more in harmony with present-day economic realities. The middle class approach has played importantly into the building of this system and has been built by it.[6]

> Thus, both for the benefit of a number of the poor themselves and for the rest of society, it would appear that, among other things, methods should be found within the democratic framework to help many lower-lower class parents raise their children in a way that, in the light of available evidence, would seem to be predictive of a greater likelihood of success and fulfillment in today's society.[7]

> The subcultural adaptation to poverty would seem to interact with the poverty situation to perpetuate lower-lower class status. For the welfare of many of the very poor, as well as for the welfare of the rest of society, it seems to be necessary to help a large group re-adapt its life styles to more effective patterns.[8]

> However, the school is also an important part of the child's social world and the low-income child in the mainly middle class school room is generally observed to be a social outcast.[9]

> As in the case of the generally accepted criteria for "good adjustment" or positive mental health, so the characteristics of the socially acceptable child are solidly middle class.[10]

> As in the case of other substantive areas discussed in this paper, the child-rearing patterns more characteristic of the very poor seem poorly calculated to develop "good moral character" in many of their children.[11]

> "No cheating in school" is often used as a criterion of honesty by researchers. With the educational cards generally

stacked against the very poor child, his failure record might well be worse than it usually is, if he consistently abstained from cheating.[12]

In addition, Dr. Chilman goes on to list no fewer than fifty-one characteristics of the way of life of the lower-lower class that are specifically handicapping to any one of them who might want to achieve such middle class characteristics as being well-adjusted, well-educated, socially acceptable, of good moral character, and involved in sound family life. Among them are (I swear!):

Fatalistic, apathetic attitudes

Magical, rigid thinking

Pragmatic, concrete values

Poor impulse control

Ambivalent attitudes toward property rights

Little value placed on neatness and cleanliness

Little verbal communication and discussion

High divorce and separation rates

Income less than $3,000 a year

Growing Up Poor can be thought of as a somewhat adulterated, but reasonably accurate distillate of the culture of poverty ideology—a popularization of this new version of the idea that poverty is a resultant of the characteristics of the poor themselves. This can be contrasted with the idea that poverty is most simply and clearly understood as a lack of money. One might formulate this idea in a more elegant way —"poverty is an economic status etiologically related to absence of both monetary input and access to income-generating resources"—but the message is the same. Being poor is having no cash in hand and damned little on the way. Put in these terms, poverty in the United States is almost a picayune problem. A redistribution of about fifteen billion dollars a year (less than two per cent of our Gross National Product that is now pushing toward one trillion dollars annually) would bring every poor person above the present poverty line. This is less than half our annual expenditure on the Viet Nam War.

But if poverty is to be understood more clearly in terms of the "way of life" of the poor, in terms of a "lower class culture," as a product of a deviant value system, then money is clearly not the answer. We can stop right now worrying about ways of redistributing our resources more equitably, and begin focusing our concern where it belongs—on the poor themselves. We can start trying to figure out how to change that troublesome culture of theirs, how to apply some tautening astringent to their flabby consciences, how to deal with their poor manners and make them more socially acceptable. By this hard and wearying method of liquidating lower class culture, we can liquidate the lower class, and, thereby, bring an end to poverty.

It all comes perilously close to putting into reality the satire of a comic greeting card that was published when President Johnson first decided to go into the poverty business. The front cover of the card showed a bedraggled old lady, with a raggedy skirt and a shawl over her head, saying, "I hear there's going to be a War on Poverty." The inside of the card shows her, arms spread wide in great concern, continuing, "Does that mean they're going to shoot me?"

II

The concept of culture has been defined many times, and although no definition has achieved universal acceptance, most of the definitions include three central ideas: that culture is passed on from generation to generation, that a culture represents a ready-made prescription for living and for making day-to-day decisions, and, finally, that the components of a culture are accepted by those in the culture as good, and true, and not to be questioned. The eminent anthropologist George Murdock has listed seventy-three items that characterize every known culture, past and present.[13] The list begins with Age-grading and Athletic sports, runs to Weaning and Weather Control, and includes on the way such items as Calendar, Firemaking, Property Rights, and Toolmaking. I would submit that even the most extreme advocate of a culture of poverty viewpoint would readily acknowledge that, with respect to almost all of these items, every American, beyond the first-generation immigrant, regardless of race or class, is a member of a common culture. We all share pretty much the same sports. Maybe poor kids don't know how to play polo, and rich kids don't spend time with stickball, but we all know baseball, and football, and basketball. Despite some misguided efforts to raise minor dialects to the status of separate tongues, we all, in fact, share the same language. There may be differences in diction and usage, but it would be ridiculous to say that all Americans don't speak English. We have the calendar, the law, and large numbers of other cultural items in common. It may well be true that on a few of the seventy-three items there are minor variations between classes, but these kinds of things are really slight variations on a common theme. There are other items that show variability, not in relation to class, but in relation to religion and ethnic background—funeral customs and cooking, for example. But if there is one place in America where the melting pot is a reality, it is on the kitchen stove; in the course of one month, half the readers of this sentence have probably eaten pizza, hot pastrami, and chow mein. Specific differences that might be identified as signs of separate cultural identity are relatively insignificant within the general unity of American life; they are cultural commas and semicolons in the paragraphs and pages of American life.

That the poor in America constitute a separate culture, then, is a manifest absurdity. At most, a claim might be made that they constitute a subculture, on the basis of a few dimensions already mentioned—values, sex and family life, child rearing, and some personality characteristics.

Before proceeding, I would like to call attention to a new book, titled *Culture and Poverty: Critique and Counter-Proposals,*[14] that was sent to me while I was engaged in writing this chapter. The author, Charles Valentine, packs into 189 pages a scholarly and devastating critique of the culture of poverty concept, which outrages his sense of anthropological propriety.

As an anthropologist, Valentine is particularly incensed by the bad habit of drawing cultural conclusions from social statistics such as census data:

> . . . census figures alone tell us nothing directly about structure or process in a cultural system. To the extent that census data are valid, they give us the statistical shape of a demographic reality. This statistical pattern is a surface phenomenon that may have a wide variety of cultural designs for living underlying it.
>
> Consider, for example, a demographic pattern in which at any one time there are many households without an observable resident adult male heading the domestic menage. This picture may reflect a system of plural marriage in which co-wives reside separately and husbands live with one wife at a time, as is the case in polygymous societies in numerous parts of the world. It may reflect a community organization

in which all adult males reside together and apart from their wives and children, as in much of the Southwest Pacific. It may be associated with a traditional family form in which male support for the household comes from kinsmen by blood, with no such social position as resident husband, as among the Nayar of South India. It may be found in societies where males are migrant laborers for periods of years while their spouses and offspring remain in the home community, as in many colonial areas. Or it may reflect a variety of systems in which multiple consensual unions involve males in various standardized obligations to women and children, not including cohabitation, as reported from Caribbean societies.[15]

Valentine also cannot swallow the validity of using the term culture in describing the life of the poor. Referring to Oscar Lewis' statement that the life patterns of the poor correspond to the traditional anthropological concept of culture, Valentino says:

Yet within this catalog of traits are quite a number that fit into this definition with difficulty, if at all. Many of these features seem more like externally imposed conditions or unavoidable matters of situational expediency, rather than cultural creations internal to the sub-society in question.[16]

The point to be made in this controversy is simply this: if the poor are different in significant ways from the rest of us, are these differences *cultural?* It is easy to be misled and to fall into the easy jargon of the day and call all kinds of minor phenomena cultures or subcultures. Consider a possible analogy: there are several million men who share certain traits, centering around an addiction to alcohol; they work irregularly, for example, show a high arrest rate, and also have high rates of family disorganization; they represent a minority of alcoholics, an even smaller minority of heavy drinkers. On the basis of such findings, would we feel comfortable in talking about a culture, or a subculture, of alcohol? A minority of the rich share many traits of the Sanchez and Rios families, and other families studied by Oscar Lewis—they are alienated from social institutions, tend to be unemployed or irregularly employed, demonstrate high rates of antisocial behavior, and have high divorce rates. Does this small group of the rich constitute a Culture of Affluence?

But, in any case, are the poor really all that different from the middle class? Take a common type of study, showing that ninety-one per cent of the upper class, compared to only sixty-eight per cent of the poor, prefer college education for their children.[17] What does that tell us about the difference in values between classes?

First, if almost seventy per cent of the poor want their children to go to college, it doesn't make much sense to say that the poor, as a group, do not value education. Only a minority of them—somewhat less than one-third—fail to express a *wish* that their children attend college. A smaller minority—one in ten—of the middle class give similar responses. One might well wonder why this small group of the better-off citizens of our achieving society reject higher education. They have the money; many of them have the direct experience of education; and most of them are aware of the monetary value of a college degree. I would suggest that the thirty per cent of the poor who are unwilling to express a wish that their children go to college are easier to understand. They know the barriers—financial, social, and for black parents, racial—that make it very difficult for the children of the poor to get a college education. That seven out of ten of them nevertheless persist in a desire to see their children in a cap and gown is, in a very real sense, remarkable. Most important, if we are concerned with cultural or subcultural differences, it seems highly illogical to emphasize the values of a small minority of one group and then to attribute these values to the whole group. I simply cannot accept the evidence. If seventy per cent of a group values education, then it is completely illogical to say that the group as a whole does *not* value education.

A useful formulation is to be found in Hyman Rodman's conception of the "lower class value stretch" which, to give a highly oversimplified version, proposes that members of the lower class *share* the dominant value system but *stretch* it to include as much as possible of the variations that circumstances force upon them. Rodman says:

> Lower class persons in close interaction with each other and faced with similar problems do not long remain in a state of mutual ignorance. They do not maintain a strong commitment to middle class values that they cannot attain, and they do not continue to respond to others in a rewarding or punishing way simply on the basis of whether these others are living up to the middle class values. A change takes place. They come to tolerate and eventually to evaluate favorably certain deviations from the middle class values. In this way they need not be continually frustrated by their failure to live up to unattainable values. The resultant is a stretched value system with a low degree of commitment to all the values within the range, including the dominant, middle class values.[18]

In Rodman's terms, then, differences in range of values and commitments to specific elements within that range occur primarily as an *adaptive* rather than as a *cultural* response.

One of the more obnoxious of the experts is Walter Miller who, unlike Oscar Lewis, sees us being inundated by the questionable behavior of the lower orders. He claims that forty to sixty per cent of Americans are partially affected by "lower class culture," and at least fifteen per cent (the "hard-core poor") are rather completely immersed in it. He is well known for having discovered the "focal concerns" of the lower class, which include such items as *excitement, autonomy, smartness,* and *toughness.* I will not inflict on the reader a detailed delineation of these concerns, but listen to this one bit of fatuous nonsense:

> "Smartness," as conceptualized in lower class culture, involves the capacity to outsmart, outfox, outwit, dupe, "take," "con" another or others, and the concomitant capacity to avoid being outwitted, "taken," or duped oneself. In its essence, smartness involves the capacity to achieve a valued entity—material goods, personal status—through a maximum use of mental agility and a minimum use of physical effort.[19]

The trouble with this kind of research and this kind of theorizing is that it lacks context. There is no comparative presentation. It smacks of the advertising slogan, "GRAB washes your clothes fifty per cent whiter!" Whiter than what? Than they were when they were dirty? Than they would be if washed in clear water? So with Miller's "focal concerns." They would only be important discoveries if they distinguished the lower class from some other group that would presumably value *boredom, stupidity, subjugation,* and *weakness.* I, for one, have never heard of any group with such a set of "focal concerns."

I am not questioning in any way that the lower class youth, whom Miller studied, demonstrated the concerns he has written about. I am merely questioning that this distinguishes them from middle class or upper class youth.

I seriously doubt that the well-to-do are any less concerned about "smartness," for example, than are the poor. Granted there may be differences in expression; the concerns may be lived out in different arenas and therefore in slightly different terms. The middle class junior executive may display his concern for smartness and "conning" in office politics rather than on the street; he may gamble with a broker rather than a bookie; he may act out his sexual aggressiveness with a girl from the secretarial pool rather than one from the next block. The differences in behavioral end-products are relatively minor and largely mediated by environmental circumstances, much more readily explainable by some concept analogous to Rodman's value-stretch idea than by such a highly inflated concept as lower class culture.

On the more specific topic of child-rearing practices, we have vastly more usable data than on the issue of value systems. Unfortunately much of the data has been contradictory. Two of the major studies, both quite old now, that illustrate the contradictions are that of Davis and Havighurst[20] and that of Eleanor Maccoby and her associates.[21] The Davis study, which has been extremely influential, indicated that middle class child-rearing was generally stricter than that of working class parents. Less than ten years later, Maccoby demonstrated precisely the opposite: that middle class parents were more permissive. A number of other studies also have shown contradictory results.

Fortunately, Bronfenbrenner[22] took on the task of trying to make sense out of all this contradictory material. He demonstrates very ingeniously that much of the disagreement can be resolved by placing the data along a time dimension (and along a geographical dimension, too). He takes some fifteen studies, carried out over a twenty-five year period, and shows that, in fact, child-rearing practices have been changing steadily, with changes among lower class mothers lagging behind those among middle class mothers. It is as if we were looking at two cyclical patterns somewhat out of phase with one another. The differences between classes are not class-rooted in any cultural or subcultural sense; that is, they are not transmitted from generation to generation, or inherent in the way of life of any particular class. Rather, we see general responsiveness to overall changes in the society—one class may be more or less rapid in responding, but the response is similar in all classes, not different between classes. He shows that the state of child-rearing practice in any one place and at any one time is much more reflective of professional opinion regarding child care and development than it is of supposed fixed class or racial patterns. In other words, Dr. Spock conquers all, something we should all find very encouraging.

The most recent, and in many ways the best information on this subject comes to us from the Hylan Lewis child-rearing studies, which I have mentioned before. Lewis has demonstrated (finally, one hopes) that there really *is* no "lower class child-rearing pattern." There are a number of such patterns—ranging from strict and over-controlled parenting, to permissiveness, to downright neglect—just as in Lewis' sample there are a variety of different kinds of families —ranging from those with rigid, old-fashioned standards of hard work, thrift, morality and obsessive cleanliness, to the disorganized and disturbed families that he calls the "clinical poor." Lewis says:

> . . . it appears as a broad spectrum of pragmatic adjustments to external and internal stresses and deprivation. . . . Many low income families appear here as, in fact, the frustrated victims of what are thought of as middle class values, behavior and aspirations.[23]

We return, finally, to where we began: the concept of Deferred Need Gratification. The simple idea that lower class folk have, as a character trait, a built-in deficiency in ability to delay need gratification has been explored, analyzed and more or less blown apart by Miller, Riessman, and Seagull.[24] They point out that the supposed commitment of the middle classes to the virtues of thrift and hard work, to the practices of planning and saving for every painfully-chosen expenditure is, at this point in time, at best a surviving myth reflecting past conditions of dubious prevalence. The middle classes of today are clearly consumption-minded and debt-addicted. So the comparison group against which the poor are judged exists largely as a theoretical category with a theoretical behavior pattern. They go on to raise critical questions, similar to those I have raised earlier in this chapter. For example, on the question of what one would do with a two thousand dollar windfall, there was a difference between class groups of only five per cent—about seventy per cent of the middle class said they would save most of it, compared with about sixty-five per cent of the lower class. On the basis of this small difference (which was statistically, but not practically, significant) the researchers, you will remember, had concluded that working-class people had less ability to defer need gratification. This conclusion may reflect elegant research methodology, but it fails the test of common sense.

One of the authors, Seagull, in examining this conclusion, conducted a very illuminating study: he used the Hershey bar paradigm that was described at the beginning of this chapter, but introduced an additional element. The added factor consisted of giving the children an experience in which the promise of delayed gratification (two candy bars next week rather than one right now) was either kept or not kept. When the experiment was repeated, this was the only factor that differentiated between those who chose immediate gratification, and those who chose to delay. Class and race were *not* related to delay. Those who had experienced a broken promise were the ones—not unsurprisingly—who were not willing to delay and thereby risk another disappointment. To generalize from an experimental classroom situation to a real life situation is of course risky, but it seems highly plausible that this kind of *experiential* determinant is much more potent in influencing delay or lack of delay in gratification. As Seagull and his associates say, "The situational variable, then, rather than class affiliation, determined the ability to delay."

As for the idea that the poor share a culture in the sense that they subscribe to and follow a particular, deviant prescription for living—a poor man's blueprint for choosing and decision-making which accounts for the way he lives—this does not deserve much comment. Every study—with the exception of the egregious productions of Walter Miller—shows that, at the very least, overwhelming numbers of the poor give allegiance to the values and principles of the dominant American culture.

A related point—often the most overlooked point in any discussion of the culture of poverty—is that there is not, to my knowledge, *any evidence whatever* that the poor perceive their way of life as good and preferable to that of other ways of life. To make such an assertion is to talk pure nonsense. To avoid making such an assertion is to admit, at least implicitly, that the culture of poverty, whatever else it may be (if, indeed, it is anything more than a catch phrase approximately as respectable intellectually as the concept of The Pepsi Generation) is, in no conceivable sense, a cultural phenomenon.

Lee Rainwater has developed perhaps the most broadly acceptable formulation of these issues. He notes that there is relatively little difference in descriptions of the *behavior* differences that characterize the poor and suggests that, from a policy point of view, the crucial issue is to view this behavior as *adaptive,* adaptive to a state of being deprived, excluded, and demeaned. He suggests that—

> . . . if lower class culture is to be changed and lower class people are eventually to be enabled to take advantage of "opportunities" to participate in conventional society and to earn their own way in it, this change can only come about through a change in the social and ecological situation to which lower class people must adapt.[25]

He suggests that the basic anti-poverty strategy must be a "resource equalization strategy," with the key goal being equalization of income.

I I I

Members of the culture of poverty cult swim almost exclusively in a stream that springs from the work of W. Lloyd Warner, whose original studies in American social stratification are now over thirty years old. As is true of many great innovators and seminal figures in the social sciences, Warner's contribution was more significant in the large questions it addressed than in the answers it produced. Warner's impact on American sociology consisted in raising the issue of social class and social stratification, a heretofore rather neglected topic. He demonstrated the somewhat unpalatable truth that there is social inequality and social ranking in American life, that some persons are in fact considered to be of more value than others. Unfortunately, his followers, rather than building on and expanding the scope of his work, bound themselves strictly within the limitations of method and concept that Warner began with.

Although Warner's approach to social stratification mixes a number of heterogeneous indices such as area of residence, occupation, income, type of house lived in, membership in clubs, etc., ultimately it focuses on associations, on participation in cliques, and most important, on personal evaluation of others. In other words, Warner was looking basically at prestige or esteem in the community. In more traditional usage, what he calls *class* would be termed *status,* what Weber called (rather elegantly) *social honor*.

This being so, it should not be particularly surprising to find that Warner and his team stayed pretty much on the lifestyle playing field, looking at such phenomena as child-rearing practices and churches attended. Warner began as an anthropologist, adapted anthropological methods for his studies, and wrote in an anthropologically-oriented style. It was a smooth transition when those who swam in Warner's wake gradually began sliding over to the use of terms like "culture."

His studies are also open to criticism on grounds of overinterpretation. Largely on the basis of community studies conducted in a few atypical towns of 10,000 to 20,000 population, Warner thought he had discovered the social stratification structure of America. Looking back from a vantage point of several decades, one wonders how he could suppose that by studying Newburyport, Massachusetts, he could thereby come to understand Boston, let alone New York; and, even more surprising, how academic colleagues could have credited claims to such knowledge.

In Warner's America, most of the components of American life are completely or virtually absent: there are no black ghettoes, no Chinatowns, no Little Italys; there is no State

Street, no Wall Street, Broadway or Madison Avenue, no Michigan Avenue; there are no big league baseball players, or numbers runners; there are no skyscrapers, and no subways.

These are some of Warner's deficiencies at the descriptive level; but of even more importance are Warner's implicit dynamic notions, particularly the idea that upward social mobility occurs through the acquisition of higher status—that is, to be blunt, through the assimilation of life style. (One can hear the first faint tinkling of the tune that Catherine Chilman was to elaborate into her sonatina on the low social acceptability of the poor.) Warner tends to ignore some of the fundamental realities of American social stratification: the brute facts about wealth, economic leverage in the marketplace, power, and the exercise of power. He did *count* some of these things, of course, such as who owned real estate, income level, whether money was "old" or "new"; but he used them almost exclusively as determinants of a static prestige-ranking and of life style. He did not really look at these items as dynamic factors in the struggle for property and position, in the battle of some trying to climb the ladder and others stamping on their fingers.

In the placid small towns of Warner's America, there seem to be no political bosses or political deals, no corrupt judges or bankers, no incompetent officeholders, no contractors with outrageously padded contracts to pave those tranquil elm-lined streets. There appear to be neither racketeers nor vice-squads to protect them. There are no strikebreakers, no stock manipulators, no generals. There is no evidence of corporation presidents struggling either to fix prices with, or to cut the throats of, their competitors.

As C. Wright Mills pointed out twenty-five years ago, Warner deviates sharply from Max Weber, who, in his classic essay *Class, Status, and Party,*[26] identified three different bases of social stratification (as against Warner's single all-purpose ranking). *Class,* according to Weber, Mills and most other observers of the phenomena of social levels, refers to *economic* ranking, to the possession and control of wealth and the sources of wealth, and to relative advantage in the marketplace. *Status,* according to this tripartite view of stratification, is applied to the results of ranking according to prestige and social honor—the esteem that one is able to command; it is reflected primarily in consumption patterns and life style. *Power*—especially as it is perceived in the conglomerate exercise of power known as *party*—means the ability to influence and enforce decisions in community life.

Thus, for example, a millionaire ranks high on the class dimension no matter what his life style may be. In this sense of the term, Howard Hughes, and J. Paul Getty, and Nelson Rockefeller, and Joseph Kennedy are all in the topmost layers of American class structure. The extent to which they are esteemed, the way they live, the influence they exert—all these may be vastly different. But each controls vast wealth and therefore occupies a very high class position. A new-rich Texas oil millionaire ranks right along with old-rich New England descendants of slave-traders and rum-distillers.

This is usually not completely true when we look at ranking according to status. On this dimension, those with the old New England slave-and-rum money are way ahead of our Texas oilman. They are expected to attend the charity balls that he is not even invited to. They may live on a street where he is not allowed to buy a house even at a premium. Similarly, even within the same family, the Barnard graduate granddaughter of a Mafia chieftain, with only a fraction of his money (and none of his power), may outrank him socially by quite a few layers.

Power—and party—is based directly on personal and group interests, which may stem from class or status factors, or both, or neither. As an example, what President Eisenhower called the military-industrial complex is, in this sense, a party which exercises great power in American life.

Class, status and party are, of course, highly correlated but they are by no means identical. Ethnic and racial minorities, for example, rarely achieve a status position commensurate with their class ranking. Political power, particularly at a local level, can be and has been accumulated and exercised by groups of relatively low status and economic class. In American cities, as one example, the police and their allies —what might be termed the "police party"—exercise considerable power in many segments of community life—power far in excess of what one would expect on the basis of class and status factors.

These are a few illustrations of the complexity that underlies the general idea of social stratification, a concept that has appeared deceptively simple to some. To deal with stratification and inequality in American life only, or predominantly, in status terms—to focus in a narrow way on life style, culture, or subculture—is to ignore many of the basic issues involved. Status certainly is almost always the last link in this three-part chain and is dependent on one or both of the other two. To have high prestige in the community, one must have—or one's family or clan must have had at one time —power, or money, or both. To suppose that the road from lower class to middle class position involves changing culture, or life style, or even social acceptability is naive. Inequality in prestige can only be corrected by altering imbalance in wealth and power, seldom by changing table manners or sexual habits.

But this is the basic logic of the culture of poverty cult.

Those who are the most devout members of this cult are say-ing, in effect, that if we can change the culture, the poverty will go away. This is where the inherent logic of this kind of thinking leads.

I V

Perhaps the most fundamental question to ask of those who are enamored of the idea that the poor have one culture and the rich another is to ask, simply, "So what?" Suppose the mythical oil millionaire behaves in an unrefined "lower class" manner, for example. What difference does that make as long as he owns the oilwells? Is the power of the Chairman of the Ways and Means Committee in the state legislature dimin-ished or enhanced in any way by his taste in clothing or music? And suppose every single poor family in America set as its long-range goal that its sons and daughters would get a Ph.D.—who would pay the tuition?

The effect of tastes, child-rearing practices, speech pat-terns, reading habits, and other cultural factors is relatively small in comparison to the effect of wealth and influence. What I am trying to suggest is that the inclusion in the analytic process of the elements of social stratification that are usually omitted—particularly economic class and power —would produce more significant insights into the circum-stances of the poor and the pressures and deprivations with which they live. The simplest—and at the same time, the most significant—proposition in understanding poverty is that it is caused by lack of money. The overwhelming ma-jority of the poor are poor because they have, first: insuffi-cient income; and second: no access to methods of increasing that income—that is, no power. They are too young, too old, too sick; they are bound to the task of caring for small children, or they are simply discriminated against. The facts are clear, and the solution seems rather obvious—raise their income and let their "culture," whatever it might be, take care of itself.

The need to avoid facing this obvious solution—which is very uncomfortable since it requires some substantial changes and redistribution of income—provides the motivation for developing the stabilizing ideology of the culture of poverty which acts to sustain the *status quo* and delay change. The function of the ideology of lower class culture, then, is plainly to maintain inequality in American life.

6
The Hydraulics and Economics of Misery

*The Society
for the Preservation of Disease*

I

Miracles of medical care fill our newspapers and magazines; American surgeons trip over each other rushing to the operating room to perform the latest incredible feat of organ transplantation. In a very real sense, Americans have the best doctoring available in the world. In the field of mental health, we may have more professionals in the United States than the rest of the world combined. But in some cities the rates of chest disease, meningitis and venereal disease are going up instead of down, thousands and thousands of mothers and babies die in childbirth, and the average emotionally disturbed person is left to struggle alone with his distress. Why aren't Americans more healthy and more sane? Let me begin by telling you what happens in mental health, the field in which I was originally trained.

Back in the late 1950's, when I was a relative beginner in clinical psychology, the psychiatric residents suddenly began using a new vocabulary. Their descriptions of patients, normally filled with "anaclitic relationships" and "anal-sadistic components," were sprinkled with references to "Class Three" and "Class Five." They had been reading a new book that had burst on the mental health scene with great impact— Hollingshead and Redlich's famous *Social Class and Mental Illness*. This was the first of a series of books and research reports[1] that called attention to the fact that emotional disorders and stays in mental hospitals were far more common among the poor than among the rich—exploding once and for all the popular belief that the rich suffer terribly from their richness in the form of neurotic symptoms, psychosomatic afflictions such as ulcers, and severe anxiety.

This great mass of research can be summarized in a somewhat oversimplified way in the following statements:

Most measures of general emotional disturbance show that the poor have much higher rates than the middle classes.

Continued disability, particularly in the form of prolonged stay in mental hospitals, is much more prevalent among the poorer groups.

Active treatment, particularly by the more "qualified" professionals, shows an opposite pattern: the middle classes are much more likely to receive effective treatment than are the poor.

There are a series of specific relationships between emotional disorder and particular components of the poverty syndrome (such as prolonged unemployment).

These findings were injected into an academic field and a field of medical practice that was undergoing great turbulence and change. From 1940 to 1960 American psychiatry was transformed from a biologically-oriented, hospital-based enterprise to a field dominated by the psychoanalytic model and the outpatient clinic. This transformation reflected a basic shift in a humanitarian and progressive direction. The image of the individual as a suffering human being in need of help and capable, with help, of growing and becoming more mature and healthy, replaced the image of the patient who was intricately diagnosed and then stored away in a huge warehouse of society's rejects. Concern for human relationship replaced the search for far-fetched analogies to the bacterial theory of infectious disease. The end result was a great flowering of humanism and liberalism in the field of psychiatry and mental health: locked doors were opened, repressive measures were abandoned, and the patient began to be treated as a social being rather than a commodity.

In such a context, the introduction of newly systematized knowledge about the linkages between poverty and mental health, between social class and emotional disorder, was followed by a great upsurge of concern and activity.

But despite all this concern, despite the unquestionably liberal and progressive credentials of most mental health professionals, Blaming the Victim has reared its ugly head. In considerations of the mental health of the poor, the theoretical —or more properly, ideological—formulations that are beginning to attain dominance show unmistakable family resemblances to the Culture of Poverty cult, and the other victim-blaming ideologies we have discussed in previous chapters.

For openers, let me quote from a widely-used psychiatric textbook:

> . . . to deal professionally with poor people . . . one must take account of their significant characteristics, particularly as these seem strange or hard to contend with . . . the deprived

are oriented toward the present and, to a lesser extent, the immediate past . . . the lower class person is handicapped in his efforts to understand change, and he may fear new adjustments . . . the disadvantaged person is likely to meet difficulties by adjusting to them rather than by attempting to overcome them . . .[2]

Then consider this statement attempting to formulate a rationale for the relationship between low social class and high rates of emotional disturbance:

". . . the low SES [socio-economic status] has (1) a weak superego, (2) a weak ego, with lack of control or frustration tolerance, (3) a negative, distrustful, suspicious character with poor interpersonal relationships, (4) strong feelings of inferiority, low self-esteem, fear of ridicule and (5) a tendency to act out problems, with violent expression of hostility and extrapunitive tendencies. . . .[3]

Some years ago, a pair of psychiatrists, Kardiner and Ovesey, produced a book that was intended to promote greater understanding of the Negro. At that time it may well have had some positive effects; but it too drew on a handful of case histories of black neurotics, and it too blamed the victim, though far more blatantly:

The result of the continuous frustrations in childhood is to create a personality devoid of confidence in human relations, of an eternal vigilance and distrust of others. . . .[4] We have seen but little evidence of rigid anal training in childhood . . . in those who came from the South, there was little emphasis on order, neatness or systematization. . . . Among the activities for bolstering self-esteem, are flashy and flamboyant dressing. . . . Narcotizing the individual against traumatic influences is effected largely through alcohol and drugs. . . . In the domain of magical aid to self-esteem, gambling takes a high place. . . .[5]

Kardiner, incidentally, developed into a first rate Victim Blamer. Before the *Saturday Evening Post* closed down, he wrote a letter to the editor rebutting an article about poverty; he said:

A large segment of the lower class, poverty-stricken Negroes suffer from the effects of a kind of emotional impoverishment that seriously hampers their capacity to take advantage of many of the opportunities Mr. Bagdikian would provide for them. This impoverishment is due to a certain manner of child rearing, which can be designated as involuntary neglect. . . . These conditions breed a type of emotional and intellectual limitation that cannot be remedied merely by housing, more jobs or improved education, etc. . . . A possible plan would be to organize neighborhood cadres of women who, after a short training program, would go into emotionally impoverished homes where they would attempt some educating and guiding of the adults as to how they can provide some of the needed nurture. . . . Whatever the plans, we must treat the causes of the disease, not the symptoms.[6]

Here we see where culturally-oriented speculation about the causes of the emotional problems of the poor can lead—not only are the emotional problems attributed to internal status-linked mechanisms, but also culturally-rooted maladjustment is viewed as a *cause* (rather than a symptom) of poverty itself.

It is, of course, difficult for a modern psychiatrist to avoid the conclusion that, since emotional disorder is the result of intrapsychic distortions and malfunctions, the excessive prevalence of such disorders among the poor must be due to differential psychic development among persons of low socio-economic rank—engorgement of the Id, peristalsis of the projective mechanisms, dysrhythmic displacement, estoppage of libidinal currents, or some similarly portentous internal events. The basic Freudian model, essentially, is hydro-dynamic; it traces, in a manner analogous to the science of hydraulics, the flow, velocity, pressure, and level of sexual and aggressive impulses through the psychic plumbing of Man—plumbing that is usually flawed by unsoldered joints, fittings of the wrong shape, pipes of the wrong size, and similar imperfections. Deviant and neurotic behavior, then, can be viewed as analogous to nerve-wracking clanging in the radiator, leaks, maddeningly slow trickles of hot water, and occasional disastrous overflowings of the toilet bowl onto the bathroom floor. Clamped inside the bounds of such a theoretical framework, the problem of the mental health of the poor is transformed into a study of the hydraulics of misery.

The final element in this ideology is the assumption that it is the early experiences of the poor—the failures of mothering, the inconsistent patterns of discipline, the exposure to deviant values and behavior patterns—that accounts for their apparent excessive vulnerability to emotional disorder. Let me return, for a moment, to Catherine Chilman and her document about how the poor grow up, not only poor, but emotionally maladjusted:

> . . . lower-lower class parental patterns, compared to middle class ones, tend to be antithetical to a child's positive mental health. . . . With generally less ego strength (lower self-esteem), the very poor individual is apt to have greater need than his middle class counterpart for security-giving psychological defenses. . . . The subcultural patterns of this group . . . suggest that their life style . . . might be termed (within the middle class frame of reference), as immature in a number of respects, such as their greater tendency toward impulsivity, lack of goal commitment, magical thinking, physical

learning and behavioral styles, low frustration tolerance, concrete attitudes, and so on.[7]

This final assumption, relating presumed cultural features to psychosexual development, is like an odd hybrid of the thinking of Freud and Warner, carrying with it the worst genetic characteristics of both parents.

I I

As we could see in Abram Kardiner's letter to the *Saturday Evening Post* as well as in Catherine Chilman's worries over the disadvantaged position of poor children, our liberal ideologist friends are very deeply concerned about these conditions and would like to do something about them. Dr. Kardiner is even willing to go to quite remarkable extremes of social engineering by training Super Mothers, or Block Captain Mothers, or Mother Gauleiters—women who would invade the homes of the poor and set lower class mothers straight on their sloppy and negligent child-rearing practices. This brand of surrogate psyche-plumbing would presumably straighten out the children, who would grow up mentally healthy at last, freed of their neurotic compulsion to be poor.

When we look at what is actually going on in the mental health business, we see the poor are almost completely absent from the scene, with one exception: they populate the large state hospitals in great numbers. In outpatient clinics, and particularly in the offices of psychiatrists in private practice, the clients ("patients") tend to be largely middle class, white, well-educated. They are either employed in rather well-paying jobs which establish them as middle class, or they are young people in school, who may be temporarily poor but who are actually undergoing their apprenticeship for middle class status. The average psychiatrist—in conformity with the Hippocratic Oath—spends half to two-thirds of his time in his private practice seeing patients who are charged substantial fees, and who pay their bills on time. The average patient is an interesting, reasonably cultured and well-educated person, rather attractive, and an enjoyable conversationalist. This complex of characteristics is summed up by the psychodynamic concept "well-motivated." With some exceptions— occasioned by deviant psychiatrists willing to see a few patients for Medicaid fees or an occasional poor patient for no fee—only those among the poor who can afford a fee of $25 or $30 an hour, once or twice a week, for three months, six months, or a year, see psychiatrists in private practice. The condition excludes the majority of the poor—those, for example, who retain a puritan unwillingness to dip into capital.

I was recently privileged to listen to a psychiatrist talking about what he called a "case"—a young lady with serious hysterical symptoms that were beginning to offer a considerable threat to her physical well-being. This Licensed Psychic Plumber indicated to the girl's father—an irregularly employed gas station attendant with an income for the previous year of $3,800—his willingness to treat the girl, at a fee of $30 an hour, with a guarantee of cure within twenty sessions. The father, of course, was thrown into an agony of indecision and despair (which our friend the psychiatrist diagnosed as "ambivalence" growing out of the unresolved Oedipal relationship) but finally had to decline the offer on the grounds that he couldn't possibly afford it. The psychiatrist tried to break through his resistance—demonstrating, at the same time, his empathy with the poor and their pitiable upside-down value system, their interest in the present concrete reality, and their reluctance to defer need gratification—by pointing out that he was proposing a fee that was merely equivalent, when all was said and done, to the price of a new color television set. The father's reply was not recorded for posterity, but I am happy to report that a colleague suggested to the psychiatrist that he return to the father and, maintaining the equivalence between fee and electronic appliance, suggest "How about a portable transistor radio?"

Information has recently come to light which indicates that the private patients of psychiatry are drawn from an even smaller segment of the population than had previously been imagined. In Boston, for example, we found[8] that the great majority of those who were in private treatment lived in a very small section of the city (it contains only three or four per cent of the population); this is the area known as the Back Bay—containing such things as the Public Library, the Ritz Carlton Hotel, the Harvard Club, and the theatres that show Scandinavian films. It is populated mostly by single persons; there are very few families with children. Most of the single population is presently, or was recently, involved in education beyond the secondary level—college or junior college or secretarial school. These young persons are scornful of phonographs with all the components made by the same manufacturer, voted enthusiastically for McCarthy and petulantly for Humphrey, and know a Jules Feiffer cartoon when they see one. A major subgroup of the population consists of single young women, twenty to thirty-five years old, with technical or professional jobs. At any one time, about one out of every twelve of these young women is in private psychiatric treatment and about half of them have been in psychiatric treatment at one time or another. Think of it! This tiny band of dedicated, tenaciously anxious young women, a few thousand in number, provide something like one-fourth of the Boston customers for this business. Talk about brand loyalty!

Areas such as the Back Bay (and it appears that each big city has a similar neighborhood—its own Patientsville, so to speak) are usually inhabited by very migratory people, remote from their own parents and families and without the usual types of stable connections binding them into the processes of the larger society. Except for the fact that most of them have jobs, people who live in Patientsville are very like people who live on the Bowery. These areas are, in a way, Skid Rows for the employed. And, in the same terms, the private practice of psychiatry might be considered the Salvation Army for the middle class.

The patient treated in a psychiatric clinic—most of which charge fees below the private practice standard or use sliding fee-scales—is not markedly different from the patient in private treatment. A sample of patients receiving treatment in such clinics will reveal that few of them are poor, very few of them are black. The poor and the black with emotional problems do come to the clinic in fair numbers, but the weeding-out process, the identification of "well-motivated" patients, the long waiting periods (what the psychiatrist who administered a clinic I once worked in called "letting them wither on the vine")—all of these processes have the effect of screening out the poor.[9]

As one might well expect, this state of affairs is subtly attributed to the characteristics of the poor, rather than the characteristics of the psychiatric service network. It is said that they are unwilling, or unable, or both, to make use of available psychiatric services.

We find a relentlessly psychodynamic viewpoint being brought to bear on the mental health problems of the poor and, even more, a relentless focusing on pathology. The latter, of course, is an occupational hazard (except that it is a hazard, not for the person in the mental health profession, but rather for those who come in contact with him). It is an event of great rarity when a person who comes in contact with a psychiatric institution is *not* given a psychiatric diagnosis. This may not seem strange at first; it is a confirmation of the common wisdom which holds that someone would have to be out of his mind to go to a psychiatrist. But consider the analogies. What would we say if everyone who walked into a cardiologist's office were told that he had heart trouble? Or if everyone—or at least every female—who walked into a gynecologist's office was pronounced pregnant? It is not unlike the test that is periodically carried out by journalists and published in some high-circulation magazine with a title like "Your Auto Mechanic is Gypping You." The journalist unhooks or removes some minor piece of his car's operating mechanism, visits a series of garages and asks what is wrong, and is almost always told that he needs extensive and expensive repair work done on his automobile.

This is not to imply that the mental health professional is trying to drum up business by deceiving his patients. Far from it. There is always more business available, more demand for mental health services, than can possibly be met; and each time a new clinic opens up, the demand increases. The explanation is more simple; it is that psychiatrists and other mental health professionals are ready to attach the label of mentally ill to almost everyone, even—or perhaps particularly—their own colleagues. They detect the deep depression hidden behind the most cheerful and sanguine faces; they perceive the boiling hostility that lies deep within the psyche of the sweetest, friendliest of persons; and they can spot the latent homosexuality which motivates the most exuberantly heterosexual young bachelor.

And their faith in psychodynamic explanation can withstand almost any evidence. Consider the following *published* case study which I quote in its entirety:

> Case 11. Psychological depression and cancer phobia preceding death from bronchiogenic carcinoma.
> A 52-year-old man was referred to a psychiatrist by an internist because of uncontrollable coughing for which no organic etiology could be ascertained. This man presented a picture of depression, although it lacked the usual features of self-accusation and self-depreciation. There were no precipitating factors to suggest a reactive depression. His manner seemed to be more a hopeless resignation than depression, and he reiterated his belief that he had a cancer for which no one could help him. Because the psychiatric picture was not typically one of depression bronchoscopy was performed with negative results. Electric shock treatment was given with a thought that this was an atypical depression with a somatic delusion. There was no relief from electric shock therapy and the patient died some months later of a bronchiogenic carcinoma.[10]

In view of this deeply ingrained style of thinking and this almost exclusive reliance on a rather narrow conceptual framework, it should not be surprising that the investigation of the mental health problems of the poor was distorted and, as a result, the facts were subtly reformulated in a way that permits and encourages the oversimplification: the problems of the poor are, at bottom, manifestations of neurosis or character disorder. That is, they are *intrapsychic* problems that can only be corrected by therapeutic intervention in the psychic processes of the poor person himself. In addition to their ideological readiness to adopt such a formulation, most psychiatrists—like most educated persons who are not directly in the social sciences (and many who are)—take their viewpoint on social class from the Warnerian line of reasoning. As I tried to point out in the previous chapter (extensively and doggedly), this view sees social stratification, not so much in terms of inequality of power and money, but in terms of status, prestige, and such questions as life style, values, behavior patterns, and child-rearing practices. This view is highly compatible with a psychodynamic and psychopathological outlook. So the mating of Freud and Warner was naturally love at first sight.

In terms of delivery of care, the intrusion of this ideology into the mental health field creates a situation of gross injustice. Through excessive concern with the classical questions of "motivation," "suitability for treatment," and "ability to profit from therapy," the poor person with *genuine* intrapsychic problems is blithely screened out and does not have anything like equal access to mental health resources. This fact has been documented over and over again, and some of the convoluted thinking underlying it has been brilliantly revealed.[11] It almost seems to boil down to the simple fact that middle class and upwardly mobile professionals don't *like* the poor, don't intend to help them, and do intend to husband mental health resources for their own kind.

The one exception to this rule is the public mental hospital which opens its doors very generously to the poor. And well it might: without the poor, the aged, the drunk, and the inept petty criminal, the state hospital would have to go out of business. There is a reason for this dramatic difference between the population of the state hospital and the population of other psychiatric facilities. The other psychiatric facilities have the clear intention—and often the capability—of *helping* people. The main function of the state hospital, on the other hand, is to store away people who are troublesome or frightening and who, in addition, have the unfortunate habit of acting crazy.

We are lately beginning to learn—to our dismay, and hopefully with many pangs of conscience—that prolonged hospitalization in such public institutions has a pronounced disabling, demoralizing, and dehumanizing effect. This is one reason why the ranks of the chronically mentally ill are so filled with poor people. They have been disabled by hospitalization in their friendly neighborhood state hospital.

The treatment situation, then, can be described as a multiple victimization of the poor. First, we blame these victims for their problems by attributing their emotional distress to faulty psychic plumbing brought about by incorrect child-rearing and deviant psychological development, as well as the acquisition of the values of poverty—all of which we attribute to life style, and other quasi-cultural characteristics.

Then, we turn around and say that their values and their culture—particular personality styles, and class-related emotional problems—make them ineligible for, and incapable of, profiting from the kind of help we have available—help which, incidentally, was created for, and is indeed specifically reserved for, our middle class peers. All of which might be called Blaming the Victim—squared!

III

I am not done yet; there is something more to say that carries us one step further. The most important sin is one of omission. In leaping so athletically onto the status and culture bandwagon, the psychiatrist and his henchmen (whom he refers to as the "ancillary" or "paramedical" services) have ignored what is most probably the heart of the matter. You will remember that we began with the fact that those at the bottom of the social stratification ladder are, at any given point in time, relatively more likely to be suffering emotional distress and to be identified as disturbed or deviant. Now, it may well be that those of very low social status do, in fact, vary substantially in their "culture" (as you recall, I doubt it); it may even be that variation in life style is a causal factor in the differentially higher rates of distress among the poor (I'm inclined to doubt this too, but I can see some plausibility in attributing a *small* differential to these factors). What is so glaringly missing from the picture are the other elements of stratification: class and power. What are the effects of lack of money and lack of power on mental health?

The late Fanny Brice may have demonstrated greater insight into this problem than most of the learned psychiatrists when she said, "I've been rich and I've been poor; and, believe me, rich is better!" Being poor is stressful. Being poor is worrisome; one is anxious about the next meal, the next dollar, the next day. Being poor is nerve-wracking, upsetting. When you're poor, it's easy to despair and it's easy to lose your temper. And all of this is because you're poor. Not because your mother let you go around with your diapers full of bowel movement until you were four; or shackled you to the potty chair before you could walk. Not because she broke your bottle on your first birthday or breast-fed you until you could cut your own steak. But because you don't have any *money*.

The connection between lack of money and emotional symptomatology is the concept of stress. Although Langner and Michaels wandered afield and dallied—unnecessarily, in my view—in the intriguing arena of speculation about cultural determinants of class-linked emotional disorder, the main core of their work consists of solid research relating stress to mental health. Their findings show beyond doubt that the more stresses a person experiences in his life, the more vulnerable he is to the development of emotional disorder. Thus, lack of money, unemployment, and similar deprivations are major stresses—occurrences associated with lower levels of mental health. In addition, of course, not only does low income invite stress, but it also makes certain events —such as a relatively minor illness—that are merely inconveniences for the middle class, disasters for the poor. Dohrenwend[12] has suggested the possibility that the apparent high prevalence of disorder among the poor may be a direct reflection of high stress levels, with no particular implications of intrapsychic causation or true rates of *enduring* disorder ("illness"). He suggests that a temporary, quasi-symptomatic reaction to stress is expectable and, indeed, normal; that stresses are more frequent and severe among the poor; and that, therefore, at any given moment, larger numbers of the poor will be encountering stress and reacting to it with signs of distress and disorder. Thus an investigation, conducted at a single point in time, would reveal higher rates of disorder among the lower class groups but would not necessarily indicate any substantially higher rates of *permanent* disorder. This is perfectly consistent with a number of research studies that show much greater class differences in rates of *mild* disorder than in rates of very severe—presumably more permanent, more "illness-like"—disorders.

Dohrenwend cites two pieces of suggestive evidence that would tend to confirm his hypothesis. He found that, in reinterviewing a group of people after two years' time, those who had experienced stress—such as prolonged illness—reported that their symptoms and disorders had *worsened;* those who had experienced a betterment of life circumstances —such as a job promotion and higher income—reported a disappearance or considerable *improvement* in their symptoms. Neither group, of course, had experienced any formal treatment. He also cites the results of an interview study conducted after the assassination of President Kennedy which revealed that about nine persons out of ten, in the days immediately following the event, had experienced what would ordinarily be defined as psychiatric symptoms—anxiety, tension, somatic symptoms—and that, several weeks later, the majority of these "symptoms" had disappeared.

It is important, then, to shift attention away from the status (or life style) question and toward the class (or money) question in considering the relationship between psychiatric disorder and low socio-economic status. The poor are bombarded with stress; they react with strain. It happens with a bar of iron; it happens—more poignantly and more relevantly—with people. To explain the mental health problems of the poor, then, as due in large measure to lack of money—although it has the undeniable handicap of being a common sense formulation—is both simpler and more parsimonious (and, therefore, perhaps more scientifically elegant) than to evoke far-fetched, hypothetical variables related to value-systems, subcultures, and child-rearing practices.

A similar point can be made with respect to the third leg of the social stratification structure—power. Here the central concept is self-esteem, which is usually deemed to be at the very core of mental health, however else that term might be defined. And self-esteem is dependent on being capable of influencing one's environment to one's own benefit. This concept is one of the few about which wide consensus can be achieved among personality theorists of a psychoanalytic bent. It has been expressed eloquently by Bruno Bettelheim in his new book, *The Empty Fortress*[13], in which he gives detailed descriptions of the tasks and events of the first months and years of life when the infant becomes a full-scale human, or, rather, *achieves* humanity. Bettelheim teaches us what the apprentice human being in the nursery *must* do: he must act in a way that affects the world about him, learn there is a self and non-self, and learn that he can influence the non-self in an understandable cause-and-effect manner. In his own terms, Bettelheim is talking about the exercise of power as a condition for self-esteem and full humanity.

A number of reports have been published suggesting that acting as a group in one's own behalf—in a sit-in, in the development and program of a block organization—does, in fact, have precisely this effect: increase in confidence, effectiveness, sense of well-being—all of the characteristics that add up to good mental health.

The elimination of stresses, then, and the opportunity to influence one's environment could be brought to bear, in a programmatic way, on the mental health problems of the poor; brought to bear in a manner that, theoretically at least, could have substantially more impact than arcane expeditions searching for the long-lost blueprint to the psychic plumbing hidden behind the walls. Program development could be turned away from the unproductive questions of status and life style and focused on the down-to-earth issues of money and power.

If the mental health scene were injected with these issues, the professional would necessarily find himself including— in his thoughts and in his programs—redevelopment as well as repression, superhighways as well as superegos, police training as well as toilet training, discrimination as well as displacement, and racism as well as autism. The mental health professional would have to confront inequality in American life, not simply group differences in breast-feeding as against bottle-feeding.

That these issues are—or, until recently at least, have been —so remote from mental health thought is testimony that, with regard to the mental health of the poor, current doctrine and theory in psychiatry and its allied fields is, indeed, ideological in nature. The purpose of thinking so exclusively about status is to *avoid* thinking about money and power; the purpose of seeking, so assiduously, to find the cracks in the psychic plumbing is to shut from one's field of vision the rents and upheavals in the world around. And to locate the cause of disorder largely inside the poor person is to absolve the surrounding society of the sins it has committed against him. The result of these intellectual exercises is the maintenance of inequality in American life.

I V

On the average, the physical health of the American people is in a shameful state. I say "on the average" because health is a typical American product in that it is distributed unequally. The majority of Americans are in rather good shape, yet in our technologically advanced, science-worshiping, pill-swallowing nation, about one-fifth of the population suffers from blatant medical neglect. This is dramatically illustrated in statistics on two significant points in the life of young people—the time of birth and the unpleasant day when a young man is called for his Selective Service pre-induction examination. Our draft-rejection rate is approximately forty per cent. The majority of rejections are on medical grounds; something like one-fourth of our young men are not healthy enough to serve in the Armed Forces. (This may be fortunate for them since, in recent years of bloody adventure abroad, service in the army has itself become a major health hazard; nevertheless, this index of the health of American youth must be viewed as alarming.)

Our infant mortality rate is also a national disgrace. Although it has declined somewhat in recent years—from 29.2 per thousand in 1950 to 23.4 in 1966—it gives every sign of leveling off, and some fear that it might begin to rise again. Relative to other nations, our infant mortality rate does not look good and, in comparison, our performance on this score is rapidly *worsening*. At one time, the United States ranked sixth among all the nations of the world in this crucial measure of effective health care. (One might well wonder why, in view of our outstanding affluence, we should have any excuse for not ranking *first,* and by a wide margin.) Today, out of a total of fifty-seven nations, we stand only fifteenth. We rank slightly better than Canada and West Germany, slightly worse than East Germany and Israel.

Our health problems are concentrated among the poor. In New York City, the central Harlem health district reports an infant mortality rate of 49.5 per thousand while the well-to-do district of Kips Bay-Yorkville has a rate of only 14.7 per thousand. According to the American Public Health Association, poor families suffer from disabling heart disease three times more frequently than others; and from visual impairment, seven times more frequently. A study of Head Start children in Boston revealed that almost one in three had major undiscovered health problems. The statistics can be cited almost indefinitely, and they add up to a formulation that is wearingly familiar—the poor man and the black man suffer and end up with the lowest health status.

Unequal health status is illustrated easily and dramatically by a contrast of racial rates. Consider the grimmest index of them all: death. Mortality statistics are the final test of a nation's health and, by this test, the black nation in America is in very poor health indeed. Negro life expectancy is now about *seven years* less than that of whites—a ten percent difference. The average Negro baby can count on about nine years of life for every ten that a white baby can look forward to. Look at it another way. Pretend you are looking into a large nursery on the maternity ward of a hospital. You see two hundred baby boys—one hundred white, one hundred black. Twenty years later, six black boys will be dead, four whites; and twenty years after that, at the age of forty, three more whites, but nine more blacks will have died: a total of 11 whites, 21 blacks. At the age of sixty-five, 66 whites will have survived, only 50 blacks. For girls, the situation is comparable: 81 out of one hundred white girls will live to be women of sixty-two, only 63 black girls. Using the white experience as a standard, we can say that one out of six black men and women will die before their time and therefore needlessly.

Two things are clear, then: that among the nations, America has rather surprisingly poor health, shockingly poor health in comparison to other industrialized and reasonably wealthy nations; and that this poor health is concentrated. Affluent white America is as healthy as Sweden. The health of the black poor American nation is comparable to such nations as Venezuela, Romania, and South Viet Nam.

How is it that the poor suffer from such poor health? They are, of course, lacking in motivation, are ignorant about health matters, delay in seeking care when they experience symptoms, and avoid any rational effort to prevent illness. They are "hard to reach" and they resist efforts to provide them with good care. As usual, it is their own fault, but not really their own fault. There is the usual stigma of social origin: they are afflicted with "cultural attitudes toward health which hinder the effectiveness of health services." And, naturally, "there is little doubt that persons who are members of the lowest socio-economic groups find it difficult to understand and to appreciate the value of preventative services." I am quoting the words of a very eminent and concerned public health physician who has done a great deal to improve the health status and medical care of the poor[14], and I am quoting, in a sense, out of context. These are not his major points, but rather side issues. Nevertheless, he wrote them; and the assumptions and ideas that they represent are endemic in the field of public health and medical care.

In a study of the organization of the health-care system, Reid, Arnaudo, and White[15] have summarized the opinions and findings of writers who hold what the authors call the "psychological point of view," which is essentially identical to what I have called victim-blaming:

> The low income person frequently lacks knowledge of or information about physiology, medical etiology, good health practices, and the work of the health-care practitioner. He often lacks ability to use information intelligently or to follow the practitioner's advice. And he is more likely than persons at other income levels to have inaccurate information concerning health and the treatment of disorders, to be more fearful of ill health and of using health resources, to be more uncomfortable in health-care facilities, and to be more distrustful of practitioners.[16]

Now, the facts are very plain, and no complicated intervening explanations about the cultural or class-based deviations of the patient are required to explain them. Medical care in the United States is primarily a *business* enterprise— the free-lance entrepreneurs we call doctors operate an artificially controlled seller's market in which care goes to the highest bidder. The reason whites live longer than blacks, middle class persons longer than the poor is very simple. They buy, at very high prices, that extra seven years of life from the merchants who have it for sale. The public and philanthropic sectors of the medical care field are downright disaster areas, in which second- third- and fourth-class care is doled out in a brutal, dilatory, negligent manner.

In America we pay approximately 200,000 practicing physicians a total of ten billion dollars a year, an amount that is rising considerably more rapidly than is the supply of physicians. Almost two-thirds of that amount comes directly from the pocket of the patient, most of the rest from insurance, and a small amount from tax funds. Only nine million, less than one-tenth of one per cent, comes from philanthropic sources. That means we spend an average of about $50 per person per year for doctor bills, of which over $30 is directly out of pocket. But the middle-income family dominates the market, spending over twice as much on health services as does the poor family, while at the same time spending a much smaller *proportion* of total income—about four or five per cent as compared with the poor family's ten and fifteen per cent of income spent for medical care. Among the poorest families, not many more than one in four have surgical insurance, while among families with over $7,000 income, six out of seven have such insurance. One result is that middle-income families are surgical patients at a rate that is proportionally two or three times as great as the poorest families; and, of course, seventy-five or eighty percent of their bills are covered by insurance, while only about one-third of the poor family's bills are taken care of by this method.

These are a handful of the many mountains of statistics available that show how the more affluent family simply crowds the poor family out of the market and uses up the relatively scarce supply of medical care. Like good cars, good homes, and good education, good health is a commodity in the American marketplace—for sale to the highest bidder. The poor are less healthy for the same reason they have less of everything else: they can't afford to buy health.

Most of the poor have to turn to tax-supported or charitable clinics and emergency rooms for their medical care, and the results are so horrifying that they scarcely need repetition. The obscenities of clinic practices and emergency room brutality are too well known to repeat in detail: the long waits, the cursory examinations, the impersonal cold world of nameless men and women in white—a cast of characters that seems to be exchanged almost daily, each set of replacements being more discourteous, prejudiced, and unsympathetic than the last.[17] Instances of the dramatic stories are known to almost everyone—the patient bleeding to death unattended while the health professionals prolong their coffee break; the misdiagnoses; the grossly incompetent treatments; the constant, obsessive concern with paying the bill.

Let me tell about a trivial incident that is, perhaps, more illustrative of the constant day-to-day indignities suffered by the poor in their encounters with the clinic and the emergency room. A friend of mine, whose baby was sick and very feverish, went looking for baby aspirin in her medicine closet and found none. It was late; no drug stores were open. She called her "family doctor"—the emergency room of the big university hospital—and asked if they could give her a few baby aspirin to tide her over until morning. "Don't have any; give him a regular aspirin." "He always throws up when I give him regular aspirin." "Well, if he throws it up, try giving him another one." Click!

Another friend happened to be there, a woman, who, unlike the first, came from a middle class family, had a college education, and could slip in and out of her "Seven Sisters" accent, tone of voice, and style at will. She called up, told the same story in her best Mount Holyoke tones, and received the reply, "Yes, ma'am, I think we have some. I'll send up to the pharmacy. Come right on down. I'll leave it at the desk."

In *Sickness and Society*, Duff and Hollingshead[18] document, in grisly detail, the story of "charitable" medical care in a major university hospital (a hospital that may well be in the vicinity of the medical school where they are employed —Yale, and the city in which they work—New Haven). Their study, similar studies, and anecdotal evidence all converge to show the vast differences between the experiences of the poor person who is sick and the middle class person. First of all, it is much harder for a poor person to get into a hospital—to cross the threshold, get admitted, and be assigned to a bed. He must be much sicker than the middle class patient; he must be very sick, preferably dangerously sick, in order to be allowed into the crowded wards. First of all, he has no "sponsor"—there is no doctor who is trying to get him in. The middle class person has a private doctor with hospital privileges and often with a university appointment. He is influential. He calls the admitting office and orders a bed. The transient intern or resident in the clinic, seeing an ill poor man who should be hospitalized, calls to inquire whether there might be a bed available for a ward patient. If yes, good; if no, he shakes his head, worries for a minute or two, writes a prescription, and turns to the next patient.

Another reason for these discriminatory admission practices is money. The middle class patient either has money in the bank or a good income, or he is protected by insurance.

He is a good financial risk. The hospital's bills will almost surely be paid promptly and fully. There is no such assurance about getting money from the poor; even if ultimately the Welfare Department were to pay the bill, their payment rates are below the extravagant costs incurred in modern hospital care. It is no wonder that patients undergoing the ritual of admission begin to believe that they are in, not a hospital, but the office of a small-loan finance company.

When the poor person does manage to get in, he gets poorer care; it is fragmented, for one thing. The more affluent person has his private doctor—his sponsor—someone who is specifically interested in coordinating the care given his patient by the many members of the hospital staff. The poor man must make do with whatever random, disconnected attention he gets. And the care he gets is almost never at the hands of an established experienced physician. He is ministered to by beginners—medical students, interns, residents —who are casually supervised by older physicians. And the care usually is given in a highly public manner. Several staff members will congregate to examine him, and talk about him, callously and contemptuously ignoring him, talking over him, not to him. Finally, the poor person, if he should get well and be discharged, almost never has his case followed up adequately.

Duff and Hollingshead vividly portray the sense of fear, frustration, and helplessness experienced by the poor person in a bed on the ward, and they also show the source of, and justification for, these feelings.

Are the poor fearful and reluctant to become involved in medical care? Definitely. Do they postpone engaging with a physician as long as they can? Without question. Is it because they are ignorant or dissuaded by the precepts of their culture from taking care of their health? Not likely. They simply detest being subjected to disinterested, second-class care. Their experiences with doctors have taught them to fear and postpone such demeaning experiences.

One of the curious facts of American economic life is the *shortage* of doctors. One would think that, in a free enterprise economy, the enormous demand for physicians would generate an increased supply. But the doctor business seems to have freed itself from normal economic patterns. We see that our health expenditures keep rising steeply. Meanwhile, all the indices of the health of the American people stay on an almost static plateau—the rate of improvement being barely detectable. Physicians' fees increased by about thirteen per cent in the two years following the establishment of the Medicare program. Hospital charges have more than doubled in ten years. Meanwhile, the number of physicians in private practice has *declined* in relation to the total population. The rate has gone from 109 per 100,000 population in 1950, to 97 in 1965. Until very recently, the American Medical Association has simply denied that there is any great problem and has been opposed to any substantial increase in the production of doctors. New medical schools appear with less frequency than new members of the United Nations, their gestation period being so super-elephantine as to guarantee a continued slow growth rate. And while the AMA now officially allows as how it might be a good idea to have a few more doctors on hand, the production rate has changed very little.

From a purely practical point of view, one can see the doctor's point: in a town of 100,000 people spending a total of $5 million on doctor bills with only 97 doctors to carve up the take, it would be quite a different matter than if there were, say, 125 doctors. Quite different. About $12,000 a year less per doctor in what businessmen call gross receipts.

So, prices of tonsillectomies, office visits, and hospital beds keep rising; the health of the middle classes gets a little better; the health of the poor remains pretty bad. The doctors get rich. And one out of five black men in America dies before his time.

This, very briefly, then, is the story on the health of the poor. The facts are plain: their health is bad. The cause is plain: health costs money, and they don't have money. The rationalization that the poor suffer from bad health because of their ignorance of health matters, their culture, or their class-linked disinterest in health is simply one more version of Blaming the Victim.

There is no culture on earth, of poverty or anything else, that voluntarily chooses death over life.

7
Taking People Out of Oak Street

Slums, Suburbs and Subsidies

I

Some time ago I watched David Susskind talking to slum landlords on his television program; they were explaining why life was so hard for them. One of them added to our previous list of eternal verities by saying, "People cause slums." By people, of course, he meant tenants, not himself and his colleagues in the slum business. In a similar vein, a well-known urban renewal expert—who has renewed at least two cities to within an inch of their lives—was reported to have said (at a cocktail party), "You can take people out of Oak Street, but you can't take Oak Street out of people." (Oak Street was—and has been for many years—an urban renewal project area.)

This theme reflects a widespread belief that, somehow or other, slum dwellers play a causative role in the creation of slums: slum tenants ruin the property through carelessness, poor housekeeping habits, neglect, or downright viciousness. Slum landlords are the most religiously committed to this point of view, of course, although it seems strange that they nevertheless keep right on buying slum property and prospering mightily. Many of them will explain their motivation by likening themselves to social workers and philanthropists, gallantly providing shelter for their impoverished fellow-man (who, they say, scarcely ever pays the rent and destroys the property in a matter of weeks).

From slum landlords, such statements are easy to understand and easy to dismiss. (They somehow just don't seem like philanthropists.) But from real social workers and real philanthropists, equivalent statements are hard to swallow.

In the old days, when immigration was at its height, there were similar explanations for the existence of slums that were even more terrible and inhuman than those we have today. The immigrants, too, were said to be ignorant about how to live in the fancy big city; they didn't know how to take care of the landlord's property. The symbolic expression, the shorthand phrase used to epitomize their sloth and ignorance, was the accusation that, not knowing what else to do with a bathtub, they kept coal in it.

The modern variation is directed, not against the European immigrant, but against what is delicately referred to as the "southern rural migrant": having grown accustomed, back on the farm, to throwing garbage out the window into the yard to feed the pigs, he continues the habit when he moves into the big city—throwing garbage out the window to feed fondly-remembered, but now imaginary pigs that are, one supposes, spiritually rooting around in the alley.

Charles Silberman has analyzed and rebutted this widespread fantasy in his book *Crisis in Black and White*. In a chapter entitled "The Beer Can in the Cotton Patch" he discusses a statement by Phillip Hauser, an eminent sociologist, that captures the heart of this mythology.[1] Hauser argues that the problem of the Negro in the city is essentially identical to that of the immigrant in the early part of the century, and he says that the Negro needs to experience, not "Americanization" (which was the treatment of choice for the immigrant), but "acculturation." Negroes, according to the good professor, "have been drawn from a primitive folk culture into a metropolitan way of life" in little more than a single generation, and this is the core of the problem. "A Negro in the Mississippi Delta tosses his empty whisky bottle or beer can into a cotton patch, and what difference does it make? But on the asphalt pavements of a city it can make a difference, esthetically and with respect to safety." Thus, we learn (with a great sigh of relief) that the problem of racial injustice in the ghetto turns out to be nothing but a special case of the larger problem of the litterbug, with which we have become so familiar.

The Ford Foundation "Gray Areas Project," which preceded and gave shape to much of the War on Poverty, was consciously aimed at the problem of acculturation—"to do in one generation for the urban newcomer what until now has taken three."

The federal government's initial approach to the problem of housing for the poor—which was only recently and partially modified—was indirectly based on these same notions. The treatment for slums was "slum clearance." A "blighted" neighborhood was identified and bulldozed out of existence —destroying not only the substandard structures in the area but also the community, removing the people as well as the buildings. The more refined techniques of urban renewal in

1970, on the other hand, emphasize "selective clearance" and "rehabilitation." The results are much the same since rehabilitation almost always involves moving out the people, repairing and remodeling the property, and renting at substantially higher rates.

Thus, whether one deals with the slum problem by destroying the housing and scattering the people or by sending in missionaries to civilize them and "acculturate" them, the implication is clear: the people living in the slums must be dealt with in some way if the slum problem is to be solved effectively. There are three separate, interconnected strands to this total mythology. The first is that there is an acculturation problem caused by hundreds of thousands of rural poor from the South flocking into the big cities of the North—Negroes and Appalachian whites. The second is that such people damage and run down the buildings they live in. The third is that there has been, in fact, a substantial and expensive effort made by the Government, the foundations, and the real estate business to do something to solve the slum problem. As usual, each of these three statements is both slightly true and enormously false.

II

It is certainly true that there has been a steady flow of black people northward from the most backward states of the South eventually coming to rest in the big city ghettoes. There has been such a migration pattern—particularly during World War I and World War II. But in most of these cities, the number and proportion of recent Southern migrants among the total ghetto population is relatively small. For example, in the five year period, 1955–1960, 7,500

Negroes moved from the South to Harlem. Now this is a large number of people, true. But, in such a huge community, it is a barely noticeable trickle. Compared to the flood of immigrants pouring into New York, Boston, and other cities of the Eastern seaboard in the early 1900's, it is insignificant. The Haryou planning report documents the true state of affairs, and shows that the great majority of Harlem's residents had been born in New York and, of those who could be classified as "in-migrants," most had lived in Harlem for many years. Fewer than five per cent were relative newcomers.

These facts are easily obscured by calculating one's data on the basis of place of birth, rather than the life history of migration. It is likely that in the majority of Northern cities —unlike the Harlem case—more than half of the Negro residents were born below the Mason-Dixon line. But large numbers of them moved to the city when they were children, others when they were young adults. In most cases, if they were born in a rural area (and many were not), they moved first to a nearby city. Later they may have moved to a city in a border state and then finally into the northern ghetto. That any substantial numbers moved directly from a farm in Georgia to Harlem, or Roxbury, or another big city ghetto is very unlikely. The more normal itinerary would be from the farm to Raleigh, to Baltimore, to Boston: or from the small town to Birmingham, to Memphis, to Chicago. There are, in fact, relatively small racial differences in migratory patterns—Americans in general are rather migratory people: one in five moves every year, often a long-distance move; the migratory habits of Southern Negroes stand out only with respect to the direction in which they travel.

A few years ago I was engaged to do a study of the problems of racial minorities, human services and citizen participation in the city of Springfield, Massachusetts. The study was part of that city's community renewal program. One of the common themes I heard in conversations with housing and social welfare officials was that of the unacculturated in-migrant. I found it advisable to do some detailed research on the migratory habits of Springfield's black population, and I reported as follows:

> The great majority of Springfield's present Negro population arrived in the city within the last twenty years; it is a population of newcomers. However, what is generally not appreciated is the fact that most of these newcomers arrived, not by way of buses from North Carolina and Georgia, but by way of the birth canal. The birth rate accounts for much more of the population increase than does the immigration rate. In particular, the majority of young people were born right in Springfield. . . . The absence of any great flooding in of immigrants is shown by the fact that, in 1960, about 80 per cent of Negroes, as compared with about 90 per cent of whites, had lived in Massachusetts for at least five years.[2]

In all cities, Negroes have a higher birth rate and a much lower average age than whites. This can be seen in the racial composition of public schools which, on the average, tends to show a black proportion that is about twice the size of the black proportion in the city as a whole.

The idea of equating the problems of racial injustice and slum housing with the issue of "acculturation," then, is plain nonsense. Newcomers from the South are relatively rare and, in any case, are often already "urbanized." The assumption that being a newcomer automatically makes one a candidate for acculturation is another issue; but since the quantitative facts upon which the theory is based are wrong to begin with, it is perhaps not necessary to deal with it. The theory is, in a sense, only a variation of the "culture of poverty" thesis.

The final demonstration that the acculturation problem has little bearing on the slum problem is a matter of simple arithmetic. In an average Negro ghetto, no more than five to ten per cent of the population are "rural Southern migrants," whereas perhaps fifty to eighty per cent live in substandard housing.

With or without the support of all the high-flown language about acculturation, however, the belief persists that "people" (that is, tenants) "cause slums." How does that belief square with facts? First, look at what constitutes slum housing. The U.S. Census Bureau is the major source of information about the quantity and prevalence of substandard housing. Every ten years they send around trained enumerators, and one of their jobs is to look at the housing in which the people they are counting live. The Census housing experts give examples of "critical" and "intermediate" defects: holes in the floors, walls or roofs; sagging floors or walls; shaky or unsafe porch or steps; rotted window sills; deep wear on floors and stairs.

When several citizens' groups in New Haven began to protest about the inadequacy of housing code enforcement, we began to hear, of course, about how terrible the tenants were, how they ruined the buildings, and how it was impossible for the landlord to keep up with their destructiveness. When we finally harassed the code enforcement agency to the point where they opened their files on uncorrected code violations, we were able to obtain a good cross-sectional view of the slum housing problem as defined, not by tenants or radical agitators, but by the trained and presumably competent housing inspectors who conducted the investigations and made out the reports. A public health student, Marian Glaser, did a detailed analysis of 180 cases of code violation.[3]

Each case represented a single building, almost all of which were multiple-unit dwellings. In these 180 buildings there were an incredible total of 1,244 different recorded violations —about seven per building. What did the violations consist of? First of all, over one-third of the violations were *exterior* defects: broken doors and stairways, holes in the walls, sagging roofs, broken chimneys, damaged porches, etc. Another one-third were interior violations that could scarcely be attributed to the most ingeniously destructive rural southern migrant in America. There were, for example, a total of 160 instances of defective wiring or other electrical hazards (a very common cause of the excessive number of fires and needless tragic deaths in the slums). There were 125 instances of inadequate, defective, or inoperable plumbing or heating. There were 34 instances of serious infestation by rats and roaches. One can scarcely imagine a newcomer to the city so naive about how to live in a house, or a poor man whose "culture" was so impoverished, that he would be motivated to climb up on the roof to chop a hole in it; jump up and down on the porch until it started to sag; run down to the basement to jam the furnace and break through a sewage drain pipe; and lure a colony of rats and cockroaches into the house.

With respect to the final one-third of recorded defects, many *could* be caused by tenants. They *could* make holes in the walls and ceilings of their apartments, or even, with some effort, in the floors. They *could* rip plaster off the walls. They *could* break windows and contribute to the accumulation of junk and trash in the yards and cellars. One would think they might have better things to do, but let us assume that at least some tenants do participate in creating slums. Using the New Haven code violation data as a guideline, it seems clear that the one-third of violations that are exterior and the one-third that consist of such defects as electrical, heating, plumbing, and vermin violations are the responsibility of the landlord. If we give the landlord the extreme benefit of the doubt of the remaining one-third and apportion the blame equally between him and the tenant, we find that, at the maximum, one violation in six can be attributed to the tenant. By the most conservative estimate, then, the remaining five out of six—eighty-five per cent—must be credited to the landlord's neglect.

But there is another factor that must be considered. After a defect has developed what is done about it? Usually, little or nothing. For example, the sample of 180 cases of code violations mentioned above represented violations that had remained uncorrected after landlords had been officially ordered to make repairs. The landlords had simply ignored or resisted these orders—for months and, in some instances, for years. In whatever way the specific conditions may have *originated,* their *continuation* (which also means their getting worse) was clearly due, first: to the failure of the landlord to keep his property up to code specifications (which are, in fact, quite lenient); and second: to the failure of the city agency to enforce the code, which provides for criminal penalties in such cases. Even in those few cases in which landlords reluctantly comply with the code, they often do so contemptuously or spitefully, so that the improvement is almost as damaging psychologically as the violation was physically. One landlord, whose failure to take care of a peeling paint problem had once led to a serious case of lead poisoning, responded to a tenant's complaint by painting each wall of the room a different color—purple, orange, red, and yellow. Others cover up holes in the walls, or the floors, or the ceilings by nailing an ugly piece of plywood or plasterboard over the hole. This meets the specifications of the housing code, but it scarcely leads to pleasant living.

Another item that makes for substandard housing is the absence of adequate plumbing. There were, according to the 1960 census, about ten million housing units that lacked a private toilet or bath. Of these, slightly over two million were occupied by black families. In comparison, of the forty-two million sound units with all plumbing facilities, forty million were occupied by whites. This most burdensome and demeaning of the features of slum living—having to share a bathroom with other families in the same building (or even in other buildings)—can scarcely be attributed to characteristics of the tenants.

As a final example, in New York City there are still close to fifty thousand "old-law" tenements with unventilated inside rooms, absence of private baths, and the ever-present danger of fire.

The latter fact is a special case of the general truth that slums are, in the most simple sense of the word, very old, worn-out, scarcely repairable buildings. Anyone who has visited a minimum of three slum tenements could hardly escape noticing that these buildings are aged, deteriorated, untended, neglected for years and years.

I've met a number of people—whites who pride themselves on having risen from poverty to prosperity—who grew up in areas that have since become Negro slums—the Hill in New Haven, Roxbury in Boston—and whose memories of their old neighborhoods are fond and glowing. "In those days," they claim, the neighborhood was beautiful—neat lawns, well-kept homes. Now that blacks have moved in, they say, the neighborhood has been ruined. How is this to be explained? First of all, these memories are partially a result of what someone once called "the old oaken bucket fallacy"; the harshest, roughest, and dirtiest part of the memories have been filtered out, leaving only the glow. I myself knew Roxbury twenty odd years ago when it was mostly white and mostly Jewish. I visited friends there and dated a couple of girls who lived there. My wife had relatives and friends in Roxbury too, and her memory jibes with mine. Roxbury wasn't all that great, even twenty years ago. The streets had fewer potholes and the trash was picked up more regularly and more neatly; there were fewer darkened street lights and broken stretches of sidewalk. But the houses, even then, were old and showed their age. In the intervening twenty years, owners, who lived in the houses and took reasonable care of them, sold out to large-scale operators who entered the houses at most once a month to collect rents, and who, if they paid carpenters and painters any money at all for work on the buildings, paid to have reasonably spacious single apartments subdivided into two or three cramped and tiny warrens. What can happen to a sixty-year-old house in twenty years under the care of a neglectful slum landlord is roughly comparable to what can happen to a sixty-year-old man growing to be eighty with never a visit to a doctor or a hospital.

No, slum tenants don't ruin good housing. The buildings are worn out and used up first, then the slum is ready for the poor and the black to move in.

III

But at least we are dealing with the problem, right? We are spending a lot of tax money on public housing and urban renewal so that the poor will have better housing, right?

Wrong. We are doing damned little, and the belief that we are doing a great deal is, though soothing to the rest of the population, infuriating to those who have to continue living in the hellholes that we call slums. At the time that New Haven had its riot (or its "disturbance" as City Hall calls it; its "rebellion," as the black militants call it), there was much clucking of tongues, both in New Haven and in other parts of the country. "After all we've done for them," said white New Haveners; outside observers said, "Even in New Haven, the model city. . . ." The basis for these remarks was the fact that New Haven had obtained enormous quantities of Federal money for urban renewal—more per capita than any other city in America. Several hundred million dollars had gone into the renewal of New Haven, which had the reputation of dealing with urban problems progressively, vigorously, and effectively. It was, in the view of many—not the least of whom were Mayor Richard Lee and his Number One Boy, Redevelopment Administrator Melvin Adams—a model city. Imagine the gall and ingratitude of New Haven's blacks! To have a riot in a model city!

Now, as a resident for three years in that unhappy city, I can testify fervently that it is no such thing. It is a model, in a sense, of two things: a monolithic structure of repression, and an uncontrollable urban renewal program that is, in fact, destroying a middling-little city on the basis of a delusional perception that it is a great metropolitan area. New Haven is a "Potemkin village," well designed by highly skilled publicists to deceive most observers, particularly those who observe from afar. To give one example: this urban renewal program, assisted by some highway construction, demolished a total of over five thousand housing units, most of which were occupied by low-income families. In the same period of time it constructed exactly twelve new units of low-income family housing.

Now, I know from experience in telling people about these figures that they have read them in one of three ways: either they skimmed over them without thinking, or they assumed there was a misprint, or they think I'm lying. Five thousand demolished, twelve built. So help me God! There was other construction: several hundred units of low-income housing for the elderly; several hundred units of subsidized middle-income housing; and several thousand units of upper-income and luxury housing. And, to be fair, there has been the rent certificate program: housing was leased for occupancy by several hundred low-income families (a portion of this was substandard, however). But, with repect to new construction, only twelve units of new low-income family housing appeared in this model city.

The effect of New Haven's urban renewal program has been a housing shortage for the poor that has to be seen to be believed. If you go to look for, say, a four-room apartment with its own bathroom, in a building that is not actually falling apart, for less than $125, you are going to have a long, long search in front of you. When we first moved to New Haven in 1966, we had to rent temporarily while we waited to move into the house we bought. We found a reasonable four-room flat—nothing fancy, no "modern" conveniences at all, and the tiny bathroom was off the kitchen. The building was formerly a single eight-room house that had been converted into a two-family dwelling. The rent was $145 a month. Three years later, when the apartment became vacant, the landlord asked $225. He had done literally nothing to the building. This was in Westville, a "nice" residential section of New Haven. In The Hill, or Newhallville, the problem is much worse. I know families, whose total income is only

$80 or $90 a week, that are paying $135 or $150 a month for housing. And their apartments are vastly, grossly inferior to the one we were renting.

The case of New Haven is only an extreme example of the effect of urban renewal on the low-income housing problem. Between the time of the passage of the 1949 Housing Act (ironically prefaced with a pious statement of the goal of decent, safe, and sanitary housing for every American family) and July 1, 1967, over 1400 urban renewal projects in over 700 American cities had accomplished the destruction of 383,000 dwelling units, almost all of which had been occupied by low-income families. During the same period—on the land thus cleared—only 107,000 new housing units were constructed, of which only about 10,000 were low-income apartments. The net effect was a loss of over 350,000 homes for low-income people. In its place went high-rise luxury apartments, a civic center, office buildings, shopping centers, and an occasional school or community center.

In the West End of Boston and in the Oak Street project in New Haven, developers cast an eye on "slum neighborhoods" that they could convert into profitable, conveniently located apartment complexes. In Chicago, urban renewal was undertaken to make room for the physical expansion of university campuses. In Newark, a new medical school was the occasion for slum clearance. In almost every urban renewal project, the objective was to get rid of a slum neighborhood (and the "undesirables" who lived there) to make room for "higher uses." The rehousing of the poor was never a matter that had the slightest priority. To continue dealing with urban renewal as if it had any remote potential for solving the slum problem is insane.

How have they been able to get away with it? How could these urban renewal people perform such prodigies of destruction and exploitation and keep their membership in the circle of progressive social actionists, or even more astonishing, be hailed as friends of the poor and the Negro? The answer is simple. They lied. And they continued to lie. And they are still lying as I write this sentence. Let me give an example. In the early 1960's, Mr. Edward Logue, fresh from his triumphs in New Haven, came to Boston to assume the post of redevelopment czar for the Hub. He was signing on to create the "New Boston." One of his first orders of business was to put into execution the Washington Park project in Roxbury. At the time, I was Urban Renewal Chairman of the Fair Housing Federation of Greater Boston, which together with the Urban League, the NAACP, CORE and other groups, had grave doubts about the Washington Park project on two grounds: the inadequacy of relocation plans, and the absence of replacement units for the low-income families that would be displaced. The redevelopment agency dealt with the relocation puzzle by drawing up an elaborate plan counting up thousands of units of nonexistent housing to which the thousands of families to be displaced would be relocated. By elaborate statistical manipulation, they found several thousands of units of sales housing in Boston— whereas the U.S. Census Bureau, in a report issued only a few months earlier on the results of the 1960 census, had been able to count only a few hundred. The statisticians of the Authority, by the most grotesque distortions of reality, were able to perceive thousands of available rental units. In reality, of the fraction of such units that really existed in real buildings on real streets, most were too high-priced for Washington Park families, and, of the remainder, only a handful were large enough. What was available was vacant substandard housing, and large numbers of relocated families ultimately went to live in such housing. They moved from one slum to another to make room for shopping centers and middle-income apartments.

This, too, is typical of urban renewal. Relocation is almost always a dreadful failure. No more than two-thirds of relocated families find "safe, decent, sanitary" housing. The remainder move into other slums. And it is no accident that four out of five families displaced by urban renewal across the country have been black. One of the most infamous projects in the whole history of this program was the West End project in Boston, involving the displacement of several thousand lower-middle class white families (the West End, despite the need for considerable upgrading of its housing, was no slum; it was so defined because greedy developers, in collaboration with city officials, had the dream of building what is now the Charles River Park apartment complex). Chester Hartman studied what happened to these families— who were far more mobile and had a far wider choice of residential areas than the typical black family that is displaced—and found that only seventy-three per cent were able to move into standard housing, despite the fact that they averaged about a twenty per cent increase in their rental costs.[4]

So the Boston redevelopment agency simply lied about their relocation plans and simply dreamed up a supply of nonexistent relocation housing. When I analyzed their figures and showed how absolutely absurd they were, they issued a whole new plan, with a whole new set of figures. All lies. By then, of course, it was too late.

The absence of relocation housing in the project area itself for families that were displaced was no problem at all. It was, in fact—as it almost always is—an integral part of the plan. Urban renewal has been called "Negro removal." Whatever else is on the agenda, public action on the issue of slums has, as its first priority, the removal of poor slum dwellers from the area; Washington Park was no exception. The standard course of action in such situations is to undertake community organization—to "plan with people." The community that is organized, however, is very carefully selected—the middle class homeowner, the professional, the small businessman are included; the low-income renters, the welfare families, the irregularly employed are carefully excluded (a very sensible and rational course of action since the former are being organized in order to drive out the latter). The results of this were evident when the Washington Park project was considered at a public hearing. The state representatives, the political bosses, the civic leaders, the lawyers, the social agency executives, and the clergymen were carefully paraded before the redevelopment board to sing the praises of the agency staff and to go into ecstasies about the proposed renewal plan. One minister got carried away and began to describe the new Washington Park in terms that would have been appropriate only for a vision of the New Jerusalem. He concluded his hymn of praise by saying, "If Jesus Christ were alive today, walking the streets of Roxbury, he would come here tonight and he would vote in favor of urban renewal."

Against the combined forces of the plan's proponents and Jesus Christ, the opponents of the renewal plan were swept away, after registering their objections at the end of the meeting as the clock ticked toward midnight.

And so it goes, all over the country. Urban renewal is to the slum housing problem approximately as a crash reducing diet is to the problem of malnutrition. In the face of a problem that can only be solved by the massive construction of new low-income housing, urban renewal keeps *destroying* low-income housing.

The other boon given to the ill-housed poor by government

action is public housing. Although Congress keeps authorizing fairly large quantities of public housing (as much as 800,000 units at one time), actual additions to the public housing supply average something like 30,000 new units a year (this is approximately one-twentieth of one per cent of the total housing stock, about two per cent of all new housing constructed). The annual federal subsidy is now on the order of $250 million a year. The net result of government action on low-rent housing programs is that, for every three housing units built for the poor, about two others are destroyed (this does not count the side effects of housing destruction caused by the federal highway program). With five million low-income families living in completely uninhabitable housing (a very low conservative estimate), it would take approximately 478 years to provide enough new housing for them at the rate we are now proceeding.

Fortunately, we *are* providing handsome housing subsidies to the rich, and this, of course, has a very beneficial effect on housing for the poor. It really does. The rich, you see, move into their new subsidized $75,000 ranch house, selling their old $50,000 Garrison Colonial to a well-to-do family that is anxious to leave the $38,000 Cape they have been living in for twelve years now, which they are delighted to sell to the middle class family whose $27,000 development house is now too small for them and for which they have a potential buyer in a family that has owned a duplex, that they can now sell to a family that has saved enough money to move out of their $225 apartment, leaving the apartment vacant for the young couple with the new baby, who want to get out of the little three-room place they have been renting for $165, which is good news to the working class family that can now afford to leave the small run-down $110 apartment, that fortunately becomes available to the family relocated out of their $85 apartment by the urban renewal project that is putting up luxury apartments, including a $700 a month penthouse which was seriously considered for awhile by the rich family that bought the $75,000 ranch house in the first place.

Thus do benefits trickle down to the poor.

IV·

The public policy on housing in the United States was clearly stated in the 1949 Housing Act: a safe, decent, and sanitary dwelling for every American family. This official statement of the policy was, of course, slightly condensed from the original and real policy, which is: a safe, decent and sanitary dwelling for every middle class American family, and everything that's left over for the poor. The government stands behind and guarantees the mortgage for about one-fifth to one-quarter of new housing that is built for the middle class. It provides community planning and facilities grants for the suburban developments where most of this housing is built, and then it shoulders ninety per cent of the cost of the new highway that makes it possible for the new homeowner to commute back and forth from his job. Most important, it encourages home ownership through a tax policy that makes real estate tax payments and mortgage interest deductible expenses. These tax advantages are not, of course, discriminatory in any way; they are available to anybody—at least anybody who can afford to own his own home. This amounts to a lot of money. I just looked up my last year's tax return and calculated that I saved $576 by owning my own home—that's the government's way of helping out on the housing problem. To a rich man who has an income of, say, $100,000 a year and who owns a home worth, say, $150,000, this housing subsidy may be worth as much as five thousand dollars a year. This is white-collar welfare on a scale that would make the average ADC mother—getting half that amount in "official" welfare —feel rich herself. Alvin Schorr has calculated that in 1962 housing subsidies in the form of tax relief to the middle- and upper-income groups amounted to about three billion dollars —with most of it (1.7 billion) going to the richest twenty per cent of the population. This three billion is about twenty times the total federal subsidy for public housing for the poor.[5]

Of course this doesn't cover everything the government does for the poor. There is another, hidden subsidy—that portion of public assistance payments that goes for rent. In 1962, by Schorr's calculations, over half a billion in federal money could be counted as housing subsidies; and he adds this in as part of the housing support for poor families. I would argue that, since many welfare recipients live in sub-standard housing, this indirect payment is subsidizing slums and slum landlords, some of whom make a fat living by renting exclusively to welfare families (adding a bit on to the take by charging a dollar for cashing the welfare check when they collect the rent).

A New York caseworker, visiting some of the families he served, reports what this kind of federally-subsidized housing for the poor is like:

> . . . roaches and rats abound; broken flooring, plumbing, windows, lighting fixtures and plasters are observable throughout. The average room size (occupied by a family) is 13 x 15, with two beds, a dresser, two chairs, a table, a refrigerator, and a closet, as the standard equipment supplied by the landlord. One community kitchen is used by seven families. Twelve toilets are intermittently in service on six floors. There is no lock on the door from the street

and vagrants, including drug addicts and alcoholics, often wander in to sleep in the unlocked kitchens and bathrooms. This is the abode of thirty families and 105 children.[6]

This, you see, is what lack of acculturation does to our neighborhoods. This is how poor families, in close collaboration with the federal government, create the slums they live in.

8
Illegal Order

The Administration
of Injustice

I

Members of several citizens' groups, led by the Hill Parents
Association, a local black militant group, were visiting the
office of Mr. Melvin Adams, redevelopment administrator of
New Haven, to protest the utterly inadequate administration
of the housing code enforcement program in this supposedly
model city. In the course of the discussion, my wife pointed
out that the enforcement agency was, in fact, coddling slum
landlords by failing to put pressure on them to correct the
demoralizing, and often dangerous conditions in their tenements. The conversation was recorded, so I am able to quote
the exchange:

Mrs. Ryan:
I want to return to talking about this double standard which
is very clear to me, and I think if you'll allow me an analogy,
I can demonstrate that. On one of these cases, I think it was

number 174, and I think the case has been on the books
nineteen months—you can correct me, you have the figures
in front of you, Irv—the notation was made "owner is seeking funds to correct property." Now let's leave the owner
waiting over there looking desperately for nineteen months
to get money—even with great feelings of . . . you know,
we're all very touched by that. Let's picture, on the other
hand the way this community and the leadership of this city,
of which you are a part—

Mr. Adams:

Yes, very happy to be.

Mrs. Ryan:

—would deal with persons of less income. For example, sup-
posing a man were arrested for failing to pay his rent or for
stealing from a grocery store, even a very large order, and
were apprehended by the police on a call from the grocer,
and the man said, "Don't put me in jail—you know, I've
got to have some time to raise some dough to pay this money
back, and if you put me in jail, I'm not going to be able to
feed my family, you know." Would you put him in jail and
slap a bail on him that would probably be prohibitive, or
would you say, "Go ahead, fella, you go out and you raise
the money, and we'll let you go, and we're not going to put
it in the paper, particularly because you're a prominent ac-
tivist in this community . . . we wouldn't slander you in the
paper. We're going to let you go and have your time to do
it because we think you'll do better and comply with the law
more if we give you a break." Now I submit that's ragtime,
that that's not what you would do, you would put him in
jail, you would probably give him a fine, and my feeling is
—may I finish—my feeling is, that that's a double standard
of justice, and that it's really not responding to the law and
is really the origin of the disrespect for law and order that
we have in this community. I suspect that the . . . that the
problem begins with the administration in not observing the

laws that are in the books, and that's where I sense that our problems begin.

Mr. Adams:

I think you're talking about apples and oranges. I think you . . . when you talk about what causes disrespect for law . . . I mean, you're entitled to your opinion; I don't think you're right, if you talked about two different legal situations. The objective—

Mrs. Ryan:

They're law violations.

Mr. Adams:

The . . . Ha! But the . . . there are law violations and there are law violations.

Mrs. Ryan:

Right![1]

We were really quite astounded to hear the man ranking second in the city administration make such a statement. I am not sure to this day whether he was being cynical or simply stating the reality as he saw it and accepted it and, as he assumed, other sensible people saw it and accepted it. That it was and is the operative reality—the way things really work out in life—there is no doubt. We were to learn this personally a few weeks later when we were arrested in a demonstration against the failure of code enforcement. I will tell that story in more detail at a later point. Here I want to underline the importance of Mr. Adams' idea—that there are two classes of law violators—as the central concept in trying to understand the problems of law enforcement and police practices, and as an area of social intercourse that has become infused with the mythology of Blaming the Victim.

There are three things that have to be understood in order to grasp the very subtle way in which Blaming the Victim is applied to problems of law and order. First, one must understand the received wisdom of the social scientists and the liberal politicians, the core of which is a seemingly praiseworthy effort to attribute the problems of crime and delinquency to unjust social conditions, poverty, family breakdown—the whole megillah. Second, one has to comprehend the staggering implications of Mr. Adams' offhand phrase —that there are law violators and law violators—and to grasp the methods by which the police and the courts operate a blatant system of two-class justice. Finally, one has to come to grips with the real function of the police—which, incidentally is to keep *order,* not to enforce *law.* Let's look at these three points one at a time.

The "progressive" view (I don't know what else to call it: the "liberal" view, the "enlightened" view, the "intellectual" view—choose one) of crime and its causation was etched out very clearly in the rhetoric of the last Presidential campaign through the contrast in the oratory of Humphrey with that of Nixon and Wallace. Wallace scarcely bothered to observe the cryptographic conventions of the Law and Order code book; he spoke openly of repressing riffraff, anarchists, looters, and what he called pointy-headed guideline writers: he even seemed eager for the opportunity to ride his limousine over any of these deviants who might be foolhardy enough to lie down in his path. His rhetoric was openly anti-Negro.

Nixon was a good deal cooler. He took a rather classical, conservative stand: criminals were immoral lawbreakers; whether or not they grew up in slums and poverty was, first of all, of doubtful relevance, and second, was certainly no basis for issuing a certificate of exemption for the consequences of their actions. By these standards of reckoning, there are two classes of people, the criminals and the rest of us. The righteous are expected—on the basis both of self-righteousness and of self-interest—to put the criminals in their place, which is usually in jail.

Poor Humphrey almost tore himself apart trying to straddle the issue, but for the most part he tried to project the classical "enlightened" position: that crime was a by-product of poverty, with some of the poor taking to crime as others take to drugs or welfare dependency. In this view, the long-range cure for crime is to improve social conditions. The short-range cure is not readily distinguishable from the standard program of the righteous middle. The main difference is that the enlightened believe that the poor criminal should be rehabilitated while the righteous believe that the immoral criminal should be locked up in jail. Since almost the only available system of rehabilitation in America is to be locked up in jail, the difference remains highly abstract.

The President's Commission on Law Enforcement and Administration of Justice[2] upholds the standard position on the relationship between crime and unhealthy social conditions such as poverty, slums, inadequate education, discrimination, and unemployment, and it makes the standard recommendation that one way to reduce the volume of crime would be to improve these conditions. Fortunately, the commission also provides an enormous amount of factual information and perceptive insights about the real problems of law and order.

The victim-blaming ideology about crime and law enforcement can be summed up rather readily, I believe—without the buttressing of numerous quotations—because it is a widely held position. The reader, I feel very sure, senses the validity of my analysis. The first point in this ideology is that crime is dramatically more prevalent in the slums and among the poor; the second point is that the criminality of the poor is a result of social conditions which, in effect, warp their character and behavior; the third point is that these lower

class criminals make up a distinct subgroup in the population; and the fourth is that the purpose of police activity—in
a manner somewhat analogous to the forceful quarantining of
persons with dangerous infectious diseases—is to control and
suppress the activity of this lower class criminal subgroup.

This set of statements is an extremely plausible and acceptable version of Blaming the Victim, perhaps the most
plausible of all the formulations I have discussed. It is also
the most outrageous collection of non-facts imaginable. But
the speciousness of the argumentation is not easy to detect.
It is difficult, in the first place, to think of the person we call
a criminal as a victim at all. In what way is the mugger, the
purse-snatcher, the thug who beat up our neighbor in Central
Park, a victim? How can the processes of criminal justice, in
any sense, be defined as Blaming the Victim?

The problem here, even more so than in the case of other
kinds of social problems, is in the nature of the facts we are
talking about and the nature of public knowledge about those
facts. The average, literate, educated citizen (provided he has
never been arrested or tried for a crime) has no sense whatever either of the method of operation or the basic function
of the police, the courts or the correctional system. The real
truth is that arrest, trial and punishment of persons accused
of breaking the law is very tenuously related to the enforcement of law and the deterrence of crime, and has only a remote relationship with any such abstract entity as justice.
As J. Edgar Hoover once said in a moment of perhaps un-
intentional candor, "Justice is incidental to law and order."

To begin with, one must consider two questions. The first
has to do with crime, its nature and quantity; the second with
criminals, their prevalence and characteristics. Everyone
"knows," of course, that America is experiencing a prolonged

crime wave. Indeed, to hear J. Edgar Hoover and the John Birch Society tell it, it is a crime whirlpool, a felony typhoon, a cataclysm of sin. Criminals are multiplying like fruit flies and growing bolder by the hour. The streets are unsafe, and the criminal element—encouraged by their pals on the Supreme Court—is overwhelming us. Is it any wonder that little old ladies skulk behind their chintz curtains, clutching shotguns in their sweaty hands and gripping switchblades between their dentures? The Hoodlums are Coming!

Each annual collection of statistics in the FBI's multi-volume detective novel[3] documents the rising crime rate. The line on the graph that reflects what they call the "Crime Index" jogs and staggers up and up like a drunkenly energetic mountain climber. Aggravated assault: up nine per cent; murder: up nine per cent; rape: up seven per cent; car theft: up eighteen per cent; robbery: up twenty-seven per cent. It's a perpetual bull market in depravity!

So it appears that the facts seem to justify the worrying. The crime-wave watchers have a lot to watch, it would seem. The facts are clear. Like that other legendary lawman, Sergeant Joe Friday, our esteemed Director Hoover marches on, interested only in the facts.

Perhaps so; it may well be true. However, the FBI Crime Report—with all its tables and charts, its fatuously precise summations (1,605,700 burglaries, indeed)—is one of the most preposterously non-factual documents ever to roll off the prim presses of the U.S. Government Printing Office. As a basis for serious discussion of social problems and social policies, it is approximately as useful as Madame Zelda's Lucky Number Dream Book. (This is not to deny its melodramatic appeal to addicted detective story fans.)

Let me illustrate. During the month of August in 1950 the Police Department of New York City recorded 110 reported robberies—rather modest in a city of some seven million. One year later, in August of 1951, the total for the month had zoomed up to 608 robberies. In the same one year period, aggravated assaults almost tripled, going from 293 to 793; and the incidents of larceny mushroomed from 634 to 5,519. There seemed to be an uncontrollable epidemic of burglaries, the number leaping from 161 to 2,913, a staggering increase of 1,772 per cent (to be precise).

One looks in vain through the newspapers of the times for any notice given to this terrifying tidal wave of misconduct. One might have expected the *Times* to have devoted perhaps a half column of dense syntax to tongue-clucking. And one would have looked forward to the *Daily News* clapping on its battered fedora to shout and shake its fist at outraged readers. Nothing of the sort happened. The famous New York City crime wave of 1951, though hardly good news, was no news.

The explanation for this is surprisingly simple. According to a study conducted by the Institute of Public Administration,[4] these phenomenal increases, far from representing a crime wave, were the result of a paper wave—that is, a drastic change in reporting procedures brought about by a new police commissioner. Previously, reports of crimes had gone unrecorded through negligence or disinterest, or the records were filed in the wastebasket (in police jargon, "assigned to Detective Can") rather than being forwarded to headquarters. It was change in bureaucratic procedures, then, that accounted for the apparent crime wave that was, quite appropriately, unnoticed and unreported in the newspapers.

The story reveals the core of the problem with crime statistics—they are dependent upon accurate police reporting, and police do not, for a variety of reasons, report accurately. To gather together hundreds and hundreds of variably reliable reports from individual police departments, and to stuff them indiscriminately into the mouth of a computer is only to guarantee that the compact summations emerging will be monumentally unreliable. This is the basic reason why most criminologists—at least privately and occasionally publicly —will admit that American crime statistics are less than useless. Yet the whole public dialogue about crime and crime waves, and about law and order is based almost wholly on these naive, useless, irrelevant crime statistics. The truth is that the Uniform Crime Reports of the FBI serve no useful purpose. They do, however, provide a guaranteed opportunity for Mr. J. Edgar Hoover to have his name on the front pages of most American newspapers on the day the annual report is released, and they do give ammunition to the police lobby and right wing extremists who scream about the Supreme Court coddling criminals and the need to support one's local police.

There are two other kinds of much more reliable information which demonstrate that crime statistics are wrong. A recent national survey, conducted for the President's Crime Commission[5] showed that the FBI Crime Index—based on the incidence of seven major crimes that are dealt with rather uniformly through the fifty states—is a gross *underestimation* of the actual crime rate. By the most conservative standards the actual crime rate is at least *double* or *triple* the rate reported by the FBI: this survey, which interviewed a large sample of the population, attempted to locate victims of crimes and to interrogate them. Those conducting the survey found that: in only about half the cases were the police notified of the crime; only three times out of four did the police come to the scene or otherwise investigate the complaint; and, of those complaints investigated, only three out of four were considered by the police to be crimes.

It is only at this point that the FBI collectors of crime statistics even pretend to pick up the thread of the story— at a point where seventy per cent of offenses and at least fifty per cent of the seven index crimes have already been excluded from the count. Further, the fact is that fewer than one in five of the major crimes (and an even smaller proportion of all crimes) ever lead to an arrest; and a large number of those arrested are never brought to trial. Perhaps this makes it quite understandable that the primary reason given why people do not report crimes to the police in the first place is their expressed belief that "the police could not do anything about the incident, would not catch the offenders, or would not want to be bothered."[6] This is perhaps the clearest statement of the real feelings of the American public about the role of the police in relation to problems of "law." (On problems of "order," however, there is, as we shall see, a completely opposite kind of reaction to the police.)

Collectors of crime statistics in the chambers of the FBI, then, may be likened to other collectors who pursue such hobbies as stamps and butterflies. Their activities are absorbing, of great interest to fellow enthusiasts, often very profitable, but add little to social progress or the relevant body of man's knowledge.

Further evidence of the great inaccuracy of official crime figures is to be found in a series of studies which show that, if one uses a simple-minded definition of a criminal as someone who breaks the criminal law, the great majority of the population are, in fact, criminals.[7] In one such study, 89 per cent of men admitted having committed larceny, 57 per cent admitted tax evasion, 26 per cent reported that they had stolen a car, and 11 per cent had committed robbery. In this study a total of 49 crimes were listed (of the hundreds on the statute books) and, although the sample was biased toward the more middle class, affluent section of the population, over 90 per cent of the respondents said they had committed at least one of the 49 crimes, with the average number for men being 18 apiece. Two-thirds of the male respondents had committed at least one serious felony that carried a penalty of more than two years' imprisonment. The average varied from one occupational group to another; for example, ministers, as one might expect, were substantially less criminal in their habits than most. The ministers surveyed committed a modest average of eight crimes apiece. Other studies have produced similar results: the overwhelming majority of the general population has committed criminal acts, many of them extremely serious. Almost all of these crimes went unreported and the criminal escaped arrest and prosecution.

This does not take into account two additional phenomena: organized crime and white-collar crime—activities which are often not even *experienced* as crimes. Much of organized crime (which makes up one of the major American industries, with gross sales estimated in the billions) devotes itself ostensibly to meeting the needs of the people, not to offending them. But retail operations in the fields of prostitution, narcotics, and gambling scarcely get counted in the crime statistics. And, of course, neither Director Hoover nor the average city police department expends much energy in dealing with organized crime.

As to white-collar crime: it is normally not even counted as *crime,* even when it is specifically known to officials. Sutherland[8] has pointed out that there is a great deal of *illegal* behavior in the world of business and commerce that is theoretically criminal—theoretically it can be sanctioned by criminal penalties such as fines and imprisonments—but it is dealt with through non-criminal regulative procedures. He investigated the records of the seventy largest American corporations with respect to court and commission findings against them on four types of laws: anti-trust, truth in advertising, labor relations, and patent and copyright laws. He found a total of 547 such adverse decisions, an average of 7.8 decisions per corporation, with each corporation having at least one such decision registered against it. Although all of these decisions indicated violation of laws that carried the possibilities of criminal penalties, only nine per cent of them were made in criminal courts. The process by which the offense was handled obscured the fact that most of the actions under consideration were, in fact, criminal in nature.

Only very occasionally—such as in the "Great Electrical Conspiracy"—when the activities of the white-collar criminal in swindling the public become grossly offensive to some sensitive prosecutor, are criminal sanctions invoked, and then they often lead to outraged sympathy for the "victims," who usually turn out to be prominent community leaders, church vestrymen, PTA presidents, and Sunday school teachers. But such rare instances demonstrate that white-collar crime is, after all, crime.

Paradoxically then, the crime wave problem is both more and less than it is said to be. Whether crime is increasing at all, or, if it is increasing, whether it is increasing at the terrifying rate certified by the FBI—these are really unanswerable questions. There are simply no reliable data. On the other hand, the real problem on the crime front is quite different from the one described by political oratory and the FBI's creative writing club. Crime is extraordinarily prevalent in this country. It is endemic. We are surrounded and immersed in crime. In a very real sense, most of our friends and neighbors are law violators. Large numbers of them are repeated offenders. A very large group have committed serious major felonies, such as theft, assault, tax evasion, and fraud. Few of them are ever arrested, still fewer tried, and only a tiny number are ever imprisoned. This "hidden crime," as it is often called, is not petty or negligible. According to the President's Crime Commission, organized crime takes in about twice as much money—from gambling and its other goods and services—as the total income from all other kinds of criminal activity combined. And unreported commercial theft losses—including shoplifting and employee theft—are more than double those of all reported private and commercial theft. The cost to the public resulting from illegal price-fixing by corporation executives is enormous. Fraudulent tax evasion costs every honest taxpayer money.

In analyzing the crime problem within the framework of the ideology of Blaming the Victim, then, I do not mean in any way to imply that crime is a trifling, or an unimportant matter. On the contrary, it is extremely important. It is a malignant infection in our society. Nor am I belittling the idea of law enforcement, and the arrest and punishment of criminals. Like most Americans, I am very much in favor of enforcing the law—so much so that I would be quite willing to support at least a pilot project to try it out somewhere.

II

The trouble with the official crime picture is that it has the effect of grossly distorting the average citizen's image of what crime is all about. It minimizes and deflects attention from one kind of crime (the common kind that one's neighbors commit) and exaggerates and spotlights another, less common, kind (the code name is "crime-in-the-street" which is presumably committed by "criminals").

Out of the total spectrum of crime, very little is committed in the streets. Even crimes of violence—particularly rape, murder, and aggravated assault—are indoor events, and the participants are usually well acquainted and often related. Robbery, however, is more typically a street crime, and the crime-in-the-street crowd are usually talking about muggings and purse-snatchings. But this sort of thing is really relatively rare. The overall chances of any single individual being killed, assaulted, raped, or robbed on the street by a stranger in the course of any given year are much, much less than one in a thousand. For the one person in a thousand who is the victim, it is of course, a very serious, damaging, and frightening experience; but for the community as a whole, there are many more widespread social problems. Consider the probabilities of being the victim in other situations involving common social problems: the chances of being injured in an automobile accident in any given year are one in sixty—sixteen times greater than the probability of being a victim of crime in the streets. One might reasonably expect hysteria about automotive safety to be sixteen times greater than the panic about street crime, and Ralph Nader to be more of a hero than J. Edgar Hoover. The chances of being divorced are five times greater, of being admitted to a mental hospital about three times greater; and the chances of a worker being unemployed for six months or more are about ten times greater. Yet, knowing these facts, can anyone seriously imagine a Presidential electoral campaign revolving around the issue of auto safety, or mental illness, or full employment, or family breakdown? It's inconceivable. Why does the American public respond so strongly to the issue of law and order?

There are at least two reasons. One is that the myopic view represented in the conventional wisdom about crime seems to provide at least some vague rationale for the tasks we set for our police; and it is comforting to keep the illusion that police are engaged in law enforcement. Another is that it permits us to keep believing that crime is fertilized by the slums and nurtured by low socio-economic status. We can then go on talking about some mythical separate group of criminals—most of whom, of course, are poor or black or both—dangerous and threatening to the life of the community. We do this through the device of defining as criminal only persons arrested by the police.

What are we to think if it can be demonstrated (as I will attempt to do a bit further on) that the chances of a poor black ghetto-dweller in the city being arrested are about three times greater than those of a thief being arrested (even though there is a slight but insubstantial overlap between these two groups)? For one thing, it means that when we draw up a composite picture of what the "criminal" is like, there will be an enormous component of poor blacks (though for most of them, their crimes are usually petty, often of a vague and undefined character, and, not infrequently, completely nonexistent), and only a small proportion of the picture will be contributed by the thief (and just a trace by the professional thief). The idea that we can know what criminals are like by studying the characteristics of convicted offenders rests on a shaky and completely insupportable assumption—that convicted criminals are a representative sample of all law violators. Nothing could be further from the truth. Consider ladies and gentlemen of the jury, a few more pieces of evidence.

Exhibit A: Of the seven major offenses that make up the FBI Crime Index—murder, rape, aggravated assault, robbery, burglary, larceny over $50, and car theft—there are about four million reported offenses annually. On the average, about one-fifth of these reported crimes are "cleared by arrest." (i.e., written off the books). These rates vary according to the type of crime: crimes of personal violence have high clearance rates, those against property have low clearance rates. When we add to this information the facts previously described—that the majority of such crimes are not reported by the victims, particularly the crimes of burglary and larceny—it is rather obvious that those arrested for serious felonies are a very small sample of those who commit felonies. Adding these two pieces of information together, we come out with the following picture: probably more than one-half of murderers and rapists are arrested, but fewer than one-fourth of those who commit robbery and only a tiny fraction—no more than five per cent—of thieves and burglars are arrested.

Exhibit B: In the police business, the felony arrest is the frosting on the cake—less than one-fifth of all arrests made. The wholesale business is pulling in drunks; this, along with other liquor offenses, accounts for about two out of five of all arrests made. Add gambling and the array of ambiguous crimes like vagrancy, disorderly conduct, and breach of the peace, and we account for about sixty per cent of all arrests.

It should not be surprising that policemen believe very firmly that criminals are lower class, marginal, unreliable, dangerous people, of whom a greatly disproportionate number are black. How could a policeman think otherwise? How could he function if he didn't believe that the group of persons he arrests and the group of persons who are criminals are essentially one and the same group? The police officer's definition of the criminal, based on his observation of the people he arrests, covers a rather narrow spectrum of law violators. On the one hand, the patrolman on the beat knows very little about the full-time thief, burglar, safe-cracker—persons who make their living from crime, and for whom crime is an occupation, indeed, a profession. At the other extreme, he knows little about the millions of criminals who are camouflaged within the general population: the embezzler, the tax-evader, the shoplifter, the employed middle class drunk, the wife-beater, the price-fixer, the briber, the grafter, the slum merchant who defrauds his customers. The group of law violators he knows (whose characteristics he uses to define the boundaries of the criminal class) are those who break the law openly, publicly, and very often, on the streets of our cities. He knows the homeless drunk who flops in doorways, but not the drunk who staggers home at eight o'clock from the corner tavern or the commuter train bar car and flops into bed in his own home. He knows, as a criminal, the young ghetto street-hustler who he picks up in a crap game in a vacant store front. He doesn't know *me* as a violator of gambling laws, though I play poker every other Thursday with a group of high class friends—doctors, Yale professors, psychologists; all of us are technically criminals just as much as the young fellow the police scoop up in the crap game. The average patrolman has no contact whatever with the bank teller who embezzles thousands of dollars from his employer or the suburban housewife who regularly steals a couple of dollars worth of groceries from the supermarket. And if he found a Cadillac or Continental belonging to someone like General Electric's former Vice-President William Ginn (one of those convicted in the "Great Conspiracy" to fix prices of electrical equipment at an artificially high level) parked in front of a fireplug, he would doubtless think two or three times before even tagging it.

Even if they tried very hard, then, to tell it like it is, the police could not do so accurately because they do not see it like it is. They recognize the black man as a criminal—or, generously, as a potential criminal—but haven't the vaguest idea what most thieves look like. This is the reason why black people are more in peril of arrest than thieves.

Let me try to demonstrate this with numbers. In a large city of, say, one million people, the police will make about 45,000 arrests in a single year. Of those arrested, about ten or twelve thousand will be poor and black. On the average, perhaps 60,000 residents of that city will be poor and black. If you are a poor black ghetto dweller, then, the odds are about one out of five or six that you will be arrested in the next twelve months. Suppose you commit larceny. According to the Ellis study, in this city there will be about 10,000 cases of larceny. As a result of police action, there will be only 700 arrests for larceny. Thus, in absolute numbers, about sixteen or eighteen black poor persons will be arrested for every thief arrested; and, in statistical terms, the poor black person is about three times more likely to be arrested than the thief. (The competent, well-trained professional thief, of course, is virtually immunized from arrest.)

As Melvin Adams tried to teach us, there are law violators and then there are law violators. The process continues as the arrested person moves from the precinct station to the court house. The court system that deals with those arrested has the function of refining the raw material, the crude oil, turned up by police operations. Theoretically, the court system is there to make a judgment about the validity of the police action—the arrested person, you will remember from eighth-grade civics class, is innocent until proved guilty. We have constructed an elaborate system of safeguards to protect the rights of those accused of crime: the preliminary hearing, the right to bail, the grand jury hearing, the right to counsel, the strict rules of trial by jury. A closer examination of the data, however, suggests that the judicial process does not seem to sort out the innocent from the guilty, so much as the well-to-do from the poor. There is a steady series of advantages accruing to the more affluent defendant.[9] He is considerably more likely to receive a preliminary hearing and, therefore, to have his case dismissed and not even brought to trial. Having money, he is more likely to be released on bail, which also has a substantial bearing on the outcome of his case. During all these procedures, he is much more likely to have his own lawyer working hard to take advantage of these many procedural protections and also working directly to influence the police and the prosecutor to drop the charges altogether.

But what about when the defendant gets into the courtroom itself? Here, certainly, it must be true that the great adversary system of pitting lawyer against lawyer in the cockpit of trial before a jury of the defendant's peers must work to finally achieve justice? Alas, it is not true. In the first place, about four out of five defendants actually brought to the point of trial plead guilty. If a trial is held, in most cases it is without a jury. Thus, despite all we have been taught— by Perry Mason, The Defenders, and other programs for educating the public—in the criminal judicial process, trial by jury is a very rare event, occurring in no more than five or ten per cent of felony cases brought to the courtroom. In the far more common cases of arrest for misdemeanors, the prevalence of trial by jury is minuscule. The likelihood of an arrested person being tried before a jury is remote indeed.

After conviction, the disadvantages of the poor continue: they are substantially less likely to receive a suspended sentence or probation, more likely to be sent to jail or prison.

The final, and most direct evidence is a set of studies that show there is no substantial relationship between social class and the commission of crimes, but that there is a very marked relationship between class and conviction for crime. Short and Nye[10] reported a specific comparison between two measures of criminalhood: one, reported behavior; the other, institutionalization. Five out of six boys in training schools for delinquents were drawn from the bottom half of the socio-economic ladder; but, judging by self-reports of behavior, there was an almost even distribution of delinquent acts among different socio-economic groups.

The lesson of all this is plain: the fact that half or more of persons arrested for crimes of personal violence, and that forty to fifty per cent of prisoners in jails and penitentiaries are black says nothing at all about the criminality of black people. And that an even higher proportion of persons arrested are poor and imprisoned sheds no light whatever on the criminality of the poor. These facts only identify the objects of police and court activity. There are law violators and there are law violators; one kind gets arrested, the other kind is usually left alone.

III

As I mentioned at the beginning of this chapter, my wife, and I, and four of our friends turned out to be the kind that get arrested; the slum landlords we were protesting against were the kind that get left alone. In New Haven, at that time—and still today as I write—slum landlords had their property inspected by city agents, got notices of violation, got warnings, and got rich, but hardly ever got arrested. The law is very clear but the law is not enforced; emergency violations are left on the books of the city agency for as long as twenty-four months after a notification to correct the violation within seven days. Members of several citizens groups —including one to which we belonged—had written, petitioned, denounced, discussed, conferred and complained about this coddling of slum landlords for months. We were, to put it somewhat ingenuously, seeking law and order. We felt that negligent landlords having failed to obey agency orders for, say, sixty days, should be prosecuted—particularly since some of the biggest slum landlords permitted such serious violations as lack of heat, infestation by rats and cockroaches, dangerous electrical wiring, and plumbing failure. Not the least of the common violations was peeling paint, often a cause of dangerous lead poisoning. The landlords continued to ignore us, and we decided to picket in front of Adams' house (which was, incidentally, only a block and a half from our own house) as a way of bringing our concern home to him.

About fifty people gathered nearby and started to walk toward Adams' house. We were met by a force of about forty policemen, some in squad cars, some on foot. This group—it looked like half a battalion to me—was led personally by the Chief of Police, handsome, soft-spoken James Ahearn. Also on hand were: the chief of the vice-squad (God only knows why), a couple of captains and lieutenants, a generous sprinkling of sergeants and detectives, and the department's ace undercover agent, a Mr. Consiglio, whose smiling face was well-known by most residents of the city (he sauntered along beside us, sheepishly pretending to be a dangerous demonstrator).

There is a theory of police work which holds that the best way to prevent crime is to use what is called "aggressive patrol." At the time I thought Chief Ahearn and his handpicked crew of crime-busters were really giving the theory a thorough testing. As we got close to the Adams' house—along with the troops defending it against us—the Chief warned us that, if we picketed, we would be in violation of statute number something-or-other and would be arrested. Six of us volunteered to continue our mission. Holding little home-made magic-marker picket signs, saying things like, "Mr. Adams! Stop Coddling Slum Landlords!" and surrounded by police, the six of us formed a single line and began to picket. Chief Ahearn warned us again, quite sternly. As we turned at the driveway and started back along the sidewalk, six stalwart law-men (one for each of us), leaped forward and laid hands on our shoulders, apprehending us in the act.

We were booked for having committed the rare crime of "picketing a residence,"—based on a twenty-five-year-old statute that had never, as far as we could determine, been used before; the statute is part of the labor code, makes a reference to labor disputes in its language, and seems either clearly inapplicable to a civil rights demonstration or, if applicable, is an unconstitutional limitation of free speech. On the first day of our jury trial, the judge seemed to be of a like mind and questioned the prosecutor quite skeptically as to how he proposed to apply a labor statute to this situation without infringement of constitutional rights. We were quite optimistic. Overnight, however, the judge either did a lot of studying or sought instruction from some wise colleague; the next day he could see every point the prosecutor made and, in his charge to the jury, defined picketing in a way that left the jury no alternative but to find us guilty. With the help of the American Civil Liberties Union, the case was appealed, and our conviction was overturned.

I cite this bit of personal history as an illustration of the selective application of the law enforcement process, and as further proof that Mr. Adams was quite right when he told us that there are law violators and law violators. We learned his lesson and another one: that the major determinant of police action is not so much the commission of a crime as the identity of the supposed criminal.

I V

The function of what we call law enforcement in our society —that is the activity of the police in arresting people—appears to be almost totally unrelated in practice to the apprehension and punishment of criminals who break the law. In the United States, at least, the great majority of us can break the law with impunity. The average reader of this book can commit a crime at will and feel just about as safe from arrest as from being struck by lightning. We know this, and we behave accordingly. Our society is a lawless and violent one, and we apparently intend to keep it that way.

Then why do we bother to hire policemen? James Q. Wilson[11] has recently shed light on this question by pointing out the fact that there are really two quite different functions that the police carry out: order maintenance and law enforcement. He also points out that the police really lack the means for accomplishing the second objective. With few exceptions —largely crimes of personal violence in which the criminal is known to, or easily identified by, the victim—"few major crimes such as burglary or robbery that are of primary concern to the citizen are 'cleared by arrest'."

I would suggest that these two objectives are, in fact, connected, and that the role of the police as law-enforcers—although it has very little to do with serious crimes, as Wilson points out—is in fact an aspect of the order-maintaining

207

function. We must judge why we hire policemen by the evidence. Presumably we hire them to do what they, in fact, do: arrest black people and poor people. In functional terms, it would be hard to evade the conclusion that the major task we give to our police is to control potentially disruptive or troublesome groups in the population.

In *Police Power,* Paul Chevigny[12] has documented in great detail the nature (although not the extent) of police abuses in New York City. Large numbers of his cases show that these abuses take place in the context of maintaining order and harassing low-status minority groups—Negroes, hippies, homosexuals. Typically, an incident begins when a citizen shows lack of respect or obedience to the forces of authority (usually embodied in the policeman himself) which inflames the policeman. There appears to be an almost ritualistic process—sometimes involving assaulting the citizen—which always ends with an arrest on a charge such as "disorderly conduct," and, if the citizen shows visible signs of having been beaten, "resisting arrest."

Other studies of police practices have confirmed the considerable prevalence of arbitrary, discriminatory, and often brutal behavior on the part of police—much of which is a violation, not simply of city ordinances or of state statutes, but of fundamental constitutional rights. The extensive use against the poor of vague, catchall charges—"loitering," "vagrancy," "breach of peace," "suspicious conduct"—is well known. It was the acknowledged excuse for arresting civil rights workers in the South; it is a major tool for exercising police control in the North today. It may be hard to believe, but approximately one arrest out of every nine is on the charge of "disorderly conduct." It is the second most common basis for arrest, the first being public intoxication.

.   .   .

We are not talking about crime, then, when we talk of law and order; we are talking about repressive control. The function of the police and of the courts cannot, by any stretch of logic, be related, in any substantial way, to the enforcement of laws or to the suppression of criminals and criminal behavior. There are obvious exceptions. Certain heinous and repulsive crimes—murder, rape, kidnapping, treason, molestation of children—elicit a vigorous and efficient reaction from law enforcement officials, and most of those who commit such crimes are found, arrested, tried, and punished. Beyond this exceptional and tiny pocket of the crime universe, law breaking, in general, leads to very little—particularly when the lawbreakers are privileged, white, and middle class.

It is not law we are concerned with when we hire our policemen, "support" them, egg them on, tolerate their lawlessness, and send hordes of them into the poverty areas of the city—areas that, ironically, are known to most anti-poverty agencies, as the "target areas." Their job is not law, but order, and all too often, order that is illegally maintained.

This is what law enforcement, as we choose to call it, is all about. To obscure it with a cloud of sentimental nonsense about the socially deprived, warped, bitter "criminal" drawn from the white slums and the black ghettoes is a shameful perversion of the techniques of social science.

Every respectable, half-way competent social scientist who has paid any attention at all to the issues of crime and delinquency knows: that crime is endemic in all social classes; that the administration of justice is grossly biased against the Negro and the lower class defendant; that arrest and imprisonment is a process reserved almost exclusively for the black and the poor; and that the major function of the police is the preservation, not only of the public order, but of the social order—that is, of inequality between man and man. To blather on and on about the slum as a "breeding place of crime," about "lower class culture as a generating milieu of delinquency"—presumably liberal explanations of the prevalence of crime among the poor—is to engage (surely, almost consciously) in ideological warfare against the poor in the interest of maintaining the *status quo*. It is one of the most detestable forms of Blaming the Victim.

9
Counting Black
Bodies

Riots, Raids and Repression

I

The upheavals in our cities have been given many different names: riots, rebellions, mass hoodlumism, and the first events in a Black Revolution. Many mutually exclusive and contradictory causes have been adduced: both poverty and the anti-poverty program; police brutality and police permissiveness; brain damage and brainwashing; Communist plots, Muslim plots, and Black Nationalist plots; speeches about Black Power; and, of course, the new all-purpose explanation —the disintegrating Negro family.

With respect to the conspiracy theory, the investigative efforts of the FBI, the Kerner Commission, and several Congressional committees have failed to produce any credible evidence of plot or conspiracy. There remain three general formulations that are most widely subscribed to by intellectuals. These are, from left to right: quasi-revolutionary rebellion, a theory exemplified in the writings of radical leftists such as Herbert Aptheker;[1] institutionalized white racism, the basic theory of the Kerner Commission;[2] and the more or less spontaneous, and almost contentless outbursts of groups of marginal Negroes—representing the *Lumpenproletariat* or "riffraff"—which is the basic theory of the McCone Commission report on the Watts disorder.[3]

Aptheker likens the Watts disorder to Nat Turner's slave rebellion of 1831: it is a particular turning point, a signal that the American black man is rebelling against injustice, is standing up, prepared to do violence to achieve his manhood and his freedom. The McCone Commission, on the other hand (along with other observers, such as Daniel Moynihan) view the urban disturbances as the work of alienated and unacculturated young black men, marginal to the society and the economy, who are frustrated to the point of constant rage, yes, but who are in no sense political in their activity. To such observers, the rioter is typically unemployed, uneducated, unskilled, the product of a broken family, often unaccustomed to city life and its institutions. In this view, the frustrated and alienated rioter is himself the generator of the riot; his frustration and alienated state prompt him to violent activity which, in a larger social sense, then, must be defined as meaningless. This formulation is the one most clearly within the mainstream of the ideology of Blaming the Victim. The Kerner Commission, on the other hand, attributes the riots to the white racism that has been—and continues to be—deeply rooted in all of America's institutions, that has segregated and discriminated against blacks, that has penned them in ghettoes, and that has deprived them of a decent life. The Kerner Report recommends rapid and extensive action as a preventive measure: the breaking down of segregation, the provision of decent jobs, homes, and education, and increased responsiveness of government to the needs and aspirations of blacks in the ghetto.

A valid explanation of urban violence must account for all of the common elements that have been reported. Journalistic descriptions have been filled with such vivid events as mobs looting liquor stores, teenagers hurling rocks and firebombs, buildings burning and firemen being shot, firefights between rooftop snipers and platoons of police and National Guardsmen, and large-scale crowd control activity including the imposition of curfews and the mass patrolling of streets. In these descriptions the central elements appear to be widespread violent actions on the part of ghetto residents which are ultimately controlled by vigorous exercise of the community's police powers.

The selective emphasis on these more sensational elements makes a neat and simple formulation possible because it eliminates other common elements that have attracted less attention. But if we are to understand the meaning of the disturbances, we must understand what happened—all of what happened. This means that a theory of civil disorder must account for certain recurring regularities—regularities in the precipitating incident, in the location, in the racial distribution of casualties, and in the course and nature of the conflict.

There is overwhelming evidence that the precipitating event—the beginning and root-point of the action—has been, in all but a few instances, a transaction between police and ghetto residents.[4] In what we might consider the prototype disorder—the Watts riot or rebellion—a seemingly simple police-citizen situation involving the arrest of a young man named Marquette Frye on a charge of drunken driving, quickly escalated into a confrontation between a gang of police and a large crowd of ghetto residents. The event included downright brutal behavior by the police, the arbitrary and illogical arrest of a girl bystander, and the arrest of Frye's mother and brother accompanied by very rough and overbearing treatment. When the police left the scene with their four prisoners, the crowd remaining behind was infuriated, seething with rage (which was expressed by a bottle hurled after the police cars as they sped away).

The Newark disorder began with the arrest of a cabdriver named—almost as if the script had been written as a heavy-handed fable of the average citizen—John Smith. Black residents of the housing project opposite the Fourth Precinct Police Station became aware of the incident when they observed police dragging Smith out of the patrol car. They inferred that he had been beaten and, while the details of the arrest and subsequent events have never been established beyond question, Smith had injuries severe enough to require his being taken from the police station to the hospital. This fact makes it highly likely that the project residents were correct in their inference (or observation—several citizens claimed to have seen the beating on the street). In any case, they gathered in protest in front of the police station and, after a time, police officers from the station charged and fought with the crowd. Shortly thereafter, rock-throwing, window-breaking and some looting took place.

In Detroit, the largest, bloodiest, and costliest disorder in the history of urban America began with a police raid on a well-known after-hours drinking place and the arrest of an unexpectedly large group—eighty-two persons. A crowd on Twelfth Street observed the movement of the prisoners into police cars and wagons, and they grew increasingly restive and angry at what they perceived to be evidence of excessive force and unnecessary brutality. As the police cars drove away, rocks and bottles smashed against the trunks and rear windows. Soon after, hundreds of people who had gathered on Twelfth Street began to break windows and loot.

In Atlanta, the disorder was attributed to an incident in which police got into a scuffle while trying to arrest a young man who was banging a broom handle on a burglar alarm outside a store. In the scuffle, a police officer drew his gun, fired, and wounded the youth.

In San Francisco, the Hunter's Point riot was sparked off when a policeman shot an adolescent boy suspected of being a car thief.

In Harlem, an off-duty policeman drew his gun on a teenager, who was said to have had a knife in his hand. The officer, a Lt. Gilligan, reported that the young man continued to approach him threateningly with the knife, and he therefore shot and killed him.

In Cambridge, Maryland, disorder was precipitated as a result of police firing into a group of people leaving a protest meeting.

In Boston, police began beating a group of ADC mothers who were sitting-in at the welfare office.

In Tampa, a police officer chased a suspected burglar who refused to halt, and the policeman shot him in the back. The young man who was shot was found dead with his hands raised over his head clutching a cyclone fence. The officer later explained that, despite appearances, he had not shot the suspect as he was trying to surrender but that, after being shot fatally in the back, the young man raised his hands above his head and clutched the fence.

In their investigations of the riots of 1967, The Kerner Commission (The National Advisory Commission on Civil Disorders) chose a sample of twenty-four cities to study in

215

great depth and detail. They identified what they called the "precipitating incident" in twenty-three of these disturbances.

In twenty-two of these twenty-three cities, the occasion of the riot—the starting point that sparked off the disorder— was police activity: making an arrest in what was perceived as a brutal manner; shooting a citizen in what seemed like an inappropriate and excessive use of force; or generalized patrol activity that was interpreted as harassment and repression of the black community. The citizenry began the activity defined as riotous or rebellious as a direct response to the stimulus of police action that was interpreted—and in many cases obviously was in fact—brutal, repressive or violent.

The initial violence that followed the precipitating incident consisted of, in descending order of frequency: looting, window-breaking, throwing of missiles at police or occasional white motorists in the community, and setting of fires. Typically, the window-breaking, rock-throwing, and scattered looting would peak during the first night of the riot, and on the following day, there would be apparent calm. In many instances, that was the end. In Newark, the active disorder seemed over after the first night—though tension was high, and a protest rally in front of the police station was scheduled to take place on the evening of the second day. During this rally, rocks and bottles began to rain against the walls of the station, the police came out once more, charging and dispersing the crowd; the people scattered and began to break windows, loot, and, in several instances, set fires.

A notable feature of most of the riots that went beyond one night was that the level of violence usually increased on following nights. It is particularly significant that, in most cases, this increase in the level of violence *followed* an increase in the level of the control forces—such as a massing of local police or the introduction of state police, National Guard or army troops to the situation. This phenomenon was most clearly illustrated in the five New Jersey cities—Elizabeth, Englewood, Jersey City, New Brunswick, and Plainfield—in which mass police patrolling of the ghetto neighborhoods, in the absence of any incident indicating disorder, was itself the stimulus to disorder. But in many other cities, the massing of more and more control forces pushed the level of violence higher. In New Haven, for example, the initial outbreak appeared to be very minor, principally consisting of several gangs of young men smashing windows. A number of police entered the area and found the situation relatively calm, except for a crowd of several hundred persons on Congress Avenue. In an unexpected manner, and for an as yet unexplained reason, the police began to use tear gas on the crowd. The violence that seemed over was rekindled and began to spread through the community. The next day, too, calm seemed to have been restored when suddenly, in the early afternoon, several hundred state police began aggressive patrolling of the streets—in specific violation of an agreement reached only hours before between the Mayor and community leaders. Again violence resumed and reached even higher levels than on the night before.

In Boston, after the beating of the welfare mothers and of a number of community leaders and community organizers who tried to go to their aid, there was no physical violence on the part of the watching crowd for a long period of time (though there was a great deal of verbal abuse of the police). Police tried to disperse the crowds several times in a very rough manner; then riot equipment was brought in, and the police moved very aggressively—pushing, and shoving, and clubbing persons in the crowd. That finally triggered the retaliatory violence of the young men in the crowd, and the

Boston riot began. *The Bay State Banner,* Roxbury's weekly newspaper, headlined its story of the event, "Police Riot in Grove Hall!"

With respect to illegal activity on the part of rioters, almost all of the serious violence was directed against property—such as breaking windows and setting fires—and by far the most common illegal action by riot participants was looting. In the major riots, looting was so widespread that it became almost a norm. Women, small children, old people, poor and well-to-do, were observed openly and blatantly stealing, walking into a wrecked store and walking out with anything from a pair of shoes, to a case of whisky, to a refrigerator. In almost all cases, the stores being looted were white-owned and, in a substantial number of cases, were defined by members of the community as exploitative and oppressive. In most cases, there was, in fact, a selective pattern in which merchants defined by the community as exploiters were looted; those defined as relatively decent and honest were spared.

Damage by fire was prominent only in Detroit and Watts. In Newark, there were thirteen fires rated as "serious." In most other cities, there were only a few major fires. Rocks and bottles were mostly aimed at police, sometimes at fire-fighters. In several places, particularly in the beginning hours, white motorists driving through the ghettoes were stoned, and some were injured—mostly as a result of broken windows or windshields. In some instances in Watts and elsewhere, a few white motorists were dragged from their cars and beaten. But, for the most part, very little physical violence was directed against white civilians. In some of the disorders, notably in Detroit, there were, in fact, documented instances of some "integration" in the disorders—white participation in looting.

In one notable case, there was direct personal violence on

the part of a crowd. In Plainfield, New Jersey, Officer John Gleason saw two white boys being chased by a twenty-two-year-old black man named Bobby Williams. Gleason intervened and began chasing Williams, who stopped and turned to meet the police officer. Gleason, for some reason, drew his gun and shot Williams, fatally wounding him. Members of the watching crowd then began to chase Officer Gleason. They caught him, threw him to the ground, and stomped him to death.

Shooting directed against the police, National Guard, and firefighters was also documented in some instances, although it is now agreed by most students of the disorders that so-called "sniping" was greatly exaggerated: that it consisted largely of police and guardsmen firing unbeknownst at each other; or that in many instances, the falling to the pavement of spent bullets, the lighting of a match, or the popping of a firecracker, was a sufficient cue for tired and panicky police or young guardsmen to begin yelling "Sniper!" There have been no successful prosecutions of citizens arrested as suspected snipers.

In all except two or three instances, police officers, troopers, or firemen who were shot and killed were the victims of accidental or mistaken firing of the guns of fellow officers.

A summation of the activities of the rioters, then, would show a balance sheet featuring: a very small amount of isolated violence directed against persons—almost all of whom were police; a large amount of window-breaking and other kinds of damage directed against the shops of white store-owners; damage by fire mostly to white-owned stores, and almost all of it in the two cities of Detroit and Los Angeles; and an enormous amount of looting.

I I

When we look at the balance sheet of the activity of the police and the National Guard, we see almost a mirror-image. Looting by the forces of law and order was not very extensive. Violence directed against property was scattered and minimal, except in two notable instances—in Newark, the police and National Guard systematically smashed windows and destroyed property in stores marked with signs such as "Soul-Brother" to identify and protect black-owned businesses; and in Plainfield, a house-by-house search for stolen rifles was the occasion for widespread wanton destruction of the furniture and belongings of the residents.

In most civil disorders, the police and the troopers appeared to concentrate on the task of shooting black people, and they were remarkably successful. In Watts, only three of the thirty-four persons killed were white—a deputy sheriff, a police officer, and a fireman. The sheriff was killed accidentally by another sheriff, the policeman accidentally by another policeman, the fireman by a falling wall while fighting a fire. According to Robert Conot,[5] who documented each of the thirty-four Watts deaths carefully and meticulously, at least twenty-eight were shot by police and National Guard troopers—twenty-two by the former, six by the latter. (There was one disputed case of a sixty-seven-year-old woman who was killed while driving her husband home supposedly because she did not stop at a barricade. No one is precisely sure who killed her; but since, of the forty-three shots fired at her, thirty-five were fired by police and only eight by Guardsmen, it seems only fair to give the police credit for the kill.)

Of the twenty-eight, nine persons were shot by policemen while—according to the unsupported stories of the police who did the killing—they were running away from a store being looted. Six were shot by police while they were *inside* stores. Five were shot when they failed to halt their automobiles at blockades set up in the street.

Two were shot as supposed snipers, in remarkably similar circumstances. In both cases, a man was standing in his own house looking out the window. Both men were dressed in white T-shirts. Both attracted attention to themselves by either moving rapidly or lighting a cigarette. Silhouetted in the window, with the white T-shirt as target, each man was an easy mark for the policeman in the street below. In neither case did a search of the premises produce any weapon that the supposed sniper might have been using or thinking about using.

One man was shot by police as a looter while he was removing clothing and household effects from his own home, which was endangered by a fire in an adjoining store.

One man was shot as a suspected criminal (of some sort) while he was standing in the midst of the shrubbery on his own front lawn.

Another man was shot by a guardsman as a suspected sniper while he was driving in his own car. No gun was found in the car.

Incredible as it may seem, in every instance of a killing, the coroner's jury reached a verdict of justifiable homicide after inquests that were shockingly brief. Even in the most blatant cases—such as the man shot carrying clothing from his own home, and the two men standing in their own windows shot as "snipers"—no question was raised that would attach blame to the killers. In a number of these cases, black resident bystanders were arrested and charged with the murder. Thirty-six such arrests were made. In thirty-five of the cases, the charges were dropped. In the case of the deputy shot by his fellow deputy, four men were arrested, one of whom was actually tried on a charge of second-degree murder; he was found not guilty.

In Watts during the first two days, there was no killing at all. On the evening of the third day, Lt. Mead, Commander of the 77th Precinct, spoke to his men; Robert Conot reports the incident:

> "I can't tell you to go out and kill," he said, "but when someone throws a rock, that's a felony. When they commit a burglary, that's a felony. When they throw a Molotov cocktail, that's a felony. And don't you forget it!"
>
> A murmur went through the ranks. The officers knew well enough that anyone resisting, or trying to escape from a felony arrest, could be shot.
>
> "Well," said Errol Lawrence to Frank Pinter, "I guess they're finally taking the clamps off. I'm gonna have myself a little surprise for one of those black bastards."[6]

Eighteen persons died in the fifteen hours following Lt. Mead's speech.

In the final days of the Watts riot, one reads of a number of instances of an episode that was to become common during succeeding summers—platoons of police and guardsmen firing into an occupied building on the grounds that a sniper might be located inside. The most famous of these incidents was the assault on the "sniper's nest" in the Muslim mosque, which, it was said, contained a cache of arms. The police attacked the mosque in force, firing hundreds of rounds into the building—it turned out that it contained twenty unarmed men, none of whom, incredibly, was seriously wounded. A search for the supposed supply of weapons was undertaken—floors were torn up, walls and ceiling broken through, and the entire interior of the mosque left in ruins.

No weapons were found.

.   .   .

In Newark, where twenty-three persons died, the black-white ratio was approximately the same as in Watts—twenty-one of the dead were black, two were white. The two whites killed—a police detective and a fireman—were both shot, supposedly by snipers.

The twenty-one blacks were shot by police and guardsmen, sometimes in bizarre circumstances. At one point in time, two columns of state troopers and National Guardsmen were directing fire at a large housing project (in the belief that a sniper was inside). They never found the sniper, but they did manage to kill three old women.

One eleven-year-old boy was shot as he stepped out of his house to empty the garbage.

A family returning home from dinner at a restaurant—mother, father, and four sons—were shot at in their car when the father panicked and swerved around a National Guard blockade instead of stopping; when they arrived home, they found that their ten-year-old son had been shot through the head.

Among the twenty-one blacks shot dead by the police and the National Guard in Newark, six were women and two were children.

Of the forty-three persons who died in the Detroit holocaust, ten were white, the rest black. Only two or three of those who died were counted as having been killed by rioters; while between twenty-eight and thirty-one were killed by police, guardsmen, and army troops, twenty or twenty-one of these were at the hands of police.

After the first two days of intensive looting and fire-bombing, the character of the events in Detroit changed markedly. The looting and fire-bombing diminished sharply, and the shooting became unbelievably intensified. Presumably, the police and the guardsmen were shooting at snipers, but subsequent events made it very clear that there was relatively little sniping going on. As in Newark, the scattered forces of order—in very poor communication with each other—were largely returning each other's fire, or shooting randomly every time they saw a flash of light, or heard a pop bottle breaking on the pavement. Of the twenty-seven persons arrested as suspected snipers, twenty-four were released when charges were dismissed at preliminary hearings—one pleaded guilty of having an unregistered gun, and two were awaiting trial at the time the Kerner Report was prepared.

As in Watts and Newark, heavy fire was frequently directed into *buildings* in which it was suspected that a sniper was lurking. This included fire from .50-calibre machine guns mounted on tanks. Many casualties resulted from this indiscriminate attack on the population of the community.

The outstanding instance of police and National Guard response to supposed sniper fire was the incident at the Algiers Motel; it has been vividly and meticulously documented by John Hersey.[7] The bodies of three young black men found in the motel were initially defined as those of snipers. Only later was it learned that they had been killed by officers, who, as they invaded the building in search of yet another imaginary sniper, found a mixed party of black men and white girls—a discovery that outraged the police. After the officers played cat-and-mouse games with their prisoners, the three young men were shot and, after being warned to silence, the others were sent out into the bullet-filled night. Although the policemen have been officially acquitted at this writing, the black community of Detroit is convinced that these three young men were neither rioters, nor looters, nor snipers, but rather plain victims of official murder—and that more than one of the others who died in the Detroit riots were victims of similar fates.

In addition to shooting by police and guardsmen, there were two other kinds of violence visited upon the black communities during the riots: indiscriminate arrest, and beatings by police. In Detroit, for example, where 7,200 persons were arrested—and often held for days before arraignment—the Kerner Report says, "Dozens of charges of police brutality emanated from the station as prisoners were brought in uninjured, but later had to be taken to the hospital." In Newark, 1,500 arrests were made; in Watts, 4,000. The overwhelming majority of arrests were of persons charged with looting or with such crimes as breach of peace, disorderly conduct, or curfew violation. Only a relative handful of persons were charged with such serious offenses as assault, carrying a weapon, or arson—less than ten per cent in Watts, about ten per cent in Newark, about five per cent in Detroit. Very few of these cases ended in convictions, and most of those were on reduced charges. The majority of burglary (looting) cases in Watts that resulted in conviction were the result of guilty pleas to the reduced charge of trespassing. One-fourth of the riot arrests in Detroit were not even prosecuted. There are endless stories of persons being arrested: undercover policemen who were black found themselves being kicked and pushed into police wagons and called "nigger" right along with their black brothers from the street; and scores of persons returning home from work or shopping were arrested by police moving along the streets and porches indiscriminately scooping up every black body in sight. And the indignities that go along with occupation by an outside power—the abusive racist language, the widespread arbitrary control of movement through curfew and patrol—all of these lesser kinds of violence affected almost all residents of the riot areas.

·   ·   ·

The racial ratio of deaths remains the most telling index of the nature of the violence. In Watts, Newark, and Detroit, one hundred persons died, of whom only fifteen were white. No more than four deaths were attributed to the action of rioters. Most of the white dead were policemen or firemen, some of whom died in fires, or from falling walls, or power lines, but most of whom were shot accidentally by their fellow officers. At least eighty of the dead—including most of the whites—were shot by police or National Guardsmen; a small number were killed by white store-owners or other white citizens, six or eight died in accidents, and a few were killed in ways that have not as yet been determined. The majority of those shot were called looters or snipers. But, in a number of cases, where there were several witnesses, it is clear that the victims were neither. In most of the remaining cases either there was no witness or the only witness was a fellow officer. Many persons were killed as the result of indiscriminate firing into buildings or crowds by police or guardsmen, sometimes with machine guns.

In summary, the overwhelming impression one gets after studying records of these three riots in detail is that: the response of law-enforcement officials was excessively violent, was directed against persons rather than property; and further, that this violent, lethal response was, for the most part, directed against the black *population,* in general, rather than against specific black *individuals.*

I I I

A final set of facts can be brought into the analytic process that are particularly relevant for testing the "riffraff" or

Lumpenproletariat theory of the riots. These relate to the question, "Who rioted?" The answer, in brief, is that those who participated in the disorders appear to be—from all the evidence—very much like other residents of the riot areas who did not participate. There are, of course, differences, but they are not extreme: the participants tend to be drawn disproportionately from the ranks of young men in their late teens and early twenties; they are more often single, unemployed, or employed in unskilled labor; they are more often born in the North, and lifelong residents of the city; they are somewhat better educated; they are more knowledgeable about the political life of the city, more militant in their racial attitudes, more involved in organized activity to achieve racial justice. The participants and the non-participants do not differ with respect to income, or with respect to having been raised in a broken family. Except for the factor of age and sex, the differences are relatively minor. The rioters clearly represent a large and significant portion of the ghetto community. Their numbers, too, were large—up to one-fourth or one-third of the population in some riot areas. And there is abundant evidence that a very large fraction of the black population was at least partially in sympathy with the rebels and viewed the riots as effective—in the sense that they called attention to problems and stimulated efforts to bring about change.

Fogelson and Hill, in summarizing the case against the "riffraff theory" say:

> If the survey research, arrest data, and impressionistic accounts are indicative, the rioters were a small but significant minority of the Negro population, fairly representative of the ghetto residents, and especially of the young adult males, and tacitly supported by at least a large minority of the black community. Which, to repeat, means that the

1960s riots were a manifestation of race and racism in the United States, a reflection of the social problems of modern black ghettoes, a protest against the essential conditions of life there, and an indicator of the necessity for fundamental changes in American society. And if the riffraff theory has not been accurate in the past, its accuracy in the future is seriously questioned. The riots appear to be gaining recruits from all segments of the Negro community.[8]

Those who discovered savages in the urban disorders, then, appear to be clearly in the wrong. The actions seemed to be, directly or vicariously, actions not of a marginal riffraff, but of very large minorities—in some cases, perhaps majorities— of the affected communities protesting in a violent way, striking back, getting even. Is it, however, correct to speak of the disorders as "revolts" or "rebellions" or "uprisings"? Did they have a revolutionary *intent?* Were they analogous to the slave rebellions in the pre-war South? There are reasons to suggest that, though in many ways having the character of rebellion and, in a sense, using revolutionary *means,* the disorders did not have truly revolutionary *ends* in mind. Unlike riots that took place in many occupied colonies, the crowds did not move against any of the institutions of society, nor did they (as *crowds,* there were individual exceptions) move in an actively violent or hostile manner against public officials. They did throw rocks and bottles at the police, resisting them and trying to drive them out. There seems little doubt, however, that if there had been a wish to do so, police could have been killed in large numbers. They were not. The action consisted of resisting and trying to drive out the police—the forces of repressive control—and "taking back" from cheating and exploiting businessmen. This does not seem, in the ordinary sense of the word, revolutionary. Moreover, the political goals of the great majority of blacks seem to be still attainable within a framework of reforms of present institutions, and they do not have revolutionary implications. It would then appear inappropriate to consider the disorders revolutionary—in the sense of being aimed at the destruction or overthrow of major social or economic institutions.

There may be, in fact, considerable danger in mistaking the actions of reform-minded citizens for open rebellion. Police all over the country have been able (with a disturbingly high degree of credibility) to arrest large numbers of militants on charges such as conspiracy; this has had a generally intimidating effect. William Worthy has brilliantly analyzed the structural and ideological weaknesses of this kind of "revolutionary" position and activity.[9]

IV

We come finally to the formulation of the Kerner Commission, which recognizes the protest character of the riot, recognizes the institutionalized racism that produces the conditions that are being protested against, and recommends a series of massive programs to correct the racial inequalities in American life. However, the Kerner Report falls short in certain respects and does not escape being tinged in some ways with a victim-blaming ideology. Principally, it does not deal effectively with the issue of power and conflict. It specifically criticizes the validity of the Black Power concept; it proposes very minor reforms of local government without coming to grips with the basic issues of community control; and, most important, it fails to fully recognize the disorders as conflict—as reflecting resistance to the exercise of unjust and repressive power in the ghetto. It implicitly defines participants as initiators—as simply rioters—and the police as controllers. (Although it hints at individual acts of police brutality and even of police homicide, the implication is that these acts represent excesses or distortions of a generally valid and legitimate function.) It emphatically does not recognize the *continuity* between ordinary police activity and police activity prior to, and during the disorders. In setting up this false balance between rioting forces and controlling forces, it fails to acknowledge that, to a very large extent, the ghetto resident continues in his role as victim *during* the disorder as well as before it.

In order to complete and extend the generally valid insights of the Kerner Commission, then, and to eliminate all traces of Blaming the Victim from a more complete formulation of the meaning of the urban disorders, it is necessary to include an interpretation of the violence of the law-enforcement participants in the disorder, and to include the concept of power, particularly Black Power.

Let us take a second look at the idea that the disorders consist of a simple dichotomy: rioting forces on one side, controlling forces on the other. The nature of the conflict really seems more subtle and more complex than is conveyed in such an image. As I have tried to document in previous sections, the core of the disorder lies in the relationship between repressive police and the community, and almost every disturbance is initiated by police action that the community finds offensive and intolerable. The escalation of the conflict is also initiated by a massive increase in the controlling forces, and subsequently there is a dwindling of the community's resisting forces. The predominant focus of violence by residents is against property, rather than persons, in what Lee Rainwater has called a primitive form of redistribution of wealth.[10] Instant, rather than creeping socialism, if you will. But the forces of law and order are truly violent to a homicidal degree. In mass formation—in tanks, in troop carriers—

the police and the National Guardsmen sweep through the occupied territory, exercising force, not against isolated and identified criminals, looters, or snipers, but, for the most part, against the ghetto population as a whole. They fire into crowds; they fire into occupied buildings, whose tenants they cannot see and will never know. Over and over again, we find the same words from the eyewitnesses: "They come in shooting."

In the sense that the controlling forces attack the total population—attacking groups rather than individuals with no effort to make their action justifiable by attempting to distinguish between law-breakers and others, the actions must be considered, in a very real sense, genocidal in nature; this is a central fact of urban violence that cannot be evaded. We have been confronted with acts of genocide which we have obscured by focusing on the characteristics and motivations of those being attacked. Our exclusive attention to these characteristics and these motivations—even when it results in as enlightened a document as the Kerner Report—is, nevertheless, subtly tinged with Victim Blaming.

The extreme violence of the lawful forces in the disorders has been seen as qualitatively different from the customary activity of the forces of law in the ghetto. The difference is, of course, very great, but it is, in fact, only quantitative. Whether or not one "believes in" police brutality, there is certainly a mass of evidence that white police in the ghetto are commonly rude and frequently use exceptional force in dealing with residents. Technical argument could go on indefinitely as to whether a policeman shooting and killing a teenager he suspects of being a car thief is, or is not "police brutality"—the policeman involved is acquitted of the charge, of course. The crucial point is that the members of the Negro community must see such an action as very close to wanton murder. A white suburbanite finds this hard to comprehend; he might find it easier if, once or twice a year, a teenage son of one of his white neighbors were found dead on the tree-lined street with a police .38 bullet in his back.

The riots have been likened more than once to war; using this metaphor, we find that they always end with the victory of the invaders over the defenders. The territory is occupied and pacified. The evening television news descriptions of the Viet Nam war have accustomed us to both the fact and the meaning of the grisly ceremony known as the body count. It answers the questions: how many did we kill? How many did they kill? The ratio is an index of who won and how decisively. Looking at the three bloodiest riots to date—Watts, Newark and Detroit—we see that the total black-white "kill ratio" has been, respectively, 31–3, 21–2, and 33–10, a grand total of 85–15. The six-to-one average compares very favorably with the feats of our soldiers in Viet Nam. It is clear, then, that in the aftermath of the urban conflicts, when the time comes for the body count, we are counting mostly black bodies.

The forces of law and order have won all the battles. Repressive control is reestablished. But has the spirit of resistance also been killed? There are reasons to doubt it.

This brings us to the final component of a theory of urban violence—the issue of timing. Why in 1965? Or 1967? Why not in 1957? Or in 1857? Police have been acting in approximately the same way in the Negro ghetto for generations—sometimes better, sometimes worse. They have killed many hundreds of black men, and not a few black women, meting out instant capital punishment for suspected misdemeanors. They have been cuffing and pushing black men around for decades. Why, suddenly, do we find a different response on the part of the black community? Why are black men suddenly determined to protect themselves against the lawless law-men who have been beating and killing them for lifetime after lifetime?

American life has always been subject to rapid changes in mood. And now it appears that the nation that cheered the black good guys in some of its favorite TV shows of 1963 are ready to boo the black bad guys on 1969's screens. A rapid shift of mood is taking place. But this time there is a very important difference: there is a corresponding shift in the mood of black people. There will be no second post-Reconstruction Era in America. The young black men of today talk together on the tenement stoops, and their faces display determination. They may live or die, but they will live or die as men. The changes in mood are ominous; they foretell a confrontation between black and white America, a confrontation that could yield a body count not of dozens, but of hundreds and thousands. Most would still be black but there would be many white bodies, too. If we are to avert this kind of confrontation—and can any sober consideration of Newark and Detroit support a denial that such a confrontation is possible?—we must strain to understand *all* that is happening and *all* that must be done.

Let me make plain what I am trying to say: that, at one level, the events of the summer riots must be seen, in a very real sense, as reflecting a basic trend in the motivational complex of white America that is murderously anti-Negro. There is a core of reality in the vision of genocide proclaimed by many black militants in what seems like a paranoid fantasy. This trend cannot be lightly dismissed. In particular, it must not be simply *equated* with one of its manifestations—such as police brutality. This cannot be written off as simply individual acts of murder by policemen. Nor can the violence of the controlling forces—or the wish for violence on the part of many whites—be viewed as merely a frustrated and repressive *response* to riots. There is primary motivation to kill blacks.

The killing that became epidemic in the urban riots of the mid-sixties have subsided to endemic, but no less lethal, proportions as we enter the seventies. The toll is steady—day-by-day, rather than sporadic—as young black men are shot down one by one in the streets of our cities, as Black Panthers are murdered in their beds in Chicago, as black patients are shot by police on the wards of Boston City Hospital. The verdict of justifiable homicide becomes monotonous in the repetition. The black body count mounts higher.

Again and again, the repression touches radical whites as students and peace demonstrators are, with greater and greater predictability, clubbed, maced, or bombarded with tear gas from helicopters; as the courts are used more and more openly as arms of political repression; and—perhaps most chillingly of all—as William Kunstler and other lawyers are sentenced to jail for the crime of trying desperately to defend their outcast clients, in a shrill and piercing warning to lawyers across America that they would be well-advised not to stand on the tracks as the engines of repression gain speed.

Meanwhile, the acceleration of more open repression is obscured by the growth of violence on the part of self-styled revolutionaries. Manic and mindless rock-throwing, and window-breaking, and bank-burning, and bombing, and random assault become another kind of every-day event. It seems almost too fortuitous, and much of it has such an aroma of irrationality that one is inclined to look for the spoor of the *agent provocateur,* the classical henchman of government repression.

The dread question—the question that should set America to trembling—is, how quickly will we escalate the murderous raids into the black community, into the headquarters of Panthers and other groups? How much more violent will assaults on demonstrating students become? How many radicals and near-radicals will be jailed? And how many lawyers will be left to defend them?

How many bodies will be counted next year, and what will be the size and power of the weapons that are brought in to kill them?

10
In Praise of Loot
and Clout

Money, Power and
Social Change

The millionaire, freshly risen from the lower class, whose crude tongue and appalling table manners betray the newness of his affluence, is a staple of American literature and folklore. He comes on stage over and over, and we have been taught exactly what to expect with each entrance. He will walk into the parlor in his undershirt, gulp tea from a saucer, spit into the Limoges flowerpot, and, when finally invited to the society garden party, disgrace his wife by saying "bullshit" to the president of the bank. When I was growing up, we had daily lessons in this legend from Jiggs and Maggie in the comic strips.

This discrepancy between *class* and *status*, between possession of economic resources and life style, has been a source of ready humour and guaranteed fascination for generations. The centrality of this mythical strain in American thought is reflected again in the strange and perverse ideas emerging from the mouths of many professional Pauper Watchers and Victim Blamers.

In real life, of course, Jiggs' character and behavior would never remain so constant and unchanging over the decades. The strain between wealth and style is one that usually tends to be quickly resolved. Within a fairly short time, Jiggs would be coming into the parlor first with a shirt, then with a tie on, and, finally, in one of his many custom-made suits. He would soon be drinking tea from a Limoges cup, and for a time he would spit in an antique cuspidor, until he learned not to spit at all. At the garden party, he would confine his mention of animal feces to a discussion of the best fertilizer for the rhododendron. In real life, style tends to follow close on money, and money tends to be magnetized and attracted to power. Those who try to persuade us that the process can be reversed, that a change in style of life can lead backward to increased wealth and greater power, are preaching nonsense. To promise that improved table manners can produce a salary increase; that more elegant taste in clothes will lead to the acquisition of stock in IBM; that an expanded vocabulary will automatically generate an enlargement of community influence—these are pernicious as well as foolish. There is no record in history of any *group* having accomplished this wondrous task. (There may be a few clever individuals who have followed such artful routes to money and power, but they are relatively rare.) The whole idea is an illusion of fatuous social scientists and welfare bureaucrats blinded by the ideology I have painstakingly tried to dissect in the previous chapters.

Although few would argue that issues of status and life style have no relationship at all to the production of social problems, it is very hard—after a close look—to evade the conclusion that issues of class and power are far more significant. Consider some of the roles of money in these processes. For example, it has been demonstrated by a number of researchers—most notably Patricia Sexton[1]—that there is a high correlation between the amount of money spent in an educational system and the quality and level of educational achievement of students in the system. This is not proof that more money causes better education: indeed, in Chapter Two, I tried to suggest that there are a number of other factors to be considered. Still, it is hardly naive to hypothesize that the reason suburbanites tax themselves so readily for their school budget is that they believe—with good reason— that they are buying better schooling for their children. To those scientists and educationists who belittle the importance of money in education, I would ask, "How would you feel about a thirty per cent cut in the number of dollars spent on *your* child in *your* suburban school system?"

And one can return to the simple relationship between low income and illegitimacy—a relationship that is most readily explained by lack of money (an explanation that fits both common knowledge and common sense). Is it possible that the sociologists, in wealthy universities, who talk so wisely about the sexual standards and behavior of the poor, do not know that flocks of their coed students swallow the Pill every day? And that they do so because they can afford to get the prescription from their private physicians? And that a poor single working girl is not going to get that service at a city hospital? And are there any of these sociologists—or readers of this book—who don't know of at least one woman who went away pregnant to Jersey City, or Oakland, or San Juan and came back with the fetus removed from her belly and five hundred dollars less in her pocketbook? How many of them were poor?

No reasonable person could spend five minutes in the out-patient clinic or emergency room of a general hospital—particularly a public hospital—and another five minutes in the waiting room of a highly competent internist, or pediatrician, or gynecologist, and not come away with some pretty strong hunches about why the rich are healthier and longer-lived than the poor.

The significance of power in these matters is parallel to and perhaps even greater than money. There are a number of suggestive examples to learn this from. For instance, the outcome of experiments in decentralization of power in public education—community control of the schools—is, at this writing, uncertain. By the time these words are being read, Albert Shanker may have killed the Ocean Hill-Brownsville experiment. It doesn't matter. The point has been made, and the lesson has been learned. Community control of the schools is now on the agenda of every black ghetto in the country.

Virtually everyone who observed the schools in Ocean Hill, who talked to the teachers and watched the excitement of the students in the classroom, who reported the exalted mood and the sense of command among the parents involved in this experimental redistribution of power—they are all persuaded that this change in the locus of control has exerted a profound change on the process of education, and that the level of teaching and of learning has jumped significantly. Obviously, there will be lessons to be assimilated, practices to develop, many more problems to solve; but if it is true that a power change results in an educational change—and it does seem to be true—then the idea of Ocean Hill-Brownsville will not die—though the Community Board may be dissolved, and Mr. McCoy may be exiled to Long Island, and Mr. Shanker's surly teachers may recapture their classrooms and their contractual privileges to erode the minds of the children. Power is something like caviar; there is no better way to develop a taste for it than to have a taste for it. There will be more Ocean Hills.

On the welfare front, we are beginning to see the effects of the exercise of power as well as the slight shift in that balance of power which has been achieved by welfare rights groups. It is a rare pleasure to observe the realization dawning among a group of welfare mothers that their potential for disruption and embarrassment through plain physical presence of numbers (often almost comically menacing) is a source of *power* that they can use in their own interest. When a welfare supervisor, after a day or a week of being surrounded by sitting-in mothers who are obviously there not for fun, but to *get* something for their children; to *force* out of that web of desks, and papers, and typewriters, and desk calendars, and file cabinets a couple of pair of pants, some new shoes, and maybe some sheets and pillow cases—when that welfare supervisor starts passing out checks or vouchers to the mothers, it is really something to behold. Those mothers have received a sliver of power, a tiny scrap of control of their own lives, and they will never forget it.

Richard Cloward and Frances Piven, the ideologists of the Welfare Rights Movement, have recently analyzed the significant changes in welfare practices that reflect, in their view, the recognition of black political power in our major cities.[2] These substantial changes in the latent political power structure provide the background, and the context, and the favorable environment for the effective activity of the Welfare Rights Movement.

The signs are everywhere that the focus on power as the major issue is absolutely correct; the only meaningful way to change the prevailing American system of liberty for the free, justice for some, and inequality for all is through shifts in the distribution of power. Here a genuine community group gets itself together and deals, and manipulates, and gains control of a piece of poverty money; there a black legislator is sent to the state capitol; up on the hill a group of wild students demands, and *gets,* a voice in the affairs of the university.

An astute observer of American society, Herbert Gans, has recently pointed out (quite correctly I believe) that America is in the throes of what he calls the "Equality Revolution"[3]— that is, that those who are excluded from the processes of control and decision-making (and they are a substantial majority), are moving and pushing for change, pressing for a shift in the pattern of unequal power. Gans is all in favor of it, though he is somewhat doubtful of the outcome. He has shrewdly noted the most telling sign that power inequality is the crucial ingredient in America's problems—the fact that the Equality Revolution has generated a far mightier backlash than all the combined civil rights activities of the early '60's.

The lesson of all this (if I may be permitted to point to a moral) is the one summarized in *Youth in the Ghetto.*[4] The primary cause of social problems is powerlessness. The cure for powerlessness is power. The criteria for effective programs to solve America's problems of race and poverty are, in fact, very simple (even though the execution of such programs would be enormously difficult and complex). They are known to most ghetto dwellers, educated or not—known perhaps most keenly to those who have never held a high school diploma in their hands. Power must be redistributed: that redistribution will then permit the redistribution of income.

The old vaudeville team of Gallagher and Shean used to sing a very popular patter song; one of the tag-lines was something like: "I didn't see it, Mr. Gallagher." "Where were you looking, Mr. Shean?" We look where the spotlight shines: one of the first tasks in breaking the ideological spell of Blaming the Victim is to shift the beam of the spotlight.

Consider another staple of vaudeville—the magician. He

does not, of course, perform sleight of *hand*. It is not the quickness of the hand that deceives the eye. The secret of magic is misdirection—getting the audience to look at the irrelevant flourishes of the right hand and to ignore the sly doings of the left. In the matters of race and poverty and social problems, the spotlight shines on the right hand, pointing our eyes to "culture" and "values" and "social acceptability." It is time to turn away and keep our eye on the left hand; to take an unblinking look at what is almost instinctively acknowledged as paramount in American life: loot and clout, money and power.

There can be little doubt that power is of overriding concern to human beings. It may be man's most central concern. What he is able to make happen by his own will and his own action determines the quality of his life, indeed, his very existence. His belief in his own ability to stay alive, to meet his basic needs, to make real at least some of his hopes, to nourish and raise his children—these are a direct reflection of his perception of his own power in the world.

And the absence of power is terribly destructive. What some are accustomed to thinking of as the enduring debilitating characteristics of the poor—such as apathy, fatalism, depression, and pessimism—are actually the straightforward manifestations of the dynamics arising from lack of power. Man powerless is not fully man.

This concept can illuminate some vexing problems. Why didn't public housing fulfill the dreams of its planners, for example? Or why cannot slum schools educate? Why are so many of our young people robotized by, or alienated from, our major social institutions? The answers to these—and to an almost endless series of similar questions—is the same: we have failed to understand the nature of humanness and to provide for its nurturance; we have restricted people's ability to act effectively on their own behalf—that is, to exercise power.

Consider the problem of public housing. The average tenant moving into the average housing project gains much: adequate space in a well-constructed dwelling, heat, light, all the material elements of decent housing. Yet, after "all we've done for him," he often remains angry or sullen or apathetic; in many cases he moves out as soon as possible, often to quarters that are objectively worse; he is frequently careless, sometimes even destructive. Exasperated housing officials get angry and complain that "these people" are "untenantable." What is it that goes wrong?

The answer is that most tenants in housing projects are prevented from acting like human beings. There is a set of uncontrollable and unpredictable barriers, sanctions, and forces; most of all, there is a sense of powerlessness. Decision-makers, who are never seen and cannot be influenced—the archetypical They—make rules that invade even the pettiest details of living in a home, forbidding, for example, both decoration and defacement with equal finality (in most housing projects the two are not distinguished). Life in a project has an eternal sense of inescapability. As a former public housing tenant (only passing through, fortunately), I can testify that we were sustained by the certainty that we would escape when graduate studies were completed. Many of our neighbors had a conscious sense of being doomed.

The solution to the problem of public housing is not to be found in the arts of administration or of architecture; neither the rationality of the rules nor the scale or beauty of the design lies at the heart of the matter. The major change required is to provide the opportunity to act like a human being—that is, to take part and to influence the events and decisions that affect one's own home, through collective action.

The tragedy of education in big city slums illustrates the same principle. The children and their parents are unable to affect the schools, cannot interact successfully with the teachers and administrators. For many children, their initiative has so often been mistaken for aggression, their spontaneity has so often been met by unexpected condemnation, their very existence seems to have called forth such disapproval and revulsion, that they retreat into a fortress; they are convinced that they are powerless, that no action of theirs can make any real difference in what goes on in this alien institution. They are anesthetized and dehumanized for the duration, and they leave school (it matters little whether as graduates or dropouts) with only a fraction of their learning capacity realized.

Their parents have almost as difficult a time. No matter how desperately they try to convince the school personnel of their concern about their children—even if they are picketing and storming the doors—they are met with the bland accusations that they ignore and devalue education, that "they don't talk to their children," and that their children fail to learn because of unwholesome family conditions—in other words, that it's the parents, not the schools, who are to blame.

One can multiply the examples. Many students in large universities have likened themselves to IBM cards—to be processed, and sorted, and punched full of information. Many of them abdicate their humanity and permit themselves to be transformed into a product, a new part of society's machine—well-tooled, shiny, fully interchangeable, equally prepared to calculate the profit on a giant box of soap or the loss from a miniaturized H-bomb. Others continue to struggle and to assert their humanity by making tiny dents in the institution. It is sad to say, but more and more seem to be turning away completely and seeking their humanity elsewhere.

I I

The first general principle to be applied in the solution of what we call social problems, then, is that the relevant dimensions are money and power. The second is that these dimensions must be applied first in the *analytic* process, and then in the development of programs. Today's crisis of inequality that imperils our nation must be understood in all its manifestations before we can deal with it effectively. We must understand its generality and extent. Before we can launch a program for social change, we must calculate change's price—which is high. It is not sufficient to be shocked when one learns from John Hersey the truth of what happened in the Algiers Motel; when one learns from Jonathan Kozol the practical procedures used in the Gibson School to achieve death at an early age; when one learns, first from television, then from David Walker and Norman Mailer, the combat methods of the Chicago police when they mount a search-and-destroy offensive against unarmed citizens. One must also come to know that these are but *examples* of what happens continually.

The Gibson School in Dorchester is only a specific instance, an example, an illustration of the generic institution known as the ghetto school. There are five, or ten, or fifty Gibson schools that you can visit tomorrow, and each one of them is destroying the hearts and minds of children—in Cleveland, and in Philadelphia, and in Milwaukee, and in your own city. Every so-called riot has been filled with more or less grisly versions of the Algiers Motel incident, and you can hear about them from the people who were there—in Watts, or New Haven, or Boston, or Plainfield, or Washington. And if you doubt what the functions of our police and our courts really are, take the day off tomorrow, go down to your nearest municipal or district court, and view the day's catch of "criminals." If you can spare the time, talk to a few of them—after they've had their two or three minutes' worth of justice—and find out about the nature of their crimes.

In the study of social problems, the analytic task is often skimped. There is a tendency to leap over and short-circuit dealing with the question of what's wrong. This is particularly true of professionals in welfare, health, and education who, in their laudable haste to do and to help, frequently draw up a premature equation: problem equals need, and need, in turn, equals the service they happen to have handy in the upper right hand drawer. A group of professionals might go into a community and note that there was an unusually large number of broken families. For one professional, this would mean that his specialized program of family life education was clearly the service required; another would conclude that his marriage counseling service was needed; a third would propose a mental health clinic. It is rare that anyone takes a close look at the situation and concludes that a new factory in the community is needed to reduce the high unemployment rate and is the most appropriate and fundamental solution —even though, in such a case, it very well might be.

Earlier I described an analytic dimension that I labeled *exceptionalism-universalism,* which is applicable to attitudes, opinions—ideology—about the causes and cures of social problems. To recapitulate briefly: the exceptionalist position holds that problems are the result of particular circumstances, unpredictable and specialized, affecting individual persons or families in unexpected ways; they are the results of unusual events, or even accidents, that produce a residue of problems that are not effectively managed by the generally satisfactory mechanisms of the social system, particularly the family and the market-place. The universalist position, on the other hand, sees social problems as rooted in social causes—the predictable, usual, even, in a sense, "normal." As I suggested previously, the basic ideological maneuver in Blaming the Victim is to apply exceptionalistic analysis to universalistic problems.

It is highly unlikely that any of the major issues I have covered—problems that affect a large proportion of the population—could have their causes rooted in the personal qualities or individual characteristics of those who are suffering from the problem. If a cholera epidemic is raging in the town, only a lunatic would study the victims to find out what distinguishes them from their healthy neighbors—to discover their personal, hypothetical, cholera-catching characteristics. The object of such a study would be to find out in what way the victims differ from the non-victims in the ways they interact with their *environment*. What kind of food have they eaten, and where do they get it? Where does their water and milk come from? What is the state of their housing and plumbing? Where do they spend their time? Doing what? With whom?

A famous public health legend—the story of the Broad Street Pump—illustrates this approach precisely. The physician who conducted the investigation was a good physician; he was anxious to do and to help, but he was also a good social analyst. He discovered that a greatly disproportionate number of cholera victims got their water from the pump on Broad Street. He concluded that there was something about the *pump* (not those who drank the water) that was causing the disease. Now, the next part of the story is very crucial.

What did he do? He did *not* apply for a research grant to study the characteristics of the pump and its water in order to develop a theory of the etiology of cholera. Nor did he publish a pamphlet urging people not to get their water from this pump. He *ripped the handle off the pump*. That particular cholera epidemic subsided.

The crucial criterion by which to judge analyses of social problems is the extent to which they apply themselves to the *interaction* between the victim population and the surrounding environment and society, and, conversely, the extent to which they eschew exclusive attention to the victims themselves—no matter how feeling and sympathetic that attention might appear to be. Universalistic analysis will fasten on income distribution as the basic cause of poverty, on discrimination and segregation as the basic cause of racial inequality, on social stress as the major cause of the majority of emotional disturbances. It will focus, not on problem families, but on family problems; not on motivation, but on opportunity; not on symptoms, but on causes; not on deficiencies, but on resources; not on adjustment, but on change.

III

Slum housing, for example, is a problem that cannot be realistically attributed to most of the causes covered by conventional wisdom—such as lack of acculturation among tenants, or even, primarily, of some especially deviant brand of businessman called a slum landlord. The city planner's explanation—"blighting" influences such as mixed uses, excessive density, or poor traffic flow—is, at best, only of secondary significance. Slum housing is due to shortage of standard low-income housing. As has been demonstrated in several European countries, creating a sufficient supply of sound low-rent housing is not merely the *way* to eliminate slums, it is the *definition* of the elimination of slums.

Existing programs, as I tried to show previously, have failed because they have not, and could not, increase the supply. What programs might be developed that would do so? In the predominantly private sphere of activity, there is the need to deal with such political and technological problems as: obsolete building construction codes; low productivity of craft union labor; development of new materials and methods of construction; and the fact that housing construction is carried out to a great extent as a high overhead, expensive small business. Just as government subsidies are used to develop new aircraft designs or new weapons designs, a similar effort could be made to subsidize research and development of less expensive housing. One or more universities might set up low cost housing institutes with governmental and foundation support. A semi-public corporation—analogous to COMSAT—could be established to deal directly with developmental problems identified in the research institutes.

The primary aim of all such programs would be the stimulation of greater and cheaper construction by the private sector. Another, a governmental program aimed at stimulation of private activity, would be *direct* housing subsidies for the poor—as opposed to the present corruption-prone rent certificate program whereby local housing authorities lease dwelling units for selected tenants. For example, among housing economists, there appears to be agreement on two issues: that it is impossible to build new housing to rent for less than $100 a month, and that people with lower income should not budget more than about twenty per cent of their net income for total housing costs. This means, as an example, that a family of four, in which the breadwinner earns $2 an hour, should not spend more than $65 a month for sound housing —an almost impossible ideal to achieve. If it were assumed, however, that $100 was a minimum realistic budget, a direct $35 a month subsidy could be paid to that family in the form of a negotiable rent certificate. Administrative costs would be fairly inexpensive—eligibility being determined readily either by affidavit or, if necessary, by a copy of income tax returns; certificates being mailed directly to tenants; and redemption of the certificates being carried out for a fee by banks. This would create a realistic demand for decent new housing and, while there would doubtless be significant seepage—at least initially—by inflation of existing slum rents, the long-term effect should be a significant increase in the housing stock. Such a program should have a certain appeal to conservatives, since it is quite congruent with our growing pattern of a subsidized economy, and since the basic transactions would occur in the private sphere between tenants and landlords, rather than through massive government action.

Another kind of governmental policy action would be required to revise our present high-priority emphasis on ownership of single-family homes. FHA insurance, income tax deductions for homeowners on mortgage interest and real estate taxes, highway construction grants, planning and facilities grants, and other subsidization primarily from Federal funds —all have shaped our national housing program for the past twenty years and have given enormous advantages to the middle-income family that wants to own a single house in the suburbs. The low-income problem, on the other hand, requires an emphasis on multiple-unit housing in the cities. To encourage this, government policy must be turned around to provide income tax deduction for *rent* paid, construction grants for public rapid-transit facilities, and tax advantages to builders that would offset the temptation to reap the advantages of building suburban developments.

The direct public action solution to the low-income housing problem is public housing—but not the kind of public housing we have become used to as another form of slum. At first glance, our American public housing appears to fit the criteria of universalistic programs; however, at second glance, the differences become apparent. First, public housing is a commodity that is dealt out exactly as if it were a form of welfare: with means tests, eligibility requirements, and caste marks of suitability or unsuitability. Second, it is provided in tiny quantities—doled out in doleful trickles—with the result that the enormous unmet need and the long waiting lists reinforce the idea that admission to such housing is a rare privilege rather than a right. Third, it is managed essentially as a custodial institution for second-class citizens. It is these characteristics, rather than design factors, or issues of high-rise or low-rise, or even issues of location, that completely vitiate the theoretically universalistic characteristics of public housing.

An effective public housing program could provide for both publicly-operated housing and housing that was publicly subsidized but operated by non-profit corporations. It would provide for rental fees based on a proportion of income (with no upper- or lower-income limits). And it would eliminate all the means tests, eligibility checks, and other screening procedures. In other words, public housing would be just that —housing that was public rather than private. The only significant distinction would be the difference between fixed rents geared to the market and rents based on a proportion of income. To have any effect on the slum problem, however, billions of dollars would have to be spent for hundreds of thousands of public housing units; public housing in tiny quantities, administered as a quasi-charity, has a seemingly inevitable tendency to be assimilated into the slum housing stock. A substantial output of this kind of public housing would also have a stabilizing effect on the private housing market—it would serve the kind of yardstick function that was originally envisioned for public electrification projects like TVA. If families entered such public housing when their income was $5,000 and their rent was $100 a month, a crucial question would be: how much would they be willing to pay to stay there? When their income rose to $7,500, would they be willing to pay $150 for the same apartment? (This would probably mean that they were then paying *more* than cost, and were helping to subsidize other tenants.) The answer to that question would be dependent on the state of the private market—whether or not there was an equivalent apartment that was either materially more attractive, or was at least of sufficient attractiveness that, coupled with that particular family's motivation to move into private housing, it would pull the family out of the public market and into the private market.

The final and most complete kind of governmental action that could be taken to solve the housing problem would require a massive redefinition of the place of housing in American life—legislation defining housing as a public utility (just as water, gas, electricity, telephones, freight movement and passenger travel are defined as public utilities). Of course, housing is a more complex matter than any of these public utilities. It has more variability—lacking the simple unidimensional structure of electricity or water supply, and is a more local issue—unlike regional or national transportation networks. As such, it would require regulation at a much lower governmental level—the level of the municipality or even the neighborhood.

Singly and in combination, all these proposed programs

and devices would contribute to the overall goal of solving the slum housing problem by producing more low-income housing.

The question of inner-city education can be approached in a similar way: providing for limited private enterprise solutions and broad public action programs, all of which would be directed at changing the *schools* rather than the children. The problem is how do we encourage, motivate, or even, if need be, *force* the schools to educate the children?

One private enterprise program has been proposed by persons as various as Christopher Jencks and Milton Friedman. This is the idea of rearranging the whole basis of the commitment to public education: making the basic unit of fiscal administration the student rather than the school system. This would be accomplished through educational vouchers attached to the child—in somewhat the same fashion that the G.I. Bill of Rights attached a financial voucher to the veteran himself, which he could use in any college, or university, or vocational training program that would accept him. *Public* education would then be carried out through a mixture of public *and* private institutions competing in a classical free-enterprise situation for the business of the student with the voucher. It would be up to the schools themselves to initiate changes and improvements—on a voluntary basis—that would make them more attractive. It would be up to the student—or, more accurately, the student's parents—to evaluate those schools and to choose which one was best.

There are, of course, obvious drawbacks to this idea. Such a laissez-faire approach to elementary education would invite efforts to exploit schooling for profit, for example, and would provide a convenient method of perpetuating racial segregation. For many conservatives, this potential should add appeal to the scheme. Moreover, the advocates of progressive education and of community schools and free schools, I suppose, would be willing to pay the price: the abandonment of the goal of integration.

I would like to propose another possible private enterprise solution to the slum school problem that, as far as I know, has not been put forth previously. Why not pay teachers on the basis of production? The task of education is to teach —to teach children to read and write, to know something about history and geography, to be able to use our arithmetical system. To apply an unfamiliar term to the situation, the *productivity* level of teachers in slum schools is abominably low. They teach very little. What if we attached a direct incentive to effective teaching? Suppose we paid substantially more money to those teachers who performed their task more effectively? Might this not have an effect on the level of ghetto education?

How might such a system work? A fourth-grade teacher is confronted with the task of teaching thirty children one year's worth of, for example, reading. Her effectiveness can be measured through standardized tests of reading achievement. (These tests are now administered under highly variable physical conditions, by teachers or guidance counselors or psychologists with minimal investment, and with highly diversified expectations; what if the results of these tests were the basis for fellow professionals' salary levels?) Under the terms of my proposal, the teacher's salary would be tied to the results of the achievement tests. If, on the average, each of her thirty pupils advanced by an increment of ten months over the previous year's testing, she would get the standard salary for her grade, education, and years of experience. If she had been an especially productive teacher, and this was evidenced by, say, an average advance in achievement test scores of *eleven* months—substantially above the norm—she would be rewarded by an appropriate bonus. If her productivity level had been low, and the pupils had advanced in their reading levels by only nine months or even eight months, her salary would be sharply reduced by an appropriate percentage. Different formulas would have to be worked out for different grade levels, weighing achievement in reading, writing, arithmetic, social studies, science, and so forth; but this would represent no insuperable problem. The two major obstacles to such a program would be the problem of differential ability and the problem of the accuracy of achievement tests. To the latter problem, my own response would be that schools are not now concerned, to any uproarious degree, about the validity of these tests. Does this mean that teachers now accept their validity but would not do so if it affected their own material well-being? What about the present and future material well-being of millions of students who, on the basis of these tests, are being labeled, packaged, tracked, and channeled year after year? If prudence dictated that the whole practice of achievement testing must be reevaluated before attaching to it the presumably far more important question of teachers' salaries, I would heartily concur. Then there is the problem of differential abilities and similar issues. What if a teacher—by unlikely chance—were confronted with thirty students who had, on the average, lesser or greater natural ability? Or, in a similar vein, what if a teacher were teaching in a particular school that—because of the administration, the principal, the atmosphere engendered by other teachers—was in itself detrimental to learning? Would it be fair to penalize a teacher for matters that were outside her control? Or conversely, to reward her for matters that were none of her doing? This might be handled by using, as the norm of the teacher's productivity, each pupil's previous average achievement through his total school experience. If it did nothing else, such an arrangement might slow down the *rate* of deterioration of academic performance in ghetto schools.

The public action style of solution would involve two components: an equalization of investment of resources for each student, and an appreciable measure of influence on the course of a child's education by the child himself, and by his parents. This formula can be translated into an increase of both centralization and decentralization. Such issues as teacher performance, curriculum *goals,* and funding would have to be drastically more centralized. We would have to work out arrangements so that the student in Scarsdale, the student in Harlem, the student in Hough, the student in Shaker Heights, the student in Newton, and the student in Roxbury would have essentially the same quantity of financial resources invested in his education (*not* in the administration of his education); and the results of his education would have to be evaluated by the same yardstick, and the *worth* of his teachers (as measured by salary) would have to be equivalent. This would have to mean extensive centralization—at least at the state level, perhaps at the Federal level. At the same time, on day-to-day issues, on questions of teacher attitude, on problems of student morale, on all the questions that might be termed operational, the school system would have to be drastically *decentralized.* Which teachers, principals, and local administrators should be hired would have to be determined by parents—or, more appropriately, by representatives of parents; detailed questions of school programs, curriculum variations, and so forth would be determined in the same way. In such a manner, the solutions of money and power could be brought to bear simultaneously on the social problem of inferior ghetto education.

. . .

Examples of both private enterprise and public action programs could be cited for all the social problems that have been discussed in the previous chapters. On the general problem of health care a private enterprise solution would be to extend Medicare so as to cover the total population, and to include preventive services, inoculations, periodic checkups, etc. A public action solution would be to institute a publicly-run National Health Service (what we shudder about when we say "socialized medicine!").

The income maintenance problem falls into two large universalistic segments: unemployment and underemployment, on the one hand, and, on the other hand, financial assistance to those who should not work—such as children, the aged, husbandless mothers, the physically and mentally disabled. (There are several small corners of the income problem where exceptionalistic analysis and programming is appropriate—for example, the functionally illiterate adult, whose inability to read prevents him from working, would need a program to teach him to read. Occupants of such corners are relatively small in number.)

Poverty that is the result of unemployment, underemployment, or very low-wage employment is obviously a universalistic problem. For example, in 1940, eight million were out of work, while in 1942, only a little more than one million were out of work. The seven million who went from a jobless status to drawing a weekly paycheck in that two year period were no different in 1940 than in 1942. When the war began, it wasn't that millions of people suddenly developed the ability to run a calculator, or a drill press, or a truck, or a riveting hammer. The situation changed, not the people. Jobs were suddenly created by the demands of the war economy, and millions of people (who were very likely identified previously as "untrained," "unmotivated," etc.) went to work. The current unemployment rate, as I write, is approximately 3.5 per cent, compared with 6.7 per cent in 1961. Over two million persons are working now who were not working then. The reason is that the economy was heated up, and more jobs became available.

The great bulk of the low-income problem reflected in an unemployment rate of more than one or two per cent, then, can be logically analyzed only in terms of the state of the economy and the consequent availability of jobs; and the solution to unemployment is not "manpower development," or "job training" (although they may be desirable or necessary supplemental programs), but *jobs*. The federal government should take ultimate responsibility for making sure that sufficient jobs are available—through fiscal policy, through subsidizing New Careers programs in the public sector, and, if necessary, as a last resort, by acting as the employer—in such direct governmental programs as housing construction, construction of health and educational facilities, water pollution abatement projects, etc.

As to low-wage employment in marginal industries and commercial activity: the income must be raised directly. The public action approach would be a universal high minimum wage (at today's prices, about $2.50 an hour). The private enterprise approach would be to subsidize low-wage industries by a direct government grant to workers—such as a family allowance with monthly payments to families determined by the number and age of children. This would, on the one hand, preserve the supply of cheap labor from the employers' point of view; but it would raise substantially the total income of the underpaid laborer.

To supply income to the "dependent"—that is, those who *should* not work—is a different matter. The occasions that produce these needs—death, desertion, divorce, illegitimate birth, accidents, prolonged illness, birth defects, mental retardation, etc.—although they occur to individuals under specific circumstances, are wholly predictable. They occur in substantial numbers year after year because we make no social provisions to prevent or minimize their occurrence. For example, there are tens of thousands of automobile accidents every year because we are very lax about safety and repair service standards for both cars and highways. Consequently, we know that many thousands of family breadwinners are going to be killed each year in this way, leaving widows and orphans in need of income. A substantial number of them will be ineligible for social security payments and will have to turn to public assistance. Because of the deprivation of contraceptive information, we know—we can predict—that tens of thousands of illegitimate children will be born to mothers who will turn to public assistance for income.

It is a waste of time, energy, and the skills of dedicated workers to deal with all these situations as remarkable, unexpected, unusual circumstances that must be investigated and evaluated to determine eligibility for financial help. The crucial point, in these situations, is that a male breadwinner is missing and no finite amount of social work, investigation, or coercion is going to change that fact. There are, therefore, millions of children, widows, old people, blind people, retarded people, and physically disabled people who cannot work and who have no one to feed them, clothe them, provide them with shelter. We can talk about getting welfare whores off their asses and into factories, we can pass laws requiring mothers of small children to undergo job training, and we can even believe that by trying to force husbandless mothers into jobs that we will solve the maid problem—but none of these issues is really relevant. Such persons should be provided with a simply-administered, steady, adequate source of income. (There may be other problems of a social service nature but such problems are separate, and easily separable, from the income problem.) The obvious solution is some form of income guarantee through one of the many means that have been proposed—such as a negative income tax. There is no need to complicate the problem with the exceptionalistic, means-testing, demoralizing practices that accompany the provision of welfare grants.

Problems of crime, policing, and law enforcement require both some redefinition of crime, and some reorganization of police practices. The first order of business is to clearly define white-collar crime as crime. The cheating, usurious slum merchant does harm to people. The price-fixing, union-busting, tax-evading corporation executive is a very costly person to the rest of us. The slum landlord causes not only physical misery, but actual disease and death. Such persons are, in the old phrase, enemies of the people; their activities should be given primary criminal definitions. If a man holds up a gas station and runs away with the day's receipts of $312, we do not send a government commissioner to bargain with him about how much of the $312 he might be willing to return, over how long a period of time, to the gas station owner. We send a cop to arrest him. Why should we bargain with the vice-president of a national corporation about the $312 million he stole from his customers? We should arrest him and charge him with grand larceny.

On the other hand, it seems almost masochistic to retain the criminal definition we apply, for example, to gambling and commercialized sex. All we are doing is guaranteeing a monopoly to organized crime, with all its associated evils of corruption of police and government officials. To define these activities as criminal is, first, to hand them over to the Mafia as private preserves, and, second, to guarantee that organized crime will have a steady source of capital accumulation for their more injurious activities. Better to take these matters away from *Cosa Nostra* and put them into the solid, middle class businessmen's world, where they could be readily taxed, licensed, and regulated. The model is that of the traffic in liquor. During the days of Prohibition, the liquor business was in the hands of the gangsters—with all the attendant evils of gang wars, Al Capone, deaths and disease from impure liquor, and widespread corruption of public officials. Now we have respectable liquor store owners and large national corporations producing not only trustworthy booze and huge investments in advertising, but also great quantities of taxes to boot.

A final problem of redefinition involves offenses against public order—public intoxication, breach of the peace, loitering, vagrancy, disorderly conduct, etc.—which, along with traffic control, constitute more than one-half of current police workloads. These offenses are not crimes in the usual sense of the word; they may be irritating, or annoying, or troublesome in general, but they are not really injurious to any one in particular. They should be bracketed together and treated as minor traffic violations are treated—offenses that violate the law, but that are neither harmful to others, nor contraventions of social goals or public policy. They can readily be removed from the realm of law-enforcement and assigned to a new category of order-maintenance; this would require the creation and definition of a wholly new community service function, quite different from that of policing as we usually think of it.

Once we separate the functions of law-enforcement and order-maintenance, the police problem and the "crime" problem are halfway solved. The police can then no longer confuse the two (in their own mind and the minds of the general public) by enforcing the maintenance of the social order under the guise of arresting criminals who are no criminals at all—who may, at most, be offenders against public order. Order-maintaining activity—such as directing traffic, tagging illegally parked cars, keeping order in the streets, dealing with drunken citizens, intervening in minor personal disputes, and undertaking community service functions such as providing ambulances—do not have to be carried out by armed officers of social control and community power. In addition, standards of community order vary greatly from one neighborhood to another, and it would seem reasonable to have the process of maintaining order conform to these varying standards. I would propose that all of these functions now vested in municipal police, should be given over to community-based, community-controlled, order-maintaining public service organizations. Partial models of such organizations are available in the functions that have been performed by air-raid wardens, meter-maids, part-time housewife traffic directors, and the improvised community patrols that have operated with generally good results in a number of cities during civil disturbances.

Real crime, on the other hand, (including now, white-collar crime) should be dealt with by skilled, trained, well-paid professional police. They should spend all their time tracking down and arresting murderers, burglars, embezzlers, stock swindlers, bribers, usurers, adulterers of food and polluters of water, rent-gougers, racists, rapists, and dishonest public officials. Since it is abundantly evident that municipal police are, first, hopelessly incompetent to perform such tasks, and, second, terribly subject to locally-inspired corruption, it is probable that law-enforcement should be organized on a regional, metropolitan, or even state-wide basis.

This would leave, as you may have noticed, no function

whatsoever for municipal police forces as we now know them. They could, consequently, be abandoned with no loss.

With policing and law enforcement thus limited in its scope to real crime, the problem of the poor and the black in the toils of justice would be reduced considerably. An effective and well-financed public defender program and a systematic application to the poor of the practice of "release on own recognizance" (often termed "R.O.R." or "no-bail" programs) would go a long way toward limiting further inequities.

I V

It's not only what you do, but, in the words of an old song, the way that you do it. More and more frequently proposals are being put forth promoting what is generally termed "social accounting." A document that emerged not too long ago from Washington is described as a first step toward this goal; it is titled *Toward a Social Report*.[5] This thinking is consciously oriented toward the model of the Council of Economic Advisors and their development of economic indicators and economic reports (providing the base for centralized decision-making that leads to adjustments in fiscal policy, tax legislation, interest rates, etc. to keep the economy humming along in good shape). The social accountants envision a Council of Social Advisors, instructing the President how to regulate the Great Society (or whatever it might be called from one Administration to another) in the same way their economic counterparts regulate the Great Economy. It is an intriguing idea, and it has some components that no one could quarrel with—notably the idea of developing sensitive social indicators, and the idea of rational planning in the fields of health, education, welfare, culture, recreation, and other human services.

The drawback to completely centralized social accounting and planning is the difficulty of dealing with the simple questions, "Who plans?" and "To whom is the accounting made?" Everything I have read would suggest that such planning will be done by highly trained technologists accountable to Presidential advisors, who are themselves perhaps even more highly trained technologists. At such centralized levels, recipients and beneficiaries of these highly complex planning processes will be necessarily left out of the equation. This is not to argue against the importance of centralized social assessment—if only because there is an absolute necessity for an overall national policy and huge national investments in the human services. The trouble is that, rational or not, centralized social accounting will do nothing to alter the powerlessness and exclusion of the poor, the oppressed, and the alienated. It will do nothing to solve the problem of what might be called the Giving Enemy.

What is a Giving Enemy? He is the agent of public service who gives us what we have to have, but seems to be against us. He patrols the streets, but acts rude, and often is brutal. He sees to it that children sit in the classroom—but he doesn't seem to like the children or understand them, and he is always scolding parents about poor home lives and lack of interest in education. He arranges for a check to come to the door twice a month, but he is nosy and unsympathetic and critical and demeaning. The Giving Enemy is the symbol of human services in the city—at the point where human being touches human being. Today, in America's cities, this touching point is frosted over with hostility and depersonalization.

No matter how kind or dedicated an individual person may

be, when he takes on the role of a worker in human services in the city, he becomes—almost inevitably, despite a few exceptions—the Giving Enemy. The reasons for this are structural and organizational, rather than personal.

There are, basically, five problems that beset human services in urban areas that make it almost impossible to provide effective help to city people. First is the problem of centralization. The welfare worker walks the streets of a neighborhood, but when he tries to act in a helpful way, his district supervisor, a county director, a state department, and finally, several hierarchical levels within the Federal government may act to impede him, or may already have acted to impede him. Calvin Gross, former Superintendent of New York's public schools, has described the essentially impossible task of influencing what goes on in a classroom through seven or eight doughy layers of administrative bureaucracy. Of course, the classroom teacher (not to mention the student or the parent) could tell an even more anguished tale of trying to influence Dr. Gross. Authority and decision-making are centralized at a point so far removed from the scene of the action—the touching point of person and person—as to appear essentially invisible.

The second problem is lack of citizen participation. The parents, teachers tell us, won't come to PTA meetings; the tenants, planners tell us, won't come to urban renewal neighborhood meetings; the residents, poverty workers tell us, won't vote in local anti-poverty council elections; the citizens, community organizers tell us, won't join their block organization. The citizens are accused of apathy at the very same time they themselves are complaining about being excluded.

The lack of effective comprehensive planning is a third problem. The local health and welfare council frenetically plans for the private social agencies; the hospital council plans for health needs; the city planning board plans for housing and zoning; and none of them influence each other; meanwhile, the largest purveyors of human services—the city departments of health, welfare, public housing, education, and public safety—go their separate ways as if they never heard the word planning.

Fourth, we have the problem of accountability—a word dear to the hearts of professors of public health and of social welfare, a word that lingers in the ears of their students like a once-heard, never-repeated melody. They would recognize the tune if the orchestra struck up the opening bars, but, in this case, the musicians have lost the music.

We deal with accountability as an abstract virtue and in much the same way that we deal with, say, chastity. An abstract virtue may be defined as one that everyone believes in, but few people practice. Financial responsibility is another matter—directly comparable to the concrete virtue of honesty. Whatever our real expectations may be about individual chastity, we are damned serious about whether or not people steal money. In the public field, the city comptroller or budget director oversees the financial affairs of public human service agencies very scrupulously, though he may not give a damn about the quality of the actual services. In like manner, we arrange to audit the books of private agencies to make sure there is no hanky-panky with the money. The people, the clients—we apparently do not count them as so important. At least we do not seem to hold agencies to strict standards of service, or really to any standards.

Finally, we have the problem of the Giving Enemy himself and how to defend ourselves against his careless ministrations, which are intentionally or unintentionally harmful to us. The innocent citizen is arrested and, what's worse, convicted; the normally bright child is taught how not to read;

the legitimate, certified, deserving welfare recipient is done out of her rightful allowances. How do we find some way of putting our hand in to stop the gears without getting our fingers cut off? This fifth problem is that of citizen defense.

It would seem obvious that one solution to the problem of centralization is decentralization; this profound truth is beginning to gain more and more credence. Decentralization of services has been recommended in recent years by any number of studies, position papers, and projects; the recommendation usually takes the form of some kind of neighborhood service center—which seems to be the new panacea in social welfare. The medical people see neighborhood health stations that draw together and coordinate what they call "the ancillary services"; public assistance people have a vision of neighborhood social welfare centers; psychiatrists, a vision of neighborhood mental health centers; and so forth. Each one views the center as an outpost of a centralized agency or— at the very perimeter of radical thinking—as an uneasy alliance of outposts of several centralized agencies, operating under one roof and depending prayerfully on the emergence of huge quantities of good will to ensure coordination.

On the question of citizen participation there is far less agreement than on decentralization. This problem has been made worse by the trend toward centralization in city government. The increasing popularity—and, we must also recognize, efficiency—of a form of city government with a strong mayor or manager, and at-large elections of legislative bodies has occurred at a certain cost, a certain diminishing of pluralistic decision-making—one might even say a loss of democracy. The mayor, or the councilman, or the member of the board of education who is elected by the city as a whole represents everyone in general, it is true. It is also true that he doesn't represent anyone in particular. It is often a case of brute rule by the majority with little concern for the minority.

Schemes for facilitating citizen participation in decision-making processes that affect their lives include, among others, the old-fashioned block or neighborhood organization; advisory committees; citizen advice bureaus; area poverty boards (both elected, appointed, and, one might say, assembled); the *ombudsman;* neighborhood city halls; community or citizens relations bureaus in (or very near) City Hall; mass organizations on the Saul Alinsky model; and the Community Foundation. Most fail of their purpose on one of two grounds: either they allow for no real participation in decision-making, or they are, at best, ambiguously representative.

Most people are familiar with block or neighborhood organization. Some have grown up spontaneously as civic-minded neighbors met together to discuss neighborhood matters. Others have been organized by community councils, redevelopment agencies, or other professional organizations. The average organization that falls into this category has limited appeal and limited membership. It might be called the Hill Neighborhood Organization, or the West Side Citizens Committee, or the Jefferson Neighborhood Improvement Association, but it is clear that it does not organize the Hill Neighborhood, it includes only a tiny fraction of West Side citizens, and many people have serious doubts as to what precisely it intends to improve in the good old Jefferson neighborhood.

The clear and obvious lack of representativeness makes it very easy for the mayor, or any other politician, to decide for himself—on the basis of his own needs—whether he will greet the delegates from such an organization as the voice of the people, or whether he will ignore them as a handful of malcontents. Most important of all, such citizen groups have nothing real to *do*—no goal to reach, no decision to make.

So they focus their attention on vague functions that exist in a virtual vacuum—organizing, improving, or often just being a committee. Since they have no work to do, they are often perceived, rather accurately (and particularly in low-income communities) as, at best, trivial, and at worst, another tool for exercising political control by the down-town representatives of the majority.

Similar criticisms can be made of most of the other devices. Consider, for example, the Scandinavian institution of the *ombudsman*. Citizens bring complaints to the *ombudsman* and he investigates them with a view to both smoothing out the complex operations of governmental functioning and identifying general defects or injustices. He acts by publicizing the problem, suggesting administrative changes, and proposing legislative remedies. The system is said to operate rather efficiently, but only with respect to a rather narrow category of well-defined administrative problems, including problems arising from illegal or arbitrary exercise of executive power. Beyond this narrow category, the *ombudsman* has no clear sanction for intervention. Although he may well be working on behalf of the people, he certainly does not *represent* them in any meaningful sense, and he has little impact on the decision-making process in many significant areas.

Advisory boards of all sorts—from urban renewal and poverty to community mental health centers—are rarely representative in any sense whatever, and they are usually asked to react to, rather than participate in, decisions.

The two exceptions I can think of are the Alinsky-type organizations, and the Community Foundation idea developed by Milton Kotler.[6] Alinsky's structural goal is a broad coalition of as many elements and interests in the community as can be brought together, that acts vigorously to correct abuses being visited on the neighborhood by public or private forces—the slumlord, the dishonest grocer, the overcrowded school, the domineering urban renewal project, etc. Kotler's notion of the Community Foundation is based on the establishment of a non-profit corporation to run one or more programs, a corporation that is potentially coterminous with the community itself. In both instances, there is usually very wide participation, and there is work to do: either defensive work of opposing exploitation or, in the case of the Community Foundation, the direct operation of service enterprises. Not *advising* about service enterprises, it should be noted, but directly *operating* them. Both of these models call for mass participation, complete inclusiveness, and election of the governing group.

I would propose, therefore, that the solution to the problem of participation requires an organization with a mass base, with elected representation, and with specific tasks to perform and primary decisions to make. The twin problems of decentralization and participation can be dealt with by a new level of city governmental machinery that meets these requirements: an elected district council in every district of a city.

If the city were divided into human-scale districts, each district could manage a great deal of its day-to-day business —particularly human service—through its own district government, the elected district council. Principally, the council would have direct operating responsibility for a set of public human services and indirect responsibility for analogous private human services. Its members would be elected by the residents of the district; those eligible to vote would include everyone who lives or works in the district and is over a given age, perhaps seventeen or eighteen. The council would directly hire its own administrative staff and, subject to personnel or civil service regulations, the staffs of public human service programs. Its funds should be protected from capricious appropriations by some system of modified per capita expenditures, or some formula based on objective measures of need.

The primary task of the district council would be to operate a decentralized and integrated system of human services including education, order-maintenance, child welfare, family counseling, public housing, neighborhood health care, etc. This program of decentralized services would, of course, have to be backed up and supported by an additional city-wide centralized system consisting of both highly specialized direct services, and supportive indirect services.

I would predict that such a system of elected district councils would stimulate very broad participation because there would be something to participate in—decisions to be made of importance to everyone. In addition, such a method of supervising and operating human services would insure greater integration and responsiveness to needs of clients and consumers because the latter would have a simple and ready mechanism for influencing the services.

With respect to the third problem area, planning: it is noteworthy that, in the past, planning for human services has been largely in the private realm—the characteristic agency for such planning has been the voluntary health and welfare council. A major drawback in this has been the separation of public and private service agencies—a separation that has been accompanied by significant differences in status, resources, and responsibilities. In more recent years we have been accepting more and more the idea of basic public responsibility for almost all human services. The step we have not yet taken is to move planning into the public sector (except in a limited way, for some public services, usually somehow related to land use).

The second proposal, then, is for the incorporation into city government of the function of social planning for human services. The Division of Social Planning should use every legal tool to incorporate private agencies into a system of mutual influence and joint planning with the public agencies. It should also provide for decentralization of certain planning functions—particularly those related to coordination and integration—in close collaboration with the proposed elected district councils.

The issues of accountability and citizen defense are, in a sense, reciprocally related. Citizen defense, seen from the citizen's point of view, is the obverse of accountability. The former (citizen defense) arises as a problem in relation to specific error or failure; the latter (accountability) around more general institutionalized efforts to avert error or failure. If citizens are to believe in and trust a structure of human services, there has to be some way in which their grievances can be not only heard, but redressed. They have to feel that there is some likelihood of being defended against unfair or abusive treatment; that errors and misjudgments are correctable; and, further, they have to feel that they can influence the process of correction.

My third proposal is for the establishment within the city government of a Bureau of Social Accountability, whose general function would be to assess the effectiveness, humaneness, and service performance of agencies. It would have the responsibility of constantly raising—and trying to answer—such questions as the following: is the agency providing service to everyone who is appropriately referred to it? More important, did the service deal effectively with the problem? Did the relocation agency, for example, provide a standard home for *every* family displaced by the renewal project? Is the school teaching *all* the children to read effectively? The

Bureau of Social Accountability should include within its orbit a set of advice and complaint centers for citizens where information about available services would be provided, and where grievances can be presented to be dealt with by the accountability mechanism. The information and complaint centers should be operated directly by the district councils, with a strong tie of communication and liaison to the Bureau of Social Accountability.

It is also important that the Bureau have a strong relationship upward, probably to a state level agency such as the office of the Governor, the Attorney General, a combined health and welfare agency, or a new state department of accountability. The state level department could provide general supervision, and consultation, and perhaps even some of the funding on a matching basis. This upward relationship would act as a counterpoise to some of the inevitable pressures the service agencies would put upon other branches of what would be, after all, a unified city administration.

These three new and interdependent mechanisms of government—elected district councils, a Division of Social Planning and a Bureau of Social Accountability—could deal rather effectively with the five issues mentioned at the beginning of this discussion: decentralization, participation, planning, accountability, and citizen defense. They would go a long way toward eliminating from the life of our cities the pervasive and eroding problem of the Giving Enemy.

V

What are the prospects? Where is the bookmaker who will give odds on the economic and political reforms substantial enough to redistribute power and income in America? It

273

seems easy. We have so much, and it would cost so little to end poverty; it would hurt so little to share some power.

But the resistance is discouragingly high. A friend of mine has been working for years to develop citizen support for the welfare rights movement. During the last months, he has been out speaking one, two, and three times a week to church groups and other organizations that might be sympathetic. He tries every approach he can think of—hard unyielding statistics, heartbreaking stories of life on welfare, patient dissection of all the myths. But most of his listeners seem unable to rid themselves of the ingrained belief that getting money without working for it—no matter how worthy and touching the recipient may be—is illicit, slothful, vaguely criminal.

We cherish poverty religiously, patriotically. It appears that poverty, too, is as American as apple pie and violence. Life would not seem natural without the poor, and we go to great lengths to make sure that we will always have them with us. Even in America in the 1970's we insist on preserving poverty when we are producing goods at such a rate that it takes a good chunk of our intellectual resources to think up ways of getting rid of them. We hire our second-best brains to labor in advertising agencies, inventing grotesque methods to consume this fountain of resources, while we employ our best brains in that great solid waste disposal agency, the Pentagon, to dream up harebrained schemes to dump the surplus on Viet Nam, into holes in the ground, or in outer space.

So the odds don't look good. Freedom is diminished daily; the excesses of reaction and repression become larger and bolder; the unthinkable glows forth on our television screens each night, and the unspeakable flows glibly from the mouths of high government officials. Scores of Black Panthers and other young black militants have been murdered, and hundreds more have been wounded and jailed. In Washington, the words "preventive detention" are no dirtier than equivalent phrases in Berlin were in 1936; resistance to desegregation is being openly led by the country's chief legal official; and the President of the United States seems not the least bit ashamed to nominate to the Supreme Court a man who appears to be a bigot and racist. Every week brings a new piece of bad news as the courts become more outrageously political, the police more blatantly violent. Worst of all, the old liberal whores from the social sciences are doing a boomtown business, the old bitches are turning new tricks every day under the baton of the madam in the White House, conducting from the score of his new oratorio, *Benign Neglect and Malignant Intervention*.

The forces on the Left, meanwhile, are in chaos. A New Exceptionalism has captured large sectors of what used to be called the radical movement. But the Right is organized, in control of most of the government, and moving inexorably.

It must be clear to most that Revolution—even if, by the gravest standards, it were judged to be necessary and desirable—is not just around the corner, nor even in sight far, far down the road. Change can only come through progressive, democratic reform that occurs, not through the achievement of a romantic life style subsidized by one's well-to-do parents, but by the hard, grinding work of organizing, analyzing, educating, and political action. We can begin to reform the inequitable distribution of wealth in our nation by well-known, tried and true methods—revision of tax structure, massive extension of social insurance, public housing, and governmental medical care; a renewal of the drive to unionize the unorganized, the establishment of a high universal minimum wage and a guaranteed income well above the poverty line for those who cannot or should not work.

Since no magic revolution will cure the inequality of power

in America, it must be put in better balance by the hard work of organizing—for welfare rights, for tenant rights, for community control, for student participation, for black equality—and by the constant insistence on strict enforcement of law—such as civil rights laws, housing codes, and, in particular, The Bill of Rights.

We cannot afford to ignore our victories; we must note them and learn from them. The social invention of New Careers has already had a greater effect on the occupational structure of this country than all the programs to promote black capitalism and economic development in the ghetto. It will continue to have a great effect, not only in this way, but also on the quality and nature of organizational and professional forms of the delivery of human services. The drama enacted in Ocean Hill-Brownsville has demonstrated the way to change our schools more meaningfully and effectively than all the privatistic free schools in the country. The organizers of a national welfare rights movement have had, and will have, more effect on the institutions of income-maintenance in America than will the burning of a hundred banks. And the legislated access to the polls provided to hundreds of thousands of black men and women has greater potential for the achievement of racial justice than fifty thousand black-white "confrontation groups" designed to expunge the stain of psychological racism from the souls of guilt-ridden white suburbanites.

These were the accomplishments of men and women who were prepared to work long hours, to do their homework, and to discipline themselves to meet a succession of related goals.

Can more of these victories be achieved? The burden rests, in the end, on the person I identified in the introduction of this book—the concerned citizen who wants and acts for constructive change, who really does believe in the values of equality and justice that, nowadays, we scarcely dare mention without an obligatory cynical smirk.

It is true that this very person has been most easily bewitched and disoriented by the ideology I have spent so many pages in trying to expose.

But if he can only get his bearings, if he can only turn his attention away from fruitless tinkering with the victim and fix his sights on the real targets—redistribution of money and power—I believe he can turn the tide.

That's why I wrote this book.

Notes

CHAPTER ONE

The Art of Savage Discovery:
How to Blame the Victim

1. Karl Mannheim, *Ideology and Utopia*, trans. Louis Wirth and Edward Shils (New York: Harcourt, Brace & World, Inc., A Harvest Book, 1936). First published in German in 1929.
2. John Seeley, "The Problem of Social Problems," *Indian Sociological Bulletin*, II, No. 3 (April, 1965). Reprinted as Chapter Ten in *The Americanization of the Unconscious* (New York: International Science Press, 1967), pp. 142–48.
3. C. Wright Mills, "The Professional Ideology of Social Pathologists," *American Journal of Sociology*, XLIX, No. 2 (September, 1943), pp. 165–80.
4. William Ryan, "Community Care in Historical Perspective: Implications for Mental Health Services and Professionals," *Canada's Mental Health*, supplement No. 60, March–April, 1969. This formulation draws on, and is developed from, the *residual-institutional* dimension outlined in H. L. Wilensky and C. N. Lebeaux, *Industrial Society and Social Welfare* (paperback ed.; New York: The Free Press, 1965). Originally published by Russell Sage Foundation, 1958.
5. For a good review of this general ideology, see I. A. Newby, *Jim Crow's Defense* (Baton Rouge: Louisiana State University Press, 1965).
6. Richard Hofstadter, *Social Darwinism in American Thought* (revised ed.; Boston: Beacon Press, 1955).
7. William J. Ghent, *Our Benevolent Feudalism* (New York: The Macmillan Co., 1902), p. 29.

CHAPTER TWO

Savage Discovery in the Schools: The Folklore of Cultural Deprivation

1. *Operation Counterpoise,* mimeograph (Boston Public Schools, 1964).
2. "A Pre-Kindergarten Program That Can Prevent Dropouts," *Boston Public Schools Review* (a report of the Boston School Committee, Division of Statistics and Publicity, undated), pp. 10–19.
3. Carl J. Dolce, "The Inner-City—A Superintendent's View," *Saturday Review of Literature,* January 11, 1969, p. 36.
4. Perhaps the most outstanding of these studies of the learning and thinking processes of poor children have been contributed by Martin Deutsch and his colleagues.
5. M. Deutsch, I. Katz, and A. R. Jensen, eds., *Social Class, Race, and Psychological Development* (New York: Holt, Rinehart & Winston, Inc., 1968).
6. James S. Coleman, *Equality of Educational Opportunity* (Washington, D.C.: U.S. Office of Education, 1966).
7. *Ibid.,* p. 311.
8. *Ibid.,* p. 296.
9. *Ibid.,* p. 218.
10. *Ibid.,* p. 316.
11. In a recent widely-noted article, Arthur Jensen did, in fact, draw on the data of the Coleman Report to support his argument that Negroes are genetically inferior in intelligence. See Arthur Jensen, "How Much Can We Boost I.Q. and Scholastic Achievement?", *Harvard Educational Review,* XXXIX, No. 1 (winter, 1969), pp. 1–123. The author makes similar use of the Moynihan Report, which is discussed in Chapter Three.
12. Coleman, *op. cit.,* p. 275.
13. *Ibid.,* p. 307.
14. *Ibid.,* p. 192.
15. *Ibid.,* p. 320.
16. *Ibid.,* p. 280.
17. E. Garrett, "The Equalitarian Dogma," *Mankind Quarterly,* No. 1 (1961), pp. 253–57; "The SPSSI and Racial Differences," *American Psychologist,* No. 17 (1962), pp. 260–63.
18. Audrey Shuey, *The Testing of Negro Intelligence* (2nd ed.; New York: Social Science Press, 1966).
19. Arthur Jensen, *op. cit.*

20. *Youth in the Ghetto* (the report of the Harlem Youth Opportunities Unlimited [HARYOU] planning project, 1964). The data on this experiment are explicated more fully in James A. Jones, "Education in Depressed Areas: A Research Sociologist's Views" (a paper delivered at the *Fourth Work Conference on Curriculum and Teaching in Depressed Areas,* Teachers College, Columbia University, June 22, 1965).

21. William Ryan, "Racial Imbalance, Cultural Deprivation, and Reading Achievement," mimeograph (Advisory Committee on Racial Imbalance and Education, background paper No. 7 [Massachusetts State Board of Education, 1965]).

22. Estelle Fuchs, "How Teachers Learn to Help Children Fail," *Transaction,* V, No. 9 (September, 1968), pp. 45–49.

23. *Ibid.,* p. 45.

24. *Ibid.,* p. 48.

25. Robert Rosenthal and Lenore Jacobson, *Pygmalion in the Classroom,* (New York: Holt, Rinehart & Winston, Inc., 1968).

CHAPTER THREE

Mammy Observed:
Fixing the Negro Family

1. *The Negro Family: The Case for National Action* (U.S. Department of Labor, U.S. Government Printing Office, Washington, D.C., 1965).

2. William Ryan, "Savage Discovery: The Moynihan Report," *The Nation,* November 22, 1965; also, "The New Genteel Racism," *The Crisis,* December, 1965.

3. Payton's influential mimeographed memorandum was published in a condensed version: Benjamin Payton, "New Trends in Civil Rights," *Christianity and Crisis,* December 13, 1965. James Farmer wrote several criticisms of the report in his column in the *Amsterdam News:* "The Controversial Moynihan Report," December 18, 1965; and "More on the Moynihan Report," December 25, 1965.

4. There have been a dozen or more published articles reviewing and criticizing the Moynihan Report. The most "neutral" and in some ways the best is Herbert Gans' "The Negro Family: Reflections on the Moynihan Report," *Commonweal,* October 15, 1965. Other important articles include: Laura Carper, "The Negro Family and the Moynihan Report," *Dissent,* March–April, 1966; Elizabeth Herzog, "Is There a Breakdown in the Negro Family?", *Social Work,* January, 1966; and Frank Reissman, "In Defense of the Negro Family," *Dissent,* March–April, 1966. Hylan Lewis' "Agenda Paper No. 5. The Family: Resources for Change" (prepared for the November planning meeting for the

White House Conference) did not criticize the Moynihan Report but rather attempted to lay out the total set of data relevant to the issues raised. It is considered by most critics to be the most thoroughgoing refutation of the Moynihan thesis.

5. "New Crisis: The Negro Family," *Newsweek*, August 9, 1965, pp. 32–35. Copyright © 1965, by Newsweek, Inc.
6. Daniel P. Moynihan, *The Negro Family: The Case for National Action*, p. 5.
7. Daniel P. Moynihan, "The President and the Negro: The Moment Lost," *Commentary*, XLIII, No. 2 (February, 1967), p. 33.
8. While awaiting a book-length report of Lewis' important child-rearing study, readers can draw on several published articles and widely-circulated mimeographed papers. The most accessible are: Hylan Lewis, "Child Rearing Among Low-Income Families," *Poverty in America*, eds. L. Ferman, J. Kornbluth and Alan Haber (revised ed.; Ann Arbor: University of Michigan Press, 1968); and Hylan Lewis, "Culture, Class, and Family Life Among Low-Income Urban Negroes," *Employment, Race and Poverty*, eds. Arthur Ross and Herbert Hill (New York: Harcourt, Brace & World, Inc., A Harbinger Book, 1967).
9. Andrew Billingsley, *Black Families in White America* (Englewood Cliffs, N.J.: Prentice-Hall Inc., 1968).
10. *Ibid.* The author reports on a good deal of unpublished research by historian Horace Mann Bond (father of Julian) reviewing the family and social background of successful Negro professional men.
11. E. Franklin Frazier, *The Negro Family in the United States* (abridged ed.; New York: Dryden Press, 1948).
12. Elizabeth Herzog, *op. cit.,* p. 8.
13. L. Scrole, T. S. Langner, S. T. Michael, M. K. Opler and T. A. C. Rennie, *Mental Health in the Metropolis: The Midtown Manhattan Study*, I (New York: McGraw-Hill, Inc., 1962).
14. Hylan Lewis, *op. cit.*
15. Moynihan, *The Negro Family: The Case for National Action*. The first three excerpts are from the Preface, the fourth from p. 30, the fifth from p. 47.
16. This theme drew an acerbic comment from Laura Carper: "I cannot here counterpose my taste in men or my concept of the good life against Mr. Moynihan's—but it seems clear to me that it is for the Negro male himself to determine his sexual and social style—whether strutting or not."

The same kind of irritation inspired me to compose a hitherto unpublished "double-dactyl" on the same topic:

> Higgledy-Piggledy
> Daniel (Pat) Moynihan
> Called on the Negro to
> Take a new tack.

Roosters and generals, he
Sociologically
Held up as models for
Men who are black.

17. Quoted by Thomas Meehan, "Moynihan of the Moynihan Report," *New York Times Magazine,* July 31, 1966, p. 58.

CHAPTER FOUR

The Prevalence of Bastards:
Illegitimate Views of Illegitimacy

1. Paul Gebhard, Wardell Pomeroy, Clyde Martin, and Cornelia Christenson, *Pregnancy, Birth, and Abortion* (New York: John Wiley & Sons, Inc., Science Editions, 1958), p. 154.
2. Theodore White, *The Making of the President, 1964* (New York: Atheneum Publishers, 1965).
3. Daniel P. Moynihan, "The President and the Negro: The Moment Lost," *op. cit.,* p. 43.
4. Jean Pakter, Henry Rosner, Harold Jacobziner, and Frieda Greenstein, "Out-of-Wedlock Births in New York City: I—Sociologic Aspects," *American Journal of Public Health,* LI, No. 5 (May, 1961), pp. 683–96.
5. William Ryan and Laura Morris, *Child Welfare Problems and Potentials, MCCY Monograph III* (Mass Fund for Children and Youth, Boston, 1967); *Help for Asking,* mimeograph (United Community Services Research Department, 1964).
6. Gebhard *et al., op. cit.* See particularly pp. 54–78.
7. *Ibid.* See particularly Chapter Eight.
8. Estelle Siker and H. M. Fritch, "Estimated Extent of Teenage Out-of-Wedlock Pregnancy in Connecticut," *Connecticut Health Bulletin,* January, 1967, pp. 3–11.
9. W. F. Pratt, "Premarital Pregnancy in a Metropolitan Community" (paper presented at the Population Association of America, April, 1965). Summarized by Adelaide Hill and Frederick S. Jaffe in *The Negro American* (see Note 11).
10. Frederick S. Jaffe, "Family Planning, Public Policy and Intervention Strategy," *Journal of Social Issues,* XXIII, No. 4 (October, 1967).
11. Adelaide Hill and Frederick Jaffe, "Negro Fertility and Family Size Preference: Implications for Programming of Health and Social Services," *The Negro American,* eds. T. Parsons and K. Clark (Boston: Houghton Mifflin Co., 1967), pp. 217–18.
12. Hylan Lewis, see Note 8 to Chapter Three.

13. Elizabeth Herzog, "The Chronic Revolution: Births Out-of-Wedlock," *Clinical Pediatrics,* V, No. 2, pp. 130–35.
14. Richard Cloward and Richard Elman, "Poverty, Injustice, and the Welfare State," Part 1, *The Nation* (February 25, 1966), pp. 230–35; Part 2, *The Nation* (March 7, 1966), pp. 264–68.
15. Richard Cloward and Frances Fox Piven, "Migration, Politics, and Welfare," *Saturday Review* (November 16, 1968).
16. Charles Lebeaux, "Life on A.D.C.: Budgets of Despair," *New University Thought* (winter, 1963). Reprinted in Ferman, Kornbluth, and Haber, *Poverty in America,* pp. 519–28.
17. *Ibid.*

CHAPTER FIVE

Learning to Be Poor:
The Culture of Poverty Cheesecake

1. For a detailed bibliography of this literature see the footnote references in Catherine Chilman's *Growing up Poor* (Washington, D.C.: Welfare Administration Publication No. 13, U.S. Department of Health, Education, and Welfare, U.S. Government Printing Office, 1966).
2. Oscar Lewis, "The Culture of Poverty," *Scientific American,* CCXV, No. 16 (October, 1966), pp. 19–25.
3. Walter Miller, "Lower Class Culture as a Generating Milieu of Gang Delinquency," *Journal of Social Issues,* XIV, No. 4 (1958), pp. 5–19.
4. Oscar Lewis, *op. cit.,* p. 7.
5. Chilman, *Growing Up Poor.*
6. *Ibid.*
7. *Ibid.*
8. *Ibid.*
9. *Ibid.*
10. *Ibid.*
11. *Ibid.*
12. *Ibid.*
13. G. P. Murdock, "The Common Denominator of Cultures," *The Science of Man in a World of Crisis,* ed. Ralph Linton (New York: Columbia University Press, 1945).
14. Charles Valentine, *Culture and Poverty: Critique and Counter-Proposals* (Chicago: University of Chicago Press, Midway Paperback Text Series, 1969).
15. *Ibid.,* pp. 6–7.
16. *Ibid.,* p. 115.

17. H. H. Hyman, "The Value Systems of Different Classes," *Class, Status, and Power,* R. Bendix and S. M. Lipset, eds., (2nd ed., New York: The Free Press, 1966).
18. Hyman Rodman, "The Lower-Class Value Stretch," *Social Forces* (December, 1963).
19. Walter Miller, *op. cit.*
20. A. Davis and R. J. Havighurst, "Social Class and Color Differences in Child-Rearing," *American Sociological Review,* XI (1946), pp. 698–710.
21. E. Maccoby and P. K. Gibbs, "Methods of Child-Rearing in Two Social Classes," *Child Behavior and Development,* eds. W. E. Martin and C. B. Stendler (New York: Harcourt, Brace and World, Inc., 1959).
22. U. Bronfenbrenner, "Socialization and Social Class Through Time and Space," *Readings in Social Psychology,* eds. E. Maccoby, T. Newcomb, and E. L. Hartley (3rd ed.; New York: Holt, Rinehart and Winston, Inc., 1958), pp. 400–25.
23. Hylan Lewis, in Ross and Hill, *Employment, Race, and Poverty,* p. 170.
24. S. Miller, F. Riessman and A. Seagull, "Poverty and Self-Indulgence: A Critique of the Non-Deferred Gratification Pattern," *Poverty in America,* eds. L. Ferman, J. Kornbluth and A. Haber (revised ed.; Ann Arbor: University of Michigan Press, 1968), pp. 416–32.
25. Lee Rainwater, "The Problem of Lower Class Culture and Poverty-War Strategy," *On Understanding Poverty,* ed. Daniel P. Moynihan (New York: Basic Books, 1969), p. 251.
26. Max Weber, "Class, Status and Party," *From Max Weber: Essays in Sociology,* eds. H. H. Gerth and C. W. Mills (Gloucester, Mass.: Peter Smith, 1958).

CHAPTER SIX

The Hydraulics and Economics of Misery:
The Society for the Preservation of Disease

1. For a thorough critical review of the research on this topic, see Marc Fried, "Social Problems and Psychopathology," *Urban America and the Planning of Mental Health Services* (Group for the Advancement of Psychiatry, Symposium No. 10 [New York, 1964]). For a more general selection of materials, see *Mental Health of the Poor,* eds. Frank Riessman, Jerome Cohen and Arthur Pearl (New York: The Free Press, 1964).
2. A. M. Freedman and H. I. Kaplan, *Comprehensive Textbook of Psychiatry* (Baltimore: Williams and Williams, 1967), pp. 155–58.
3. Thomas Langner and Stanley Michaels, *Life Stress and Mental Health:*

The Midtown Manhattan Study, XXII (New York: The Free Press, 1963), p. 438. This is not the primary emphasis of the authors, who also demonstrate the relationship implied in the title.

4. A. Kardiner and I. Ovesey, *The Mark of Oppression: Explorations in the Personality of the American Negro* (New York: World Publishing Co., n.d.), p. 308.

5. *Ibid.,* p. 313.

6. A. Kardiner, letter to the editor of the *Saturday Evening Post,* August 24, 1968, p. 10.

7. Chilman, *Growing Up Poor,* Chapter Four.

8. William Ryan, "Distress in the City: A Summary Report of the Boston Mental Health Survey," *Distress in the City: Essays in the Planning and Administration of Urban Mental Health Services,* ed. William Ryan (Cleveland: Case Western Reserve University Press, 1969).

9. Daniel Levinson, John Merrifield and Kenneth Berg, "Becoming a Patient," *Archives of General Psychiatry,* XVII (December, 1967), pp. 385–406.

10. Roy R. Grinker and Fred P. Robbins, *Psychosomatic Casebook* (Philadelphia: Blakiston Company, 1954), pp. 72–73.

11. Paul Adams and Nancy McDonald, "Clinical Cooling Out of Poor People," *American Journal of Orthopsychiatry,* XXXVIII, No. 4 (April, 1968), pp. 457–63.

12. Bruce Dohrenwend, "Social Status, Stress, and Psychological Symptoms," *American Journal of Public Health,* LVII, No. 4 (1967), pp. 625–32.

13. Bruno Bettelheim, *The Empty Fortress* (New York: The Free Press, 1967).

14. Alonzo Yerby, "The Problems of Medical Care for Indigent Populations," *American Journal of Public Health,* LV, No. 8 (August, 1965), pp. 1212–16.

15. O. Reid, P. Arnaudo, and A. White, "The American Health-Care System and the Poor: A Social Organization Point of View," *Welfare in Review,* VI, No. 6 (1968), pp. 1–12.

16. *Ibid.,* p. 2.

17. For a vivid summary description of what medical care is like for the poor, see Anselm Strauss, "Medical Ghettoes," *Trans–action,* May, 1967, pp. 7–15.

18. R. Duff and A. Hollingshead, *Sickness and Society* (New York: Harper & Row, Publishers, Inc., 1968).

CHAPTER SEVEN

Taking People Out of Oak Street:
Slums, Suburbs and Subsidies

1. Charles Silberman, Chapter Three of *Crisis in Black and White* (New York: Vintage Books, 1964), and especially pp. 36–37.
2. William Ryan and Laura Morris, *Social Renewal for Springfield,* mimeo (Massachusetts Commission on Children and Youth, Boston, 1966). An adaptation of this report was included in Springfield's Report on Community Renewal, City Planning Dept., 1967.
3. Marion Glaser, *Code Violations in New Haven,* mimeograph (Coalition of Concerned Citizens, New Haven, 1968).
4. Chester Hartmann, "The Housing of Relocated Families," *Journal of the American Institute of Planners,* XXX (November, 1964), pp. 266–86.
5. Alvin Schorr, "National Community and Housing Policy," *Social Service Review,* XXXIX (December, 1965), pp. 433–43.
6. James Dumpson, "The Human Side of Urban Renewal," *The Welfarer,* XIII, No. 10 (October, 1960), pp. 1–4.

CHAPTER EIGHT

Illegal Order:
The Administration of Injustice

1. From a taped conversation.
2. *The Challenge of Crime in a Free Society* (President's Commission on Law Enforcement and Administration of Justice [New York: Avon Books, 1968]).
3. J. Edgar Hoover, *Crime in the United States: Uniform Crime Reports —1967* (U.S. Government Printing Office, 1968).
4. *Crime Records in Police Management* (Institute of Public Administration, New York, 1952).
5. P. E. Ennis, "Crime, Victims and the Police," *Trans-action,* IV, No. 7 (June, 1967), pp. 36–44.
6. *Ibid.,* p. 40.
7. James Wallerstein and Clement Wyle, "Our Law-Abiding Lawbreakers," *Probation,* April, 1947.

8. Edward Sutherland, "Is 'White Collar Crime' Crime?", *American Sociological Review*, X, No. 4 (1945), pp. 132–39.
9. S. S. Nagel, "The Tipped Scales of American Justice," *Trans–action*, III, No. 4 (May–June, 1966), pp. 3–9.
10. J. F. Short and F. I. Nye, "Reported Behavior as a Criterion of Deviant Behavior," *Social Problems*, V (1957), pp. 207–13.
11. James Q. Wilson, "Dilemmas of Police Administration," *Public Administration Review*, XXVIII (September–October, 1968), pp. 407–17.
12. Paul Chevigny, *Police Power: Police Abuses in New York City* (New York: Pantheon Books, 1969).

CHAPTER NINE

Counting Black Bodies:
Riots, Raids and Repression

1. Herbert Aptheker, "The Watts Ghetto Uprising," *Political Affairs*, Part I (October, 1965), Part II (November, 1965).
2. *Report of the National Advisory Commission on Civil Disorders* (New York: Bantam Books, 1968). Called the Kerner Report.
3. *Violence in the City—An End or a Beginning?* (Sacramento, Calif.: Governor's Commission on the Los Angeles Riots, 1965).
4. For a detailed report of the events of many of the disturbances see: *The Kerner Report*. For instructive detailed reports on disturbances in individual cities, see Robert Conot, *Rivers of Blood, Years of Darkness* (New York: William Morrow & Co., Inc., 1968); John Hersey, *The Algiers Motel Incident* (New York: Alfred A. Knopf, Inc., 1968); Peter Green and Ruth Cheney, "Urban Planning and Urban Revolt: A Case Study" (New Haven Disturbance); *Progressive Architecture* (January, 1968); "The Night of June 2: A Report on Roxbury" (Boston: Commission on Church and Race, Massachusetts Council of Churches, 1967). Digests of specific disturbances and statistical summaries are contained in the several numbers of *Riot Data Review*, Lemberg Center for the Study of Violence, Brandeis University, Waltham, Massachusetts.
5. Conot, *op. cit.*
6. *Ibid.*, p. 243.
7. Hersey, *op. cit.*
8. Robert Fogelson and Robert Hill, "Who Riots? A Study of Participation in the 1967 Riots," *Supplemental Studies for the National Advisory Commission on Civil Disorders* (Washington, D.C.: U.S. Government Printing Office, July, 1968), p. 243.

9. William Worthy, "The Decline of the Black Militants," *Boston Globe Magazine,* July 13, 1969.
10. Lee Rainwater, "Open Letter on White Justice and the Riots," *Transaction,* IV, No. 9 (September, 1967), pp. 22–32.
11. "Plotting a War on 'Whitey,'" *Life,* August, 1966.

CHAPTER TEN

In Praise of Loot and Clout:
Money, Power and Social Change

1. Patricia Cayo Sexton, *Education and Income* (New York: Viking Press, 1964).
2. Richard Cloward and Frances Fox Piven, "Migration, Politics, and Welfare," *Saturday Review,* November 16, 1968.
3. Herbert Gans, "The 'Equality' Revolution," *New York Times Magazine,* November 3, 1968.
4. *Youth in the Ghetto.*
5. *Toward a Social Report* (U.S. Department of Health, Education and Welfare, U.S. Government Printing Office, Washington, D.C., 1969).
6. Milton Kotler, *Neighborhood Government* (Indianapolis, Ind.: Bobbs-Merrill Co., Inc., 1969).

Index

Abortion, 18, 72; effect on illegitimacy rates, 96–7
Accountability, for human services, 266, 272–3
"Acculturation": myth of relation to slum problem, 166–70
Achievement, educational, 37, 44–47; family background and, 45–6, 48–9; effect of educational background on, 49–50; effect of educational motivation on, 49, 50–1
Adams, Melvin, 185–7, 205–7
Administrative bureaucracy, 265
Adoption, of illegitimate babies, 102–3
AFDC program (Aid to Families with Dependent Children), 17–18; expanding rolls, 92, 104; aid to unmarried mothers, 103; low per-person monthly grants, 107–8; "budgets of despair," 108–9
Algiers Motel incident, 224, 245, 246
Alinsky, Saul: community organizations, 268, 269–70

Allport, Gordon, 39
American Medical Association, 161
Analytic process, in study of social problems, 245–8
Aptheker, Herbert, 212
Arnaudo, P., 157
Arrest, rates of, 199–200

Bettelheim, Bruno: on exercise of power as condition for self-esteem and full humanity, 152–3
Billingsley, Andrew: on relationship between black family and larger social systems, 81–2
Birth control, 18, 72; see also Family planning
Black Families in White America (Billingsley), 81–2
Black Power concept: criticism of validity of, by Kerner Commission, 229–30
Blaming the victim: process of, 4–6; reasons for, 25–9
Block organizations, 268–9
Boston: integration battle in, 31–2,

291

Boston (*cont.*)
38–9; 1964 school boycott in, 38–9; Freedom School in, 38–39; inadequacy of relocation housing plans, 178–9
Breeden, Rev. James, 38
Broken homes: Hylan Lewis on, 66–7, 77–8; Midtown Manhattan Study on, 75–6; effect of, on mental health, 76–7
Bronfenbrenner, U.: on child-rearing practices, 125–6
"Budgets of despair" (Charles Lebeaux), 108–9

Carper, Laura, 282–3 *n.*
Centralization, of human services, 265, 267
Chevigny, Paul: on police abuses in New York City, 208
Child-rearing practices, studies on, 125–6
Chilman, Catherine: on growing up poor, 115–17; on lower-lower class way of life, 117; on emotionally maladjusted lower-class, 141–2
Citizen defense, 265–6, 271–2
Citizen participation, in human services, 265, 267–71
Clark, Kenneth, 53, 54
Class, 130, 133, 236–7, 238; defined, 132
Class, Status, and Party (Weber), 132
Cloward, Richard, 104, 240
Coleman, James S., 42–52
Coleman Report (*Equality of Educational Opportunity*), 37, 42–52; on levels of achievement among children, 44–7; criticisms of, 44–52; on relationship of family background and school achievement, 48–9; on "educational background," 49–50; on "educational motivation," 49, 50–1
Community Foundation idea of of Milton Kotler, 268, 269, 270

Compensatory education programs, 8
Connecticut Mental Health Center (New Haven), 105–6
Conot, Robert: documentation of Watts deaths by, 220–2
Cosa Nostra, 261
Court system: inequities in, 202–4
Crime: relating poverty to, 188–90, 199; conclusion of policeman that criminals are lower class and most often black, 200–2; need for redefinition of, 260–1; programs to solve problems of, 260–3
Crime, organized, 195, 197, 261
Crime, white-collar, 195–6, 260
Crime Index (FBI): *see* FBI Crime Index
Crime Records in Police Management (Institute of Public Administration), 192
Crisis in Black and White (Silberman), 165–6
Cultural deprivation theory, 31, 34; as explanation for inner-city school, 4; political and ideological use of, 31–2, 34; discrepancies between theory and research findings, 35–7, 53–5; acceptance of, as excuse for low level of achievement, 48–9
Culture: defined, 118–20; items that characterize, 119; lower class, Walter Miller on, 123–4
Culture of poverty, 114–15; Oscar Lewis on, 115; Charles Valentine's critique of concept of, 120–1; *see also* Lower class culture; Poverty
Culture and Poverty: Critique and Counter-Proposals (Valentine), 120–1

Davis, A.: on child rearing practices, 125
Day, Noel, 38
Day care centers, need for, 109–10

Death at an Early Age (Kozol), xii, 245
Decentralization, of human services, 267
Deferred Gratification Pattern (D.G.P.), 113–14; lack of relation between class and race and, 127–8
Deutsch, M., 36, 37
"Different Ones," the, 9–10
District councils, proposal for, 270–271
Duff, R.: on "charitable" medical care in major university hospital, 160–1

Education: enormous commitment to learning by Negroes, 37–40; importance of money in, 238; Ocean Hill-Brownsville experiment, 239–40; *see also* Cultural deprivation theory; Ghetto education; Schools, slum
"Educational background" and "educational motivation," 49–51
Emotional disturbance: research and assumptions about the poor and, 137–42; *see also* Mental illness
Empty Fortress, The (Bettelheim), 152–3
Equality of Educational Opportunity (Coleman): *see* Coleman Report
"Equality Revolution," 241
Exceptionalistic analysis: application of, to universalistic problems, 19, 247
Exceptionalistic and universalistic solutions for social problems, 16–19, 246–8

Family planning services: eagerness of poor to have and use, 99–101
Farmer, James, 61
FBI Crime Index, 191; gross underestimation of actual crime rate by, 193; rates of arrest for major offenses, 199–200
FBI Crime Reports, 191; no useful purpose served by, 193
Fluoridation, 18
Fogelson, Robert: on inaccuracy of "riffraff" theory of riots, 227–228
Ford Foundation "Gray Areas Project," 166
Frazier, E. Franklin: on history of Negro families, 69–70
Freedom Budget, of A. Philip Randolph, 83
Freedom schools (Boston), 38–9
Friedenberg, Edgar, 59
Friedman, Milton, 253
Fuchs, Estelle, 56–7, 59

Gans, Herbert, 241
Garrett, E., 53
Ghetto children: *see* Slum children
Ghetto education, xiii; tutoring programs in big-city ghettos, 38; *see also* Schools
Gibson School, 245
"Giving Enemy," 264–5, 266–7, 273
Glaser, Marian: on housing code violation in New Haven, 170–171, 172
"Gray Areas Project" of Ford Foundation, 166
Gross, Calvin: on administrative bureaucracy, 265
Growing Up Poor (Chilman), 115–117

HARYOU (Harlem Youth Opportunities Unlimited) Planning Project, 53–6
Hauser, Philip: on Negro's need to experience acculturation, 166
Havighurst, R. J.: on child-rearing practices, 125
Head Start program, 35; good results of, 36; gains of, washed

Head Start program (*cont.*)
away in inferior slum schools, 37
Health, physical: *see* Physical health
Health care: *see* Medical care
Hersey, John: on Algiers Motel incident in Detroit, 224, 245
Herzog, Elizabeth: summary of arguments against "heritage of slavery" theory by, 73; on illegitimacy rates, 104
Hicks, Louise Day, 30, 31
Hill, Adelaide, 100–1
Hill, Robert: on inaccuracy of "riff-raff" theory of riots, 227–8
Hill-Dwight Moms, 105–6
Hofstadter, Richard: on Social Darwinism, 19–21
Hollingshead, August: on "charitable" medical care in major university hospital, 160–1
Hoover, J. Edgar, 190, 191, 193; and organized crime, 195
Hospitals: discriminatory admission practices in, 160–1
Hospitals, state: mental health treatment in, 142, 148–9
Housing, low-income: *see* Low-income housing
Housing, slum: *see* Slum housing; Slum problem
Housing code violations by slum landlords, 23, 170–2
Human services in urban areas: problems, 265–7; solution to problems, 267–73
Humphrey, Hubert: on crime as a by-product of poverty, 189

Illegitimacy, 25, 87–111; welfare and, 5–6, 88–90, 92–3, 103–110; comparison of Negro and white rates of, 72–3, 93–5; beliefs about Negro poor and, 88–92; Social Security proposals for reduction of, 88; under-reporting of white illegitimacy, 94–5; effects of abortion on rates of, 96–7; effect of marriage before birth on rates of, 97–8; attitudes of low-income families toward, 101–2; "hard to place" Negro and poor babies, 102–3; small percent of illegitimate children receiving AFDC support, 103; relation of low income and, 238
Illegitimacy rates, 104
Infant mortality rate, 155
Inner-city children, 33–4
Inner-city education: suggested programs to solve problems of, 253–6; *see also* Schools, slum

Jacobson, Lenore, 59
Jaffe, Frederick, 100–1
Jencks, Christopher, 253
Jensen, Arthur, 53
John Birch Society, 191
Jones, James, 53, 54
Justice, two-class, 188, 202–4

Kardiner, Abram: on emotional disturbances of Negro, 139; plan to help emotionally impoverished, 140, 142
Kerner Commission (National Advisory Commission on Civil Disorders), 211; institutionalized white racism theory, 212; recommendations of, 212–13; on police activity as precipitating incident in urban violence, 215–16; faults of, in report, 229–30; criticism of validity of Black Power concept, 229–30
Kohl, Herbert, xii, 59
Kotler, Milton: Community Foundation idea of, 269, 270
Kozol, Jonathan, xii, 59, 245

Landlords, slum: *see* Slum landlords
Larner, Jeremy, 59

Law enforcement process: selective application of, 205–6; programs to solve problems of, 260–3

Lead paint poisoning, 172; 205; placement of blame for, 22–4

Lebeaux, Charles: on "budgets of despair," 108–9

Lewis, Hylan: on results of broken homes, 66–7, 77–8; on attitudes of low-income families toward illegitimacy, 101–2; child-rearing studies of, 126

Lewis, Oscar: on culture of poverty, 115, 121, 122

Logue, Edward, 178

Long, Russell, 88–9

Low income: programs to solve problem of, 257–9

Low-income housing: slow progress in creation of, 180–1; lack of, as cause of slums, 248–9; suggested programs to increase supply of, 249–53; effective public housing program as solution to problem of, 251–2

Lower class culture, 114, 118, 129; see also Culture of poverty

"Lower class value stretch," 123

"Lumpenproletariat" or "riffraff" theory of riots, 212, 227; case against, 227–8

Maccoby, Eleanor: on child-rearing practices, 125

Mailer, Norman, 245

Maney, Catherine, 32–3

Mannheim, Karl: on maintaining the status quo, 10

Marital separations, and unemployment, 70–1

"Marshall Plan for the Poor" (Whitney Young), 83

Massachusetts Freedom Movement, 38

Matriarchy in Negro and white families, 67

McCone Commission, 12; report of, on Watts disorder, 212

McCoy, Rhody, 239

Medical care system: and the poor, 157–61; domination of services of, by middle-income families, 158–9; "charitable" care in major university hospital, 160–1; discriminatory admission practices in hospitals, 160–1; shortage of doctors in, 162

Medicare, 257

Mental health: effects of lack of money on, 150–2; effects of lack of power on, 152–4; and self-esteem, 152–3; see also Emotional disturbance; Mental illness

Mental health treatment: in large public mental hospitals, 142, 148–9; in outpatient clinics, 142, 145; in offices of psychiatrists in private practice, 142–5; of the poor, by psychiatrists in private practice, 143–4; "screening out the poor," 145, 148

Mental illness, 15, 25; summary of research on the poor and, 137–40; see also Emotional disturbance

Midtown Manhattan Study, 75–6

Miller, S., 127

Miller, Walter: on lower class culture, 123–4

Mills, C. Wright, 131–2; on ideology of those who write about social problems, 13–14

Mills, Wilbur, 88

Money: importance of, in education, 238; relation of low income and illegitimacy, 238

More Effective Schools, 35

Mortality rates: for infants, 155; other than infant, 155–6

Moynihan, Daniel P., 61–2, 64; proposed remedy for family pathology, 83, 282–3 n.; on illegitimacy and welfare, 90; on urban disturbances, 212

Moynihan Report, 61–4, 70–1, 80–81; critique of, 61

Murdock, George, 119

National Advisory Commission on Civil Disorders: *see* Kerner Commission

Needs, gratification of, 113–14

Negro children: "educational background" of, 49–50; "educational motivation" of, 49, 50–51; tutoring programs for, in big-city ghettos, 38; myths about effects of fatherless homes on, 73–5; "hard to place" babies, 102–3; *see also* Slum children

Negro community: social, economic, educational and cultural variability within, 54

Negro equality: elimination of racism as necessary element in achievement of, 82

"Negro family": connotations of phrase, 5, 24–5, 64–5

Negro Family, The: The Case for National Action: see Moynihan Report

Negro family, arguments disproving following myths about: unstable, tending toward matriarchal form, 65–8, 71; present status is rooted in experience of slavery, 68–70, 73; distortions in structure have been maintained by high Negro unemployment, 70–1; weakened family produces sons who are "damaged" by family experience, 73–5; efforts to change ghetto schools and discriminatory employment practices will have little effect on patterns of inequality of status, 80–1

Negro family pathology: Andrew Billingsley on those who place emphasis on, 82

Negro-white comparisons: broken homes, 66–8, 71–3, 78; illegitimacy, 72–3, 93–5; abortions, 96–7; forced marriages, 97–8; mental health treatment, 142–3; mortality rates, 155–6, 158; persons killed in urban riots, 220, 223, 224, 226

Negroes: enormous commitment to learning, 37–40; beliefs about sexual behavior of, 88–92; research and assumptions about emotional disturbances of, 137–42

Neighborhood organizations, 268–269

New Careers programs, 258

New Haven: faults in integrated schools of, 34; housing code violations in, 170–1; housing shortage for poor as result of urban renewal in, 175–7; protest by citizens' group for failure of slum landlords to correct violations, 205–6

New York City: police abuses in, 208

Non-deferred Gratification Pattern (N.G.P.), 113–14

"Nonverbal" poor children, mythology of, 40–2

Nye, F. I., 204

Ocean Hill-Brownsville experiment, 239–40, 276

O'Connor, William, 31

Old-age pensions, 16

Ombudsman, 269

Organized crime, 195, 197, 261

Ovesey, I.: on emotional disturbances of the Negro, 139

Payton, Benjamin, 61

Physical health: of American people, 154–5; draft-rejection rates, 154; infant mortality rates, 155; poor health of the poor, 156–8, 163; *see also* Medical care

Piven, Frances, 240

Planned Parenthood Federations: eagerness of poor to use services of, 99–100

Planning, lack of, in human services, 265–6; solution to, 271–2

Police abuses: studies of, 208; *see also* Urban violence
Police Power (Chevigny), 208
Poverty, 112–35; relating crime to, 188–90, 199; programs to solve problem of, 257–9; *see also* Culture of poverty
Power, 133, 237, 238; defined, 132; effects of lack of, on mental health, 152–4; exercise of, as condition for self-esteem and full humanity, 152–3; significance of, in community control of schools, 239–40; shifts in distribution of, 239–41; exercise of, as achieved by welfare rights groups, 240; tenants' lack of, in public housing, 242–4; children's lack of, in slum schools, 244
President's Crime Commission, 193; on relationship between crime and unhealthy social conditions, 189; on organized crime, 197
Private enterprise, solutions to problem of slum schools, 253–256
Problems, social: *see* Social problems
Programs, development of : to change the victim, 7–8; to "solve" social problems, 14–16
Programs to solve problems of: supply of low-income housing, 249–53; inner-city education, 253–6; health care, 257; low-income and poverty, 257–60; crime, policing and law enforcement, 260–2
Psychodynamic viewpoint of mental health profession, 145–8
Public health, 16
Public housing: slow progress in creation of, 180–1; powerlessness of tenants in, 242–4; as solution to low-income housing problem, 251–2; *see also* Low-income housing

Racism: elimination of, as necessary element in achievement of Negro equality, 82
Rainwater, Lee: on lower class culture, 128–9; on primitive form of redistribution of wealth, 230
Randolph, A. Philip, 83
Reid, O., 157
Relocation, in urban renewal programs, 178–9
Riessman, F., 127
"Riffraff" theory of riots: *see* "Lumpenproletariat"
Riots: *see* Urban violence
Rockefeller, John D.: on survival of the fittest, 20, 21
Rodman, Hyman: on "lower class value stretch," 123
Rosenthal, Robert: report of, on teachers' expectations as determinant in child's performance, 57–9
Roxbury, Mass.: *see* Boston
Russell, Bill, 39
Rustin, Bayard, 65

Schools: tracking system of, xiii, 34; compensatory education programs in, 8; integration battle in Boston, 31–2, 38–9; faults in integrated schools of New Haven, 34; 1964 boycott of, in Boston, 38–9; significance of power in community control of, 239–40; *see also* Coleman Report; Education; Schools, slum
Schools, slum: miseducated child in, 3–4; inadequacies of teachers and, 35, 37; gains of Head Start washed away in, 36–7; expectations of teacher in, as major determinant in child's performance, 53, 55–9; powerlessness of children and parents in, 244; private enterprise solutions to problem of, 253–256; public action solution to problem of, 256

Schorr, Alvin, 183
Seagull, A., 127–8
Seeley, John: on defining a social problem, 11
Self-esteem, and mental health, 152–3
Sexton, Patricia, 238
Sexual behavior, beliefs about Negro poor and, 88–92
Shanker, Albert, 239
Short, J. F., 204
Shuey, Audrey, 53
Sickness and Society (Duff and Hollingshead), 160–1
Silberman, Charles, 165–6
Slavery: "justification" for, 19; arguments against myth that present form of Negro family is derived from, 68–70
Slum children, 33; miseducation of, 4; "cultural deprivation" of, 31, 34; mythology about, as "nonverbal," 40–2; see also Inner-city children; Schools, slum
Slum housing, xiii, 5; and lead paint poisoning, 23; absence of adequate plumbing in, 173; description of apartment in, 183–4; cause of, 248–9
Slum landlords, 260; violations by, 23, 170–2; view that tenants cause slums, 164–5, 170; ignoring orders to make repairs, 172, 185, 204–5; coddling of, by enforcement agency, 185–187, 204
Slum schools: see Schools, slum
Slums: landlords' explanations for cause of, 164–5; myth about acculturation problem and, 166–70
Social Class and Mental Illness (Hollingshead and Redlich), 137
Social class and social stratification, 129–33; W. Lloyd Warner on, 129–32; Max Weber on, 132
Social Darwinism, 19–21

"Social pathologists," 13–14, 18
Social problems: identification of, 11–16; John Seeley on definition of, 11; C. Wright Mills on pathologists of, 13–14; described according to predetermined norms, 13–14; exceptionalistic and universalistic solutions for, 16–19, 246–8; absence of power as primary cause of, 241; principles to be applied in solution of, 245; analytic process in study of, 245–8; crucial criterion by which to judge analyses of, 248; private enterprise and public action programs that could be applied to, 257–63
Social stratification, 129–34, 148
Southern rural migrant, 165
Spencer, Herbert, 20
Status, 130, 131, 133, 236–7; defined, 132
Status quo, maintaining of, 10–11; role of Social Darwinism in, 19–20
Stokes, Bishop, 39
Sullivan, Marguerite, 31, 32
Sumner, William Graham: on Social Darwinism, 20, 21
Sutherland, Edward: on white-collar crime, 195–6

Tax evasion, 197
Tax relief, for middle- and upper-income home owners, 182–3
Teachers: inadequacies of, 35, 37; expectations of, as major determinant in child's performance, 53, 55–9
36 Children (Kohl), xii
Toward a Social Report (Dept. of Health, Education and Welfare), 263
Tracking system, in schools, xiii, 34
Tutoring programs, for Negro children, 38

Unemployment insurance, 16

Unemployment: relationship between marital separation and, 70–1

Universalistic and exceptionalistic solutions for social problems, 16–19, 246–8

Universalistic problems: applying exceptionalistic analysis to, 19, 247

Urban renewal: as creators of slums, xiii; housing shortage for poor as result of, 175–7; inadequate relocation plans in, 178–9; destruction of low-income housing by, 178–9, 180

Urban violence: "lumpenproletariat" theory of riots, 212, 227–229; precipitating events of, 213–16; in Watts, 213–14, 218, 224, 225, 226; in Newark, 214, 224, 225, 226; in Detroit, 214–15, 218, 223–4, 225, 226; in Atlanta, 215; in San Francisco, 215; in Harlem, 215; in Cambridge, Maryland, 215; in Boston, 215, 217–18; in Tampa, 215; police activity as precipitating incident in, 215–16; initial violence following precipitating incident, 216; level of violence pushed higher by presence of police, 216–17; looting during, 218; damage by fire during, 218; act of direct personal violence in, 218–19; property damage by police and National Guard during, 220; Negroes killed during, 220, 223, 224; indiscriminate arrest and beatings by police, 225; police brutality during, 231

Valentine, Charles: critique of culture of poverty concept, 120–121

Violations by slum landlords, 23; see also Slum housing; Slum landlords

Violence, urban: see Urban violence

Walker, David, 245

Wallace, George, 188

Warner, W. Lloyd: on social class and social stratification, 129–132

Watts Riot, 12, 213; McCone Commission report on, 212; documentation of deaths, 220–2; instructions to policemen during, 222; see also Urban violence

Weber, Max: on social stratification, 130–1

Welfare: and illegitimacy, 5–6, 88–90, 92–3, 103–10; proposed ceiling on support for dependent children, 88; major defects of system, 104; increase in caseloads, 104–5; organization of welfare mothers, 105–6; see also AFDC program

Welfare rights groups, exercise of power by, 240

Welfare Rights Movement, 105, 240

White, A., 157

White, Theodore: on sexual life of ghetto Negro, 90

Wiley, George, 105

Wilson, James Q.: on dilemmas of police administration, 207

Worthy, William, 229

Young, Whitney, 65; proposed "Marshall Plan for the Poor," 83

Youth in the Ghetto (Haryou Planning Project), 53–6, 241